SACRED
DREAMS

SUNY series in
Women in Education

Margaret Grogan, editor

Sacred

Dreams

Women and the Superintendency

Edited by
C. Cryss Brunner

STATE UNIVERSITY OF NEW YORK PRESS

Published by
State University of New York Press, Albany

For information, address State University of New York Press,
State University Plaza, Albany, NY 12246

Production by Laurie Searl
Marketing by Anne M. Valentine

Library of Congress Cataloging-in-Publication Data

Sacred dreams : women and the superintendency / edited by C. Cryss
  Brunner.
       p.   cm. – (SUNY series in women in education)
    Includes bibliographical references and index.
    ISBN 0-7914-4159-8 (hc. : alk. paper). – ISBN 0-7914-4160-1 (pbk.
  : alk. paper)
    1. Women school superintendents—United States. I. Brunner, C.
  Cryss. II. Series.
  LB2831.72.S23 1999
  371.2'011–dc21   98-36545
                                                                                 CIP

10 9 8 7 6 5 4 3 2 1

To all women who have ever been, who are, or who ever will be

superintendents of schools;

and to Patricia Nehm,

whose assistance with this book kept it alive.

Contents

Foreword

In 1986, when my friend Roberta Hutton resigned her position as superintendent of an Oregon school district, the percent of women superintendents in grades K-12 districts declined by 25 percent. Today, in Oregon, seventeen women, or 8 percent, are superintendents in grades K-12 districts, and there are three women among the five largest districts in the state. In the latter half of the twentieth century, women have been invisible in the superintendency. Yet, earlier in this century, women were quite visible as superintendents, primarily as county superintendents in the West. Advocacy groups, such as the National Council of Administrative Women in Education, increased the political clout of women in education earlier in this century. Today, organizations such as the Northwest Women in Educational Administration and the Northeast Coalition of Educational Leaders have inspired and supported women to seek the superintendency (see Blount in this book; Gribskov 1987; Schmuck 1995). Again, there is a momentum for women to achieve superintendent positions; women's representation nationally has changed from the 1974 figure of .01 percent to about 7 percent in 1993. Interestingly, however, data about sex representation in educational administration are somewhat unreliable; Tyack and Hansot argue that there is a "conspiracy of silence" concerning these data (1982, 21; see also Tallerico in this book). In the latter twentieth century, the almost invisible woman superintendent is again claiming a visible space.

This book pays attention to women of color in the superintendency; several chapters address issues of race and ethnicity. Black women (who are mostly in primarily black urban centers) and Hispanic women (who are primarily in the Southwest) each constitute about 1.5 percent of superintendents, with other minorities accounting for another .5 percent (see Alston, Ortiz, Méndez-Morse, Jackson, and Tallerico in this book). While the feminist movement has been, in large part, a white, middle-class movement, the literature on women of color has been growing and leads to our understanding that race and ethnicity are also factors in the gendered construction of schooling. While the representation of women of color and other ethnic minorities is small among women superintendents, the fact is there is proportionally more diversity among women superintendents than among the 93 percent males who occupy the superintendency. Superintendents have not only been primarily male; they have been primarily Caucasian, Protestant, married with children, and Republicans. Women superintendents are, more often than men, people of color, Catholic or Jewish, never married, divorced or widowed, and Democrats. There is more variation among the 7 percent of women superintendents than among the 93 percent of male superintendents. It is as though selection committees say unconsciously, "Since we've gone out on a limb to hire a woman, we might as well forget the other usual attributes as well." Sue Paddock, in a national study of female superintendents and high school principals, said, ". . . gender may be the most difficult career contingency. . . . Once women surmount this barrier, the other attributes may no longer carry weight as a precondition for employment" (1981, 190).

Brunner asserted that this " book specifically about women superintendents is long overdue and certainly needed" (p. xx in this book). I agree. I have searched the literature about superintendents for my course on the superintendency, offered at The Institute for Executive Leadership, a course I have taught for the last decade (Schmuck 1992). Literature about the superintendency is sparse, however, good literature about the superintendency is even more difficult to find. Although I respect and admire the work of Blumberg (1985), Cuban (1976), and March (1978), their work is derived from studies of male superintendents and from a traditional scientific management perspective on administration. Their work focuses on issues of power "over." Brunner's book focuses on power "with/to" (Follett 1942, Hurty 1995).

The discussion about power "with/to" and power "over" reflects one of the current debates within the feminist research community. Does the gender of the role taker make a difference in leadership? Do women and men lead differently? Does gender matter? The debate about whether females and males are more different than alike or more alike than different goes back as far as Plato, who argued that women could be governors because gender was the difference that made no difference.

Those who take an essentialist position argue that women lead differently than men because of "essentially" different qualities that come from socialization. In fact, some argue that women's socialization gives them a leadership advantage; they argue that women have been already trained to be the kind of leaders we are looking for today—facilitative, communicative, empowering—women are socialized to have power "with" (Helegson 1990; Rosener 1990). Others would take a role theory argument and say that the role prescribes behavior, and that gender is merely one of the many variables that may account for differences between individuals.

Paradoxically, I believe both to be true. I believe women and men are more alike than different, and I believe that women and men lead differently. I trust the earlier findings of Maccoby and Jacklin, that gender alone cannot account for variation between groups of males and females (1974). But females and males will lead differently. They will lead differently for at least two reasons: 1) Males and females live in different realities in our gendered society and have learned different socially appropriate behaviors, and 2) Gender, the social meaning given to being female or male, includes a transactional relationship between people. Others' expectations and one's sense of self will be formed through the construction of being female or male.

Schools are gender-bound institutions. Women superintendents do not experience the same reality as men superintendents. Even if a female and a male behaved identically, those behaviors would not be received in the same way. Gender is the mediating force in superintendents' selection, effectiveness, and retention. Thus, we need to understand women's experience; what has been written about men superintendents does not necessarily apply to women.

I find it hopeful that many women superintendents in this book are cognizant of their gender; too many women in leadership roles proclaim their disaffection with feminism. I have heard too many women superintendents begin a sentence with, "I am not a feminist, but . . ." (Bell 1995; Matthews 1995). Brunner's study of women superintendents shows that while on the surface women superintendents did not appear to be paying attention to the fact that they are women, they "articulated and carried out gender-specific strategies which created, in part, their support while in the superintendency" (Brunner, chapter 11 in this book). These women did not try to act like men; they learned that women who act like men quickly get labeled "bitches." Men can get away with being directive and authoritarian; women cannot; this is well confirmed in the literature (Eagley and Johnson 1990; Riehl and Lee 1996). Marshall argues that women in administration are "abnormal"; they do not meet the social gender expectations of being a leader, nor do they meet the gender expectations of femaleness (Marshall 1985).

Fortunately, the women superintendents represented in this book no longer consider themselves abnormal: they have developed a sense of self, so that they are comfortable with the fact that they are women, and they are comfortable with the fact that they are the chief executive officer of a school district.

This book indicates that women are finding their way in the superintendency; it seems that more and more boards, as well as "headhunters" are not using female sex as a negative characteristic for inclusion in the administrative pool (see Kamler and Shakeshaft in this book). We must still wonder, however, about issues of retention. Thirteen out of twenty women superintendents studied left, due to nonrenewal of their contracts (Tallerico, Burstyn, and Poole 1993).

I recently talked with the president of an urban university who is exiting her position voluntarily, making a lateral move to a comparable university in another state. I asked her why she was leaving. She said the best piece of leadership advice she had received in her early years as an administrator was to "be sure you know when it's time to leave." Although her exit was voluntary, she knew full well that she, as a woman, could not fit into the "stable" of the chancellor of the state system. In this volume, Beekley studied women who were exiting the superintendency. It is a beginning. One of the needed areas of study is more information about why women exit, voluntarily or involuntarily, positions of leadership in education.

I have been studying women in school administration for over twenty years. It has been an incredible journey of celebration, frustration, delight, hope, and despair. In 1974, I identified the "Who, ME?" woman; this woman, when asked to take on a position of authority and responsibility, responded self-deferentially with the words, "Who, ME?" In 1999, I do not think that there are any "Who, ME?" women in public school administration. The women reflected in this book know their strength, trust their capabilities, and understand that their femaleness makes a difference in how they must operate in gendered organizational cultures. It gives me hope about women reaching positions of the superintendency; and it gives me hope that women leaders, with their tendency to be more communicative, facilitative, and to share power "with/to," may help meet the incredibly difficult challenges that face school districts now and into the twenty-first century.

PATRICIA A. SCHMUCK

REFERENCES

Bell, C. 1995. If I weren't involved in schools, I might be a radical. In D. Dunlap and P. Schmuck (eds.), *Women leading in education*. Albany, N.Y.: State University of New York Press.

Blumberg, A. 1985. *The school superintendent: Living with conflict*. New York: Teachers College Press.

Cuban, L. 1976. *Urban school chiefs under fire*. Chicago: University of Chicago Press.

Eagley, A. H., and B. Johnson. 1990. Gender and leadership style: A meta-analysis. *Psychological Bulletin* 108: 223–56.

Follett, M. P. 1942. *Creative experience*. New York: Longmans, Green, and Co.

Gribskov, M. 1987. Adelaide Pollock and the founding of NCAWE. In P. Schmuck (ed.), *Educators: Employees of schools in Western countries*. Albany, N.Y.: State University of New York Press.

Helegson, S. 1990. *The female advantage: Women's ways of leading*. New York: Doubleday.

Hurty, K. 1995. Women principals: Leading with power. In D. Dunlap and P. Schmuck (eds.), *Women leading in education*. Albany, N.Y.: State University of New York Press.

Maccoby, E., and C. N. Jacklin. 1974. *The psychology of sex differences*. Palo Alto, CA: Stanford University Press.

March, J. 1978. American public school administration: A short analysis. *School Review* 86: 217–89.

Marshall, C. 1985. From culturally defined to self-defined, career stages of women administrators. *The Journal of Educational Thought* 19(2): 134–47.

Matthews, E. 1995. Women in educational administration: Views on equity. In D. Dunlap and P. Schmuck (eds.), *Women Leading in Education*. Albany, N.Y.: State University of New York Press.

Paddock, S. 1981. Male and females paths in school administration. In P. Schmuck, W. Charters, and R. Carlson (eds.), *Educational policy and management: Sex differentials*. New York: Academic Press.

Riehl, C., and V. Lee. 1996. Gender, organizations, and leadership. In K. Leithwood, J. Chapman, D. Corson, P. Hallinger, and A. Hart (eds.), *International Handbook of Educational Leadership and Administration*. New York: Kluwer Academic Publishers.

Rosener, J. B. 1990. Ways woman lead. *Harvard Business Review* 68 (6): 119–25.

Schmuck, P. 1992. Preparing superintendents for the unexpected, the unanticipated and the untoward: The institute for executive leadership. *Educational Leadership* 49(5): 66–71.

———. 1995. Advocacy organizations for women school administrators. In D. Dunlap and P. Schmuck (eds.), *Women leading in education*. Albany, N.Y.: State University of New York Press.

Tallerico, M., J. N. Burstyn, and W. Poole. 1993. *Gender and politics at work: Why women exit the superintendency*. Fairfax, Va: National Policy Board for Educational Administration.

Tyack, D., and E. Hansot. 1982. *Managers of virtue*. New York: Basic Books.

Preface

> For years women who carry the mythic life of the Wild Woman
> archetype have silently cried, "Why am I so different: Why was I
> born into such a strange [or unresponsive] family?" Wherever their
> lives wanted to burst forth, someone was there to salt the ground so
> nothing could grow. They felt tortured by all the proscriptions
> against their natural desires. If they were nature children, they were
> kept under roofs. If they were scientists, they were told to be moth-
> ers. If they wanted to be mothers, they were told they'd better fit the
> mold entirely. If they wanted to invent something, they were told to
> be practical. If they wanted to create, they were told a woman's
> domestic work is never done. (Estés 1992, 193)
>
> —Clarissa Pinkola Estés, *Women Who Run With the Wolves*

If women wanted to be superintendents, they were told to remain teachers.
The fact that most superintendents of schools are men bears this out. Do
women even want the job? Our research indicates that they do. For many reasons, however, the road to the superintendency is extremely difficult for most
women. We, as researchers and practitioners, have noted this particular difficulty
and have decided that it deserves our attention. Each of us, at times, believed herself to be the only one focusing on this dilemma. In fact, there are very few people doing research on women in the superintendency.

Paradoxically, we have taught and experienced leadership preparation
classes, including superintendency courses, in which half of the students were
women. We are aware, as well, that the discourse on the superintendency has
been articulated, in no small measure, by men. Given these two actualities, we
believe that a book specifically about women superintendents is long overdue
and certainly needed.

Finally, given the nationwide concern that superintendency positions will be
emptied faster than they can be filled during the next decade (Brockett 1996), we
believe that it is important to make more public this neglected area of study. In
addition, we believe that the greatest untapped pool of capable candidates for the
position of superintendent of schools is that group of women of all races who is
credentialed and trained, but not hired into positions because of gender and
racial bias. As those women candidates think about, seek, and take superintendency positions, they need to understand women superintendents' experiences.

Such an understanding has the potential to not only increase the number of women in the position, but also to increase the likelihood of their success once in the position.

To the ends outlined above, we collectively offer our voices to encourage and support all women who dare to think about becoming superintendents. We vow to provide fertile soil rather than "salt the ground" beneath their dreams. We insist that it is not only natural, but also important that women become superintendents, if that is what they want to do.

REFERENCE

Brockett, D. 1996. Boards find fewer good superintendent candidates. *School Board News* 16 (10): 1, 10.

Introduction

"Scattered All over the Road"

C. CRYSS BRUNNER

They left dreams scattered all over the road.

—Clarissa Pinkola Estés, *Women Who Run With the Wolves*

With the research of Patricia Schmuck, Flora Ida Ortiz, Charol Shakeshaft, and others, a foundation was laid for a previously neglected area of study—women in educational administration. As a result, many have joined those interested in the obvious question: If women have dominated the teaching ranks at all levels since the turn of the century (Tyack and Hansot 1982), why do men occupy 93 percent of superintendency positions? This question has driven a number of research studies focused specifically on women in the superintendency.

Not surprisingly, the research undertaken on women in the superintendency has been done primarily, if not only, by other women. This in itself is problematic. If only women find the topic important enough for further investigation, the cries for change will remain marginalized. The normative assumption, that only men can be superintendents, is far stronger than any female voice advocating that women of all races belong in the position.

Hope is not lost. Hope remains because recent research that has focused on reform efforts has drawn attention to the role of the superintendent. This new attention to the role is not a result of concern about inequalities surrounding gender and race, but rather because of the realization that the office of superintendent plays an important part in advancing reform agendas, including parental choice and site-based decision making (Carnoy and MacDonell 1990; Murphy and Hallinger 1993). Even with this realization, there is very little in the literature that informs or supports specific ways that the superintendency may change or is changing (Crowson 1988).

There are at least two reasons for this lack of analyses. First, reform action has been focused on the local school community and on state and federal change initiatives (Cuban 1990; Smith and O'Day 1990), with the widely held belief that reform can happen without concern for the superintendency (Murphy 1995). Second, some reformers believe that superintendents are not only a major cause of the problems with schooling, but also are unwilling to relinquish their control over education (Chubb 1988). Thus, research aimed at helping superintendents as they consider transforming their practice becomes extremely pertinent.

A review of the literature on women in positions of power clearly shows that women bring to their practice many of the characteristics noted as currently missing and necessary for reform. With this in mind, research on women in the superintendency becomes vastly more important to anyone interested in educational administration. To be sure, calls for public school reform fall at all points along the ideological continuum. Decentralized decision making is one major thrust of certain reforms, such as site-based management, teacher empowerment (Hallinger 1992; Mohrman 1993; Wohlsetter, Smyer, and Mohrman 1994), joint problem diagnosis (Beer, Eisenstat, and Spector 1990), high-performance schools (Odden 1995), and connecting schools and communities (Crowson 1992). A small portion of the literature on decentralized decision making focuses on administration and points out how successful superintendents spend time enhancing and supporting various collaborative decision-making efforts (Murphy 1995) that facilitate reforms, which in turn advance high academic achievement for all students (Odden 1995).

A second major thrust of reform highlights the moral issues facing public school educators. Some of the issues dealt with are social justice (Purpel 1989), with an emphasis on academic achievement for every child (Capper 1993); higher-order democratic values, exemplified by equality of input and equality of opportunity (Tyack 1974); and the notion of an "ethic of care" (Noddings 1984, 1992), which combines caring, administration, and academic achievement (Beck 1994). This literature admonishes superintendents and other administrators to care enough about people—children and adults—to listen to them, suggesting the replacement of the current pyramidal governance structure with a circle model within which no point is in a superior position (Beck 1994, 84). Despite this thrust, there is no literature to help superintendents transform their practice in a way that addresses these moral issues.

We believe that research on women in the superintendency would inform and sensitize all people, men and women, either seeking or already in the position of superintendent, to issues raised by the two major reform thrusts discussed above. Further, we believe that drawing attention to the worth of women's practice in the superintendency would increase the number of women in the position. Given these goals and those outlined in the Preface, this book addresses many topics of importance for women and men as they consider, seek, and then step into the role of superintendent of schools.

Without a doubt, research on women in the superintendency is as scarce and scattered as the women themselves. In an effort to unify and solidify this body of literature, this book pulls together, for the first time, leading scholars who focus on this specific topic. The book is organized into four sections. Using quotes from Dr. Clarissa Pinkola Estés (1992) as an organizer, the sections are arranged in a sequence that follows the thoughts and life of a woman who becomes a superintendent of schools. The first section contains information a woman might want when her thoughts first turn to the idea of becoming a superintendent. Estés' compelling quotes are an appropriate organizer because they communicate a deeper sense of what women superintendents express about their work and lives. The second part discusses issues of interest to a woman as she decides to pursue a position. The third division covers facets of the life a woman might experience while in the position, and the fourth section offers her reflection on the connection between research and the actual superintendency practice.

The representative sampling used by the researchers, when doing their studies, ensures a range of diverse contexts and perspectives. Further, several pathbreaking insights can be drawn from across the chapters which assist women as they traverse the unfamiliar terrain of the superintendency. Five of the most important of these insights include: 1) the affirmation that most women, even in the most powerful position in public school education, are strongly inclined and willing to share power; 2) the confirmation that women superintendents experience gender bias, and that they acknowledge the experiences; 3) the overt recognition that an articulation of the complexities, difficulties, and strengths brought to the superintendency by women of color is critically important to all people; 4) the fact that women in the superintendency have ways to talk about how they have succeeded in the role, and that their strategies of success are useful to other women; and 5) the collective opinion of women superintendents that they are at their best when the needs of children come first. This collective insight suggests that women in the superintendency provide the type of leadership needed to keep all educators focused on basic moral essentials during this period of school reformation.

The first part of the book, "Crawling Through the Window of a Dream—Surveying the Terrain," centers on what the superintendency looks like for women, historically and in general, as they consider the position. In the first chapter, Jackie M. Blount uncovers historical events that shaped the terrain in ways that made it more difficult for women to enter the superintendency. Marilyn Tallerico follows with a comprehensive review of the literature on women in the superintendency. She not only provides a fuller view of the position from the

perspective of gender, but also identifies gaps in the literature that require further research if women are to understand the role.

The second part of the book, "Do It Anyway—Gaining Access," makes clear
gender and racial issues surrounding the selection of women for the position of
superintendent. Women wishing to gain access face numerous constraints and
need information in order to seek the position in spite of barriers—in other words,
to "do it anyway." Estelle Kamler and Charol Shakeshaft open the section with a
chapter devoted to the impact search consultants have on the selection process and,
in turn, the careers of women administrators. C. Cryss Brunner's chapter is
broadly cast around the issues of power, gender, and the selection process. Next,
Judy A. Alston writes about the difficulties that African-American women face
when seeking positions. She focuses specifically on constraints and facilitators that
black female superintendents encounter en route to the superintendency. Continuing the focus on race, Flora Ida Ortiz's chapter addresses two areas: how the
search and selection process leads to the appointment of Hispanic female superintendents, and how Hispanic female superintendents prepare for the position.

The third part of the book, "Small but Brilliant—Living the Life," captures
snapshots from the "small [in number] but brilliant" lives of women superintendents, from the beginning stages to times when they may choose to "stop" living the life. Barbara Nelson Pavan opens the section with a chapter aimed at
exploring the beginning years as experienced by four women in the superintendency. Sylvia E. Méndez-Morse's chapter follows four Mexican-American women
as they sought and stepped into the role of superintendent of schools. She highlights the transformation of these women as they gained confidence in their own
strengths and capabilities. Barbara L. Jackson's chapter includes information
about thirty-two African-American female superintendents, including their career
paths and views of their positions. In the last chapter in this section, Cynthia
Beekley discusses issues that caused women in her study to leave the position of
superintendent. The issues are organized into three frames: cultural/social, orga-
nizational/ professional, and personal/family.

The final part of the book, "One's True Song—Authenticating Research,"
addresses our goal as researchers to do work that reflects the "true song" of the
women we study and crystallizes what they have taught us in a way that makes
our work useful to women seeking or occupying the superintendency. To that
end, this section includes three interactive chapters that examine the usefulness
of the work of two researchers through the eyes of a woman superintendent currently in practice. This section brings the reader full circle from the introduction,
where we offered our voices in support of women desirous of the position of
superintendent, and puts our voices to the test. We put our work under the looking glass, and ask a woman superintendent to examine it closely for its worth.
We ask if we are building a foundation of strength for women, or missing the

mark. What is it we have done? In C. Cryss Brunner's chapter, narrative data from a woman superintendent, Debra Jackson, is analyzed, using a framework, "strategies for success," that Brunner constructed in previous research.

Margaret Grogan's chapter analyzes the same data that Brunner collected from Debra Jackson (in addition to narrative data from another woman superintendent), using a feminist poststructuralist lens. In the last chapter, Jackson responds to Brunner's and Grogan's individual analyses and poses additional questions. The interaction among these chapters is a model for future dialogue focused on authenticating research in ways that may enable us, as researchers, to keep the promises we make to those in practice. Susan Chase closes the book by reminding us that having women in the superintendency serves the larger purpose of social justice.

Women wishing to become superintendents or women superintendents who seek the promise of support deserve a "promise kept." These women have often faced difficulties in their lives because of their courage to think and act outside of social norms in our culture.

> Sometimes they tried to be good according to whichever standards were most popular, and didn't realize till later what they really wanted, how they needed to live. Then, in order to have a life, experienced the painful amputations of leaving their families, the marriages they had promised under oath would be till death, the jobs that were to be the springboards to something more stultifying but better paying. They left dreams scattered all over the road. (Estés 1992, 193)

And while leaving "dreams scattered all over the road" may be the cost to women who aspire to positions most often filled by men, we hope that our research helps keep one of their sacred dreams in place; that is, that women can and should be superintendents of schools.

REFERENCES

Beck, L. 1994. *Reclaiming educational administration as a caring profession.* New York: Teachers College Press.

Beer, M., R. A. Eisenstat, and B. Spector. 1990. Why change programs don't produce change. *Harvard Business Review* 68: 158–66.

Capper, C. A. (ed.). 1993. *Educational administration in a pluralistic society.* Albany, N.Y.: State University of New York Press.

Carnoy, M., and J. MacDonell. 1990. School district restructuring in Santa Fe, New Mexico. *Educational Policy* 4 (1): 49–64.

Chubb, J. E. 1988. Why the current wave of school reform will fail. *Public Interest* (90): 28–47.

Crowson, R. L. 1988. Editor's introduction. *Peabody Journal of Education* 65 (4): 1-8.

———. 1992. *School-community relations, under reform.* Berkeley: McCutchan Publishing Corporation.

Cuban, L. 1990. Reforming again, again, again. *Educational Researcher* 19 (1): 3-14.

Estés, C. P. 1992.*Women who run with the wolves: Myths and stories of the wild woman archetype.* New York: Ballentine Books.

Hallinger, P. 1992. The evolving role of American principals: From managerial to instructional to transformational leaders. *Journal of Educational Administration* 30 (3): 35-48.

Hargreaves, A. 1994. *Changing teachers changing times.* New York: Teachers College Press.

Mohrman, S. A. 1993. *School based management and school reform: Comparisons to private sector organizational renewal.* Paper presented at annual meeting of the Association for Public Policy Analysis and Management, Washington, D.C.

Murphy, J. 1995. Restructuring in Kentucky: The changing role of the superintendent and the district office. In K. Leithwood (ed.), *Effective School District Leadership* (pp. 117-33). Albany, N.Y.: State University of New York Press.

Murphy, J., and P. Hallinger. 1993. Restructuring schooling: Learning from ongoing efforts. In J. Murphy and P. Hallinger (eds.), *Restructuring schooling: Learning from ongoing efforts.* Newbury Park, Calif.: Corwin/Sage.

Noddings, N. 1984. *Caring: A feminine approach to ethics and moral education.* Berkeley: University of California Press.

———. 1992. *The challenge to care in schools: An alternative approach to education.* New York and London: Teachers College Press.

Odden, A. 1995. *Educational leadership for America's schools.* New York: McGraw-Hill, Inc.

Purpel, D. 1989. *The moral and spiritual crisis in education: A curriculum for justice and compassion in education.* Granby, Mass.: Bergin & Garvey.

Smith, M. S., and J. O'Day. 1990. *Systemic school reform.* Palo Alto: Stanford University Center for Policy Research in Education.

Tyack, D. B. 1974. *The one best system: A history of American urban education.* Cambridge: Harvard University Press.

Tyack, D., and E. Hansot. 1982. *Managers of virtue.* New York: Basic Books.

Wohlsetter, P., R. Smyer, and S. A. Mohrman. 1994. New boundaries for school-based management: The high involvement model. *Education Evaluation and Policy Analysis* 16 (3): 268-86.

PART ONE

"Crawling through the Window of a Dream"

Surveying the Terrain

C. CRYSS BRUNNER

> Don't be a fool. Go back and stand under that one red flower and walk straight ahead for that last hard mile. Go up and knock on the old weathered door. Climb up to the cave. Crawl through the window of a dream. Sift the desert and see what you find. It is the only work we have to do.
>
> —Clarissa Pinkola Estés, *Women Who Run With the Wolves*

As researchers studying women superintendents, we are "crawling through the window of a dream." It is not surprising that all of the authors of this book are women, but it is sad. It is not surprising that our work often remains unseen, but it is disappointing. We are "knocking on the old weathered door" of the position of the superintendency. We desire a window of opportunity for women like ourselves—women who have dared to dream differently.

We, as authors and researchers, meet ourselves when we do research with women superintendents. Often we have begun with a vague curiosity and found ourselves in the middle of a deep outrage—an outrage that lives in the gut of women who have overtly faced and acknowledged gender and racial bias. Often we ask anyone who will listen, "What do I do when a woman superintendent— a powerful, capable, brilliant, successful woman—breaks down and cries?" We recoil. We see ourselves, hear ourselves. We quietly become mainstream feminists—women who believe in fairness for all people. We cannot *not* do our work—"It is the only work we have to do."

Women seeking the superintendency are doing the same work. They, too, are "crawling through the window of a dream" in order to survey the terrain of the superintendency. That window is usually small, too small, to see much of the terrain. In this section we connect multiple windows to create a larger view. We wish to give women seeking the position a better view of the superintendency through the eyes of other women. We want women to be able to "sift the desert" to see what they find for themselves, but we want them to see the position of superintendent as one that welcomes women rather than one that is unfriendly to things considered feminine.

CHAPTER ONE

Turning out the Ladies

Elected Women Superintendents and the Push for the Appointive System, 1900-1935

JACKIE M. BLOUNT

E arly in the twentieth century, ambitious women seeking school leadership positions briefly enjoyed broad-based and enthusiastic support from a powerful emerging political constituency of women. Suffrage activism and the larger women's movement effectively propelled women into school leadership positions. During these years, hundreds of women waged successful campaigns for superintendencies, and by 1930, women accounted for nearly 28 percent of county superintendents and 11 percent of all superintendents nationwide (Blount 1998, Appendix). Activists such as Ella Flagg Young, the superintendent of Chicago schools from 1909 to 1915, hoped that women would eventually dominate school leadership, just as they had teaching. Once swept into office, they might purge corrupt administrative practices, bring an elevated moral purpose to schooling, and improve public education much as they believed women already had improved teaching. During these years, women found boundless cause for optimism.

Victories would not always come easily, however. As women won the right to vote on school-related matters in individual communities and then eventually full national suffrage, superintendent groups sought to change superintendencies from elected to appointed positions. Schools needed expert administrators, they argued; and experts could hardly be chosen in public, politically charged contests. Rather, they believed that popularly elected politicians should select superintendents from pools of qualified, well-trained experts. On the other hand, newly enfranchised women activists doubted that such an appointive system maintained the spirit of American democracy. As they eagerly prepared for their duties as voting citizens, they confronted a growing movement to take the superintendency out of politics.

9

WOMEN, EDUCATION, AND SUFFRAGE

The 1848 Seneca Falls meeting was one of the earliest gatherings of American women to improve their own conditions as a group rather than those of others, a focus critics thought selfish. They came together to identify and explore the myriad forms of their oppression. One focus of discussion concerned women's lack of full access to institutions of higher education. Even though some academies and seminaries had opened their doors to women, most secondary and post-secondary institutions barred their admission. Ironically, as school boards hired ever greater numbers of women teachers, male students enjoyed better educational prospects than their female teachers ever would (Stanton et al. 1881, 70–71). Attendees insisted that women be allowed full access to all institutions and programs so that they might eventually break free of their otherwise certain dependence on men.

Clearly, education weighed heavily on the minds of women at the Seneca Falls meeting. Some had attended women's educational institutions and developed a certain pride in their academic accomplishments, as well as a strong faith that women's continued education would eventually bring their full independence and equality. No doubt, these women could articulate their conditions partly because they had come to enjoy formal learning, and they continued to educate themselves informally by reading, discussing, and writing about works such as Margaret Fuller's 1845 provocative feminist classic, *Women in the Nineteenth Century*.

Beyond their desire for empowerment through education, however, some of the women at the Seneca Falls meeting and many of the earliest women's rights activists also were interested in education because they had been schoolteachers. At the time, teaching offered perhaps the only profession women could pursue that utilized, and, in fact, required, their formal education. The venerable Susan B. Anthony, for example, taught school for a few years before launching into full-time political activism (Barry 1988, 39–45). Decades later, Carrie Chapman Catt, who eventually led the National American Woman Suffrage Association (NAWSA) through to enactment of the suffrage amendment in 1920, started her public career as a teacher and then later served as superintendent of the Mason City, Iowa, schools from 1883 to 1885 (Noun 1993). In the years between Anthony and Catt, a host of other women educators devoted their efforts to the women's suffrage movement, including Betsey Mix Cowles, superintendent of the Canton, Ohio, schools from 1850 to 1855. Cowles, known statewide as a gifted teacher and leader for women's rights, served as president of the first Ohio Women's Convention in 1850 (Sicherman et al. 1980). Voters in Wyoming elected Estelle Reed to be the State Superintendent of Instruction in 1894, which made her the first woman in the country to hold a state office. In this capacity, she addressed the 1898 meeting of the NAWSA convention (Larson 1980, 9).

Teachers generally played active roles in organizing and sustaining the suffrage movement. For example, late in the nineteenth century, 5,000 Indiana teachers signed a petition asking for women's vote (Anthony and Harper 1900, 37). Teachers formed a significant constituency of local, state, and national gatherings of suffragists. They also played key roles in the proliferation of women's rights periodicals, which offered an important forum for discussing the ramifications of the Seneca Falls Declaration of Sentiments. Magazines such as *The Woman Voter* effectively lent coherence as well as a sense of community to widely scattered groups of woman's rights activists. Of the twelve papers championing women's rights from 1849 to 1920, schoolteachers edited nine of them (Butcher 1986).

Anne Firor Scott traces one of the most important links between the suffrage movement and education when she describes how the rise of female seminaries in the early 1800s eventually catalyzed the women's rights movement. The bold, intelligent, and diligent women who founded these institutions created unique social spaces for young women to develop their academic abilities, build warm friendships with one another, draw inspiration from the model of admirable women educators, and to come to believe that women deserved equal rights. Emma Willard, who established the Troy Female Seminary, was by various accounts a powerful, wise, and deeply compassionate person who inspired the hundreds of students with whom she worked. Willard long contended that "justice will yet be done. Women will have her rights. I see it in the course of events" (Scott 1979, 8). Graduates of the Troy Female Seminary frequently became influential teachers and leaders themselves, and some even established their own female institutions.

Many of these women also worked for women's rights. For instance, Elizabeth Cady Stanton attended the Troy Seminary, where she developed a deep admiration for Willard. Stanton later joined Susan B. Anthony in organizing the Seneca Falls meeting and providing critical leadership for the larger women's suffrage movement. The influence of the Troy Seminary and other institutions like it expanded outward to touch many women indirectly. Scott concludes that "education appears to have been a major force in the spread of feminism" (1979, 20).

Not all advocates of women's education supported the movement for women's rights, however. Catharine Beecher, a tireless advocate of women teachers, consistently spoke out against women's suffrage, insisting that the development of teaching as a woman's profession was more important than fighting for full citizenship (Burstyn 1974, 386). She blasted suffragists for seeking male prerogatives where instead she believed they should aspire to developing their own inherent feminine qualities for nurturance and accommodation (Norton 1979, 145). Beecher's position militated against suffrage because she believed that societies were civilized by the degree to which they made distinctions between the responsibilities of men and women (Burstyn 1974, 387). Women therefore should not seek privileges reserved for men. Because of her views, suffragists regarded Beecher as an enemy (Norton 1979, 145).

Advocates of women's education clearly diverged in their political views and willingness to agitate for women's rights. Regardless of the roiling public debates, many graduates of female educational institutions took their activism directly to the schools. There they labored to improve opportunities for girls by founding their own women's seminaries, or by venturing out on their own to teach in remote schoolhouses to ensure that the next generation of young women would be educated. May Wright Sewall, an Indiana teacher and chair of the executive committee of the National Woman Suffrage Association (NWSA), described this sense of mission in 1885: "Naturally, so far, woman's best efforts have been given to the young of their own sex, for the educated woman's first feeling, I might almost say her primary conviction, is that her duty binds her to her own sex, that she may make to them possibilities for such training as was denied to her" (1885, 155).

SUFFRAGE AND ELECTED WOMEN SUPERINTENDENTS

As school districts began hiring women teachers in the mid-nineteenth century, women's suffrage advocates discovered important new strategies for leveraging their right to vote. First, women's increasing property ownership opened the possibility for their suffrage. Because women teachers earned salaries, low as they may have been, and because women teachers usually were single, they sometimes possessed their own property. Property owners were entitled to vote; therefore, women teachers who owned property were thought to need suffrage (Sewall 1887; Phelps 1912, 77–78).

Second, since communities elected school officials who in turn directed teachers' work, then teachers should have a voice in choosing school officials, the reasoning went. Male teachers could vote; however, because increasing numbers of teachers were women, and women could not vote, then many teachers effectively had no voice in or control of their own working conditions or salaries. To remedy this unjust situation, a few Midwestern and Western communities granted women school suffrage, or the right to vote in school-related elections. Eventually, entire states formalized the practice by passing legislation assuring women the right to vote on school matters. By 1910, twenty-four states had granted women school suffrage (Blackwell 1904; Grenfell 1904; Price 1898; Woody 1929, 2, 441–44).

Suffrage activists then argued that if women exercised their franchise responsibly for school-related matters, they also should be trusted with full suffrage.

They further contended that because the political process could be corrupt, then women's full suffrage might lend a moral tone to democracy. Women could safeguard moral principles in the sometimes-tainted political realm. In 1869, the male citizens of Wyoming concurred with this reasoning and voted to extend full suffrage to women. Other Midwestern and Western states followed suit over the next fifty years in a development that gradually offered women significant new power in civic affairs (Bjrkman and Porritt 1917; Anonymous 1914a). Women's work in public schooling, then, provided important justification for their eventual right to full suffrage.

Enfranchisement was not women's only means of affecting the political process, however. The citizens of some states not only believed that women should vote, but that they also should be eligible for some public offices. They especially should be allowed to hold positions for which there was a shortage of competent men, such as in school supervision. United States Commissioner of Education John Eaton wrote in 1873: "The difficulty experienced in finding fully-educated men for the various departments of school-work has for some years past led to an engagement of women in this work on the ground that cultivated women are more frequently available for the performance of such duty than equally cultivated men" (Eaton 1874). A number of states passed legislation permitting the employment of women in various school offices. For example, in 1888, California passed the following law: "Women over the age of 21 years, who are citizens of the United States and this state, shall be eligible to all educational offices within the state, except those from which they are excluded by the constitution." Voters in eleven counties elected women superintendents soon afterward (Anonymous 1896, 960; Woody 1929, 1, 516).

Occasionally women won school elections even before laws clarified their right to do so. Julia Addington's friends persuaded her to run for a county superintendency in Iowa, though she initially resisted. When she won the seat, her opponent challenged the victory because, as a woman, she was not legally a citizen, and only citizens could hold public offices. The state attorney general, however, issued a strong statement favoring Addington's right to hold office, and in 1876, the state passed the following law: "No person shall be deemed ineligible, by reason of sex, to any school office in the State of Iowa" (Anthony and Harper 1900, 627-28, 1417).

In some cases, schools needed women's leadership services so desperately that citizens sometimes elected women to offices even before these candidates could vote for themselves. In 1879, sixteen states allowed women to hold elected school offices before granting them suffrage (Woody 1929, 2, 443). To protest this situation, a member of the New Hampshire legislature in 1878 argued in house debate: "If women are capable of holding office they are also capable of saying who shall hold it." The legislature then passed a bill granting school suffrage to New Hampshire women (Anthony and Harper 1900, 375).

Once women could vote and then run for school offices, they started winning. Some campaigns offered them easy victories, because previous incumbents either obviously had neglected their duties or had succumbed to the temptation of political corruption. Even with competent and honest opponents, though, women sometimes succeeded in their campaigns with the active help of groups of women. For instance, in 1890, Sarah Christie Stevens won her race for the superintendency of the Blue Earth County schools (Minnesota) because, as reporters suggested, the "ladies worked in getting out voters with the energy of male politicians" (Christie 1983, 250).

When women assumed their newly won positions, they quickly discovered that the public held them to a higher standard of performance than men. Two years after winning the county superintendency, Sarah Stevens lost her bid for reelection because the man who challenged her charged that she had neglected to visit every school in her district each year. Although school visitations constituted one of the county superintendent's most important duties, officeholders found it exceedingly difficult to travel to each of the many remote one-room schoolhouses, especially since the bitterly cold, long winters of the Northern prairie made rural travel impossible for months at a time. Few county superintendents managed to visit every school annually, and when they did, it usually only happened in small or urban counties. Sensing that her opponent was gaining an advantage with these attacks, Stevens appealed to the state superintendent for endorsement of her reelection because he had witnessed the improved conditions of schools under her leadership. He wrote back: "You asked if [women] are in every way as well qualified as men. I think not. While in most particulars I think they accomplish their work as well as men in similar positions, they are not as well able to endure exposure in the winter in riding over prairies and through the woods to visit schools." Finding little support from the state superintendent, Stevens endured the blistering attacks of her opponent, who defeated her handily. Interestingly, once in office, he succeeded in visiting far fewer schools than Stevens, a shortcoming for which he was not criticized. In the end, he had won the position by exploiting the perception of women's physical frailty (Christie 1983, 252). Even though Stevens had performed notably better than her opponent in this respect, she would have been above reproach only if her record had been flawless, a standard to which he fell far short.

Political ordeals such as Stevens' were repeated in districts around the country and contributed to women's reluctance to run for office. Carrie Chapman Catt described the problem when she wrote, "The candidate is likely to be forced to wade through mud to her victory, to make concessions to interests which nauseate her soul and to arrive at the goal with a reputation in tatters" (1924). Their opponents routinely barraged women candidates for school offices with a wide range of criticisms. One minister justified this treatment when he explained: "If woman steps out of her sphere, and demands to be and to do what men do, to enter political life, to enter the professions, to wrestle with us for office and employments and gains, she must understand that she will have to take the low prices as well as the high places of life. If she goes to Congress, she must also go to the heavy drudgery of earth" (Todd 1887).

In spite of these challenges, after the Civil War, women began winning superintendencies, mainly elected county positions. They tended to invest themselves fully in their work to prove that women could excel in positions of public responsibility; however, voters in some states regarded the employment of women school superintendents as a temporary expedient or an experiment. As a result, some early women superintendents faced critical evaluations to determine the worthiness of their continued employment. In 1873, when Illinois first allowed women to hold school offices, ten women won county superintendencies. At the end of their four-year terms, the president of the state teachers' association wrote an evaluation of their performance in four fundamental areas.

First, he explained that the women had handled the financial aspects of their work with great care and competence. "In many of these counties the financial affairs were in the greatest confusion when the ladies came into office, strange irregularities were discovered. In every instance these crookednesses have been straightened out, the finances put upon a surer basis, hundreds, we believe thousands, of dollars of bad debts have been collected, treasurers and directors have been induced to keep their books with greater care and in better shape, reckless expenditure of school funds has been discouraged, and directors encouraged to expend the money for things which will permanently benefit the schools." Second, the women handled their legal concerns with skill and diplomacy, where, as he explained, "scores of controversies were referred to her, and there has never been a single appeal from her decisions." Third, because all ten of the women had been teachers, they comfortably worked with teachers and capably offered practical suggestions. Finally, the evaluator indicated that all of the women managed the details of their work in an outstanding manner. He said, "In looking after the details of official work, those tiresome minutiae so often left at 'loose ends,' producing endless confusion, woman has shown great aptitude." He concluded that every woman superintendent had doubled the efficiency of the office, and some had produced four- or even ten-fold increases (Anthony and Harper 1900, 575–78).

Hardworking, diligent women superintendents eventually won valuable support from a variety of places. Women in Colorado won suffrage in 1893, and within a decade, women accounted for the majority of the state's county superintendents. Many of these individual women were hailed as "the most efficient officer we have ever had in this county" (Woodbury 1909, 128–44). The Commissioner of Education in 1880 applauded women's service to education:

> Carefully considering the position of woman in the work of educa-
> tion, what she has done and may do as a teacher, what her nature
> and experience may fit her to do better than man as an officer,
> inspector, or superintendent, as facts have illustrated these points in
> this and other countries, I have favored the extension of suffrage to
> her in all matters relating to education and the opening of appropri-
> ate offices to her in connection with institutions and systems of
> instruction. (Anonymous 1901, 26)

With such a strong endorsement from the commissioner, as well as with broad-
ening bases of support, women made rapid gains in the superintendency in the
late 1800s and early 1900s. They especially won elected county positions in Midwestern and Western states where women had enjoyed suffrage long before their
Eastern sisters.

As women won increasing numbers of county superintendencies, several
state superintendencies, and a few city executive positions, women's rights
activists lauded these victories as harbingers of women's eventual equal rights.
Enthusiastic writers filled suffrage publications with tallies of elected women
school officers and other evidence of women's growing political clout. The Blue
Book (1917) contained concise summaries of women's political victories around
the country so suffrage activists could propound these speaking points at rallies,
in congressional hearings, and in newsletters (Bjrkman and Porritt 1917,
30–40). The 1917 Woman Suffrage Yearbook concluded that women accounted
for half of the county superintendents in the United States, and most of them
served in Western equal suffrage states. By that time, seventeen different women
had served as state school superintendents as well (Anonymous 1917, 166). In
reviewing the records of these women state officers, one suffragist noted that
"Miss Permeal French has been several times re-elected as state superintendent
of public instruction of Idaho. Governor Steunenburg declared her to be the best
the state ever had. The same compliment by the people and by the governor was
paid Mrs. Helen Grenfell, of Colorado. She had the largest vote ever cast for a
candidate in the state, ran ahead of the ticket for governor, and for president of
the United States" (Cooley 1904, 129–30). Clearly, women's victories in superintendent races were a source of great pride and hope for suffragists around the
country.

The overall number of women superintendents increased quickly around
the turn of the century. In 1896, women held 228 county superintendencies, two
state superintendencies, and twelve city superintendencies (Woody 1929, 1,
517). Just five years later, the Report of the Commissioner of Education indicated
that 288 women held county superintendencies for a 26 percent increase
(Anonymous 1902, 1228–29). By 1913, there were 495 women county superintendents—more than doubling the 1896 figure in less than twenty years. Also,

women had won state superintendencies in Colorado, Idaho, Washington, and Wyoming (Woody 1929, 1, 517; Anonymous 1917, 165-67).

The rapid increase in women superintendents occurred as the women's suffrage movement entered its most active phase in the early decades of the twentieth century. By this time, many states west of the Mississippi had already granted women full suffrage. Women's suffrage associations in the Northeast sponsored important public demonstrations and vigorously campaigned for national suffrage. Since school superintendencies were among the first public positions for which women were eligible, the strengthening suffrage movement effectively translated into votes for women superintendents.

MUTUAL OBLIGATIONS: WOMEN SUPERINTENDENTS, TEACHERS, AND WOMEN ACTIVISTS

Women's suffrage was not the only focus of organized women and their allies, though. In their exhaustive, multivolume account, *The History of Woman Suffrage*, Susan B. Anthony and Ida Husted Harper detailed the rise of an immense variety of women's associations in the late 1800s. Some groups addressed social problems like alcoholism, child labor, and poverty, all of which plagued an increasingly industrialized, urban America. Others were strictly social in nature. Eventually, women's groups appeared in virtually every community, and many of these were affiliated with state and national organizations. By 1900, well over a million women belonged to clubs that comprised the National Council of Women (Anthony and Harper 1900, 1042-44). Beyond the organizations represented by this umbrella group, around 3 million women belonged to other similar groups. Altogether, Anthony and Harper estimated that well over 4 million women belonged to women's clubs and associations in 1900, representing over one-tenth of the 37 million females reported in the U.S. census. And women's association membership continued to climb (1900, 1043-44).

Women joined associations for a variety of reasons. They came to know each other, enjoy each other's company, and understand concerns uniting women generally. The club movement broke the isolation that many middle-class women experienced in their daily lives and fostered a connection among women beyond their circles of neighbors and kin. In addition to the social contact of club meetings, women felt enriched by the intellectual stimulation of educational programs, guest speakers, journals, and association conferences.

Women also developed important public leadership skills by participating in these groups, since the growth of associations required members to understand social organizations, develop persuasive speaking and writing skills, devise strategies for political action, manage finances, and master other skills routinely required of men by their work, but generally denied to women (Anthony and

Harper 1900, 1042–43). Historian Joan Burstyn further explains that the leadership skills developed in women's associations were not cast simply from the mold of traditional patriarchal organizations. Rather, members of women's associations tended to minimize hierarchical power configurations while instead fostering cooperation and shared power. This is because women as a class understood what it felt like to be excluded in decision making, especially in the political and legal realms (Burstyn 1980, 71).

At first, however, women hesitated to engage in political work because it seemed foreign to their experience, inappropriate, uninteresting, or even beneath their moral dignity. Most groups eventually discovered that they needed political power to accomplish their aims. In time, women's associations became quite powerful, adept forces on a number of political issues (Anthony and Harper 1900, 1071–72).

Although women's associations initially dedicated their efforts to their specifically stated causes, by the turn of the century, many of them actively supported suffrage. Because these organizations had already discovered the importance of political lobbying, they knew that women would have far more political clout if they had full enfranchisement. The Women's Christian Temperance Union (WCTU), for instance, resisted championing women's suffrage at first, but in the late 1800s, members of the organization became convinced of the need for women's vote to advance their crusade. Members became tireless advocates of women's suffrage, leading Anthony and Harper to explain that "considered as a body there are no more active workers for woman suffrage [than are in the WCTU]" (1900, 1071). As women's clubs and suffrage organizations increasingly joined forces, the larger women's movement became a formidable national political force in the early decades of the twentieth century.

When women first won suffrage in individual states and then full national suffrage in 1920, their power in some respects escalated to new levels. The political pressure of women's associations could no longer be dismissed as an irritating inconvenience, or as irrelevant. Women members voted, and they cared.

Women also frequently voted in concert. And many women were determined to bring to the polls their concerns for social improvement and moral elevation. An editorial from the *Los Angeles Express* captured something of the sense of moral victory as well as victory for morals represented by women's enfranchisement in California: "Those who were formerly in the habit of claiming that the ballot in the hands of woman would only multiply the number of ballots without altering the moral bearing of the ballot-box for either weal or woe were clearly mistaken. Woman has added a great moral force to the ballot in California. She has added very materially in humanizing the party platform and vitalizing the issue" (Anonymous 1914b).

Women teachers remained an active component of the larger women's movement during this time. This is not surprising, because by 1910, around a half million American women worked in education in some capacity (U.S. Government, Office of Education 1921, 10). Teachers' organizations also expanded rapidly during these years as they rallied for such causes as improved classroom conditions and equal pay for women teachers. Beyond women teachers' clubs and associations, publications sprouted bearing such names as *The Women's Voice* and *Public School Advocate*. Teachers' unions also organized in many cities and some became mighty political forces.

Not only did teachers participate actively in the women's movement, but so did women superintendents. Their records of achievement demonstrate that women superintendents typically valued their service in women's associations (Sicherman et al. 1980). Some women superintendents viewed their official duties as a means of advancing the various goals of the women's movement. One certain cause of women's activism was the elimination of political corruption. When Ella Flagg Young served as the superintendent of Chicago schools, as well as the president of the National Education Association (NEA), she endeavored to root out the ploys of dishonest officials who skimmed money from public and association coffers. In both the NEA and Chicago, she met with considerable resistance from entrenched forces. Shortly after her election to the presidency of the NEA, Young discovered that a trust fund of membership dues had been invested in questionable deals by Nicholas Murray Butler, president of Columbia University, and a man who "controlled" the NEA. Butler responded by hatching a campaign to overturn her election, alleging that many newly enfranchised female teachers in the association had cast votes illegally. His effort failed, but then he blocked an investigation of the trust fund. He even resorted to personal threats when he sent one of his associates to Chicago to tell Margaret Haley, the president of the Chicago Teachers Federation, and Young's friend, that if Young did not back off the investigation, "They're going to kill Mrs. Young. I mean it. They're going to kill Mrs. Young." Young toned down her pressure, but within a short time, Butler resigned as trustee of the fund. Young had won this battle. However, through the rest of her career, she continued to feel the aftershocks of this encounter with Butler's nationwide NEA network of supporters (Smith 1979, 164–73).

In Chicago, Young also faced serious opposition from members of the school board who had regularly received kickbacks from textbook publishers. She sought to end these kickbacks and instead chose texts by their quality alone. Some board members also wanted to use school land for personal speculative business ventures rather than for school purposes. Again, Young prevented these misuses of public school properties, especially because schools needed funds desperately for teachers' salaries and other educational expenses. Her resistance to these corrupt efforts eventually led the board to vote her out of office in 1913 (Bass 1915).

Young was not without her resources, though. Social activist Jane Addams rallied thousands of women in a public demonstration of support for Young when the board initially ousted her. In the end, Young was reinstated shortly after her dismissal, but grumbling board members vowed that they should get rid of the political influence of women altogether (Bass 1915). By 1915, the cumulative animosity of board members had taken its toll and, again, Young was forced to step down, this time for good (Mead 1914).

Female superintendents found support not only from groups of women such as the one led by Jane Addams, but also from teachers and teachers' organizations. For example, teachers elected Susan Dorsey president of the California Teachers' Association (Southern section) before she served as the Los Angeles superintendent. During her nine years as superintendent, she maintained ties with teachers by laboring tirelessly for their higher salaries, right to sabbatical leaves, and job tenure. Ella Flagg Young, while serving as the director of the Chicago Normal School, regularly held social and professional meetings at her house for all of the teachers in her school. Once appointed superintendent, Young remained connected with teachers by campaigning for their higher salaries and greater participation in school administration. She developed strong friendships with many of the teachers in the Chicago schools, including members of the Chicago Teachers' Federation. Teachers trusted Young to the extent that at times they called on her to mediate disputes within the Federation (Bennett 1915, 261–77; Smith 1979, 122–27).

Josephine Corliss Preston, elected to the Washington state superintendency in 1913, offered single women teachers an even more personal form of support for their work. Having been a teacher for eleven years before moving into administration, Preston understood firsthand the problems women faced in having to board with families in the school district. She firmly believed that women needed privacy, places of their own so that they could relax and think. When she became the Walla Walla County superintendent, she devised a plan for women to have their own homes, or "teacherages." Then she made sure that every teacher in her district had such a place to stay. She enlisted the help of the National Federation of Women's Clubs to expand the project to the entire state. The Federation not only launched the Washington state teacherage campaign, but Women's Federations around the country also joined the effort. Women in Texas, for example, were so inspired with the idea that they "built more 'teacherages' in one year than Washington did in ten." In time, even the U.S. Commissioner of Education took up the cause, so that by the early 1920s, large numbers of teacherages had been built around the country (Griswold 1923).

Teacherages meant a great deal to the women who lived in them. For the first time, tens of thousands of single women could live comfortably on their own without having to board with their own or another community family. Preston regarded it as an essential part of her personal and work responsibilities to foster strong, mutually supportive relationships between herself and the teachers. These relationships were then fortified with the assistance of the larger community of women. Eventually, teachers nationwide rewarded Preston's efforts by electing her president of the NEA (Griswold 1923; Maxcy 1979).

Women school administrators not only maintained close connections with teachers, but in time they also established a national association for themselves. During the 1915 NEA meeting in Oakland, California, a group of women administrators gathered to form the National Council of Administrative Women in Education. Thereafter, the group met twice a year, once during the regular NEA meeting and again during the NEA Department of Superintendence meeting. Eighteen states formed affiliates of the national group, some of them quite active.

In the end, women school superintendents emerged as part of the broad-based women's movement of the late 1800s and early 1900s. The discrimination women faced as they attempted to expand their sphere of influence into public service and even into school leadership was generally too great for them to conquer alone; yet the strong, supportive constituency provided by the women's movement gave many aspiring women administrators the boost they needed to win their positions. In turn, women superintendents endeavored to uphold the moral ideals of women's activism. The complex, mutually supportive relationships among women superintendents, teachers, women's association members, and suffrage activists provided the essential network for women's rise to school leadership positions. Historian Margaret Gribskov summarizes: "The rise and fall of the woman school administrator approximates the peaks and valleys of the first American feminist movement of the late 1800s and early 1900s, and the feminist movement was a crucial factor in producing the large numbers of women administrators of that period" (1980, 77). After enactment of suffrage, however, the activity of women's groups continued, but much less feverishly. A steady dissipation of women's support networks presaged the eventual decline in the number of women superintendents, and new efforts to erode women's hard-won political gains would meet with little resistance.

TURNING THE LADIES OUT: THE APPOINTIVE SYSTEM

The women's suffrage movement had sparked the emergence of women school administrators for at least two reasons. First, the quest for women's rights had triggered the larger movement of organized women's groups, many of which actively supported the candidacy of women for school offices. Second, suffrage had given women power at the ballot box, which allowed them to affect the political process directly, to become, as some had hoped, a political constituency.

Democracy, as a concept as well as a practice, clearly meant a great deal to newly enfranchised women.

As women cast their first ballots, however, groups of superintendents began pushing for reforms in school district governance and the superintendency that would have the effect of removing school administration from the electoral process. Threatened by suffrage era gains in women's rights, and stinging from widespread criticisms of school inefficiency, many superintendents sought to bolster their collectively sagging image. An important means of maintaining their public viability involved adopting the methods and trappings of well-trained scientific experts, much like the Taylor-inspired efficiency engineers popularly deployed in industries of the time. If superintendents could become clipboard and stopwatch toting efficiency experts and convince the public of their merit, which, incidentally, would not be determined directly by the ballot, then they might be able to deflect much criticism (Callahan 1962).

The problem with experts, though, was that many superintendents believed the public could not be trusted to recognize and choose expert talent. They argued, therefore, that the superintendency should become strictly an appointed rather than an elected position for which candidates were selected based on their expert credentials. Democracy would be preserved through this system because the public would elect representatives, such as school board members or commissioners, who then would appoint superintendents. Since this strategy emerged just as women were winning suffrage and some elected school leadership positions, it is plausible that the movement toward the appointed superintendency was partly inspired by the fear of women's vote.

Iowa, for example, granted women school suffrage in 1893, though a number of women had already been elected as superintendents. However, immediately after school suffrage was enacted, superintendents began protesting. The *Journal of Education*, in 1894, reported that one county superintendent said: "The principal need was that the superintendent should be a better trained man and should be divorced from politics. There are forty-nine changes this year, and it would no doubt be better if many of these officers could have been retained" (Anonymous 1894e).

Colorado granted women full suffrage in 1893. Women quickly established their political presence around the state, and elected officials knew this change had the potential to alter the face of politics in every locality (Anonymous 1894b). When State Superintendent Murray addressed the winter meeting of county superintendents that year, he indicated that thirty-eight out of fifty-six county superintendents had just been defeated, including "some of the best men of the state" (Anonymous 1894d). In response, male educators organized and devised strategies for negotiating these changes. The *Journal* subsequently noted that a select committee of twenty-one persons had met with the state superintendent to consider "How to Remove the Schools from Politics," a discussion led by Aaron Gove, superintendent of Denver schools (Anonymous 1894a). Meanwhile, women around the state voted in their first election, and their enthusiasm and high turnout led the *Journal* to explain the great excitement: "Unquestionably woman did it" (Anonymous 1894c). That same year, State Superintendent Murray—who had been concerned about the recent heavy turnover of superintendents—was defeated by a woman candidate, Mrs. A. J. Peavy, who was later succeeded by a long line of women state superintendents (Anonymous 1917, 165; Woodbury 1909, 122-46; Brown 1898, 16-52). No doubt, the move to take the Colorado superintendency out of politics was inspired by the fear of women's significant collective power at the ballot.

A 1909 editorial, printed in the *Fresno Republican*, demonstrated a similar concern among California school officials:

> If there is any public place that ought not to be elective, it is that of any sort of school superintendent. But there is only one policy in regard to a school superintendent or a school teacher, and that is to get the most competent person available, regardless of other considerations. Popular election is notoriously not the way to do that. When an educational office is elective, it is always filled by a local man. Other things being reasonably equal, the local man is, of course, entitled to the preference, on account of his advantage of local knowledge. But teaching is a profession, and its largest places should be filled by its men of largest professional knowledge and tested capacity. If this happens under the elective system, it is an accident, and a rare one. Under the appointive system, it is the usual result. Our city superintendents and principals, and our university and normal school presidents and teachers, are usually the best of their kind. The exceptions are rare enough to be regarded as remarkable. Yet not one in ten of them could have got his place by election. Probably not one in three of the county superintendents could have got his place by any other process. This is the sober fact, and if we want our state and county school systems put under the leadership of the real educational leaders we must change the system. (Anonymous 1909)

Though the author made no overt mention of women and used only masculine pronouns, his ideas had important implications for women superintendents. When he penned this piece, women held nearly 40 percent of county superintendencies in California (a little over "one in three"), the elected position about which he complained, and their numbers were rising. On the other hand, women held none of the thirty-three appointed city superintendencies, which he believed were filled by men who were "the best of their kind." When this piece was printed, the campaign for women's suffrage in California was well under way and would succeed two years later. Woman's suffrage clearly formed the contextual backdrop for his words. With momentum quickly building for electing women to school superintendencies, it appeared that women might take over the county superintendency, just as they had in other Western states.

An appointive system, however, would effectively halt women's progress into school leadership positions. Women rarely received appointments to superintendencies because they tended to be excluded from the male political networks responsible for placing most superintendent candidates. This superintendent selection method quietly and effectively removed women from contention for school leadership opportunities. A more public means of selection, or one that explicitly invoked gender as a factor, would have raised the ire of organized women's groups.

Decades later, the NEA formed the Committee on the County Superintendents Problems, which released its report in 1922, two years after enactment of the national suffrage amendment. Committee members lamented that "one does not have to study the rural-school problem long until he becomes convinced that its success or failure centers in and around the office of the county superintendent." Their report concluded by strongly suggesting that future county superintendents receive academic and professional training—available to men, but rarely to women—and that the office should be removed from politics "by having him selected very much as a city superintendent is now selected by a board small in number, selected especially for the purpose of conducting school affairs." Further, the committee urged the NEA to "lend its force, energy, and prestige to the support of such a campaign" (Driver 1922).

CONCLUSION

Turn-of-the-century women's activists drew much of their strength from and centered many of their aspirations around education. Education helped them prepare for greater roles in public work. Educated women created a profession for themselves, one complete with positions of public power and influence, such as the elected school superintendency. Ella Flagg Young even dared to proclaim in her 1909 acceptance speech for the Chicago superintendency that women eventually would come to dominate school leadership, much as they already had come to dominate the ranks of teachers. With the monumental nationwide energy of women's activists supporting women candidates for elected superintendencies, it appeared that women might eventually control their own profession.

Women's assumption of power in school affairs would not come without resistance, though. As women increasingly won superintendencies, therefore displacing men—some of whom were quite powerful in organized superintendency associations—the move to make the superintendency an appointed position quietly gained support. Traditionalists justified this change with public rhetoric describing the need for qualified, expert school superintendents. They did not dare speak publicly about removing women from politics, which would have risked powerful backlash from organized women's groups. Yet the tight linkage between women's suffrage victories and regional efforts to remove the superintendency from politics suggests the possibility that, in fact, the appointive system was less about expertise and more about limiting women's growing power in school affairs.

REFERENCES

Anonymous. 1894a. Colorado. *Journal of Education*, May 3, p. 284.

———. 1894b. Colorado. *Journal of Education*, May 31, p. 348.

———. 1894c. Colorado school election. *Journal of Education*, May 17, p. 312.

———. 1894d. Colorado teachers. *Journal of Education*, January 11, p. 28.

———. 1894e. Iowa teachers. *Journal of Education*, January 18, p. 44.

———. 1896. School legislation in the United States. *Report of the Commissioner of Education, 1894–1895*. Washington, D.C.: Government Printing Office.

———. 1901. Women as voters and school officers. *Report of the Commissioner of Education, 1880*. Syracuse, N.Y.: C. W. Bardeen, p. 26.

———. 1902. *Report of the Commissioner of Education, 1900–1901*, vol. 2. Washington, D.C.: Government Printing Office.

———. 1909. Out of politics. *American School Board Journal* 38 (March): 6.

———. 1914a. Woman suffrage a success. *The Woman Voter* 6 (11): 14–16.

———. 1914b. *The Woman Voter* 5 (1): 26.

———. 1917. *The woman suffrage yearbook*. New York: National Woman Suffrage Publishing Company, Inc.

Anthony, S. B. and I. Harper (eds.). 1900. *History of woman suffrage*. Vol. 4. (Reprint Salem, N.H.: Ayer Co., 1985).

Barry, K. 1988. *Susan B. Anthony: A biography of a singular feminist*. New York: Ballantine Books.

Bass, Mrs. G. 1915. Mrs. Young and the Chicago schools. *School and Society* (October 23), pp. 605–06.

Bennett, H. C. 1915. *American women in civic work*. New York: Dodd, Mead, and Co.

Bjrkman, F. M. and A. G. Porritt (eds.). 1917. *The blue book: Woman suffrage history arguments, and results*. New York: National Woman Suffrage Publishing, Co., Inc.

Blackwell, A. S. 1904. Progress of equal suffrage. Political equality leaflets. Warren, Ohio. National American Woman Suffrage Association.

Blount, J. M. 1998. *Destined to rule the schools: Women and the superintendency, 1873–1995*. Albany, N.Y.: State University of New York Press.

Brown, J. G. 1898. *The history of equal suffrage in Colorado, 1868-1898.* Denver: News Job Printing Co.

Burstyn, J. 1974. Catharine Beecher and the education of American women. *New England Quarterly* 47: 386-403.

————. 1980. Historical perspectives on women in educational leadership. In S. K. Biklen and M. Brannigan (eds.), *Women and Educational Leadership.* Lexington, Mass.: Lexington Books, pp. 65-75.

Butcher, P. S. 1986. Education for equality: Women's rights periodicals and women's higher education, 1849-1920. *History of Higher Education Annual* 6: 63-74.

Callahan, R. 1962. *Education and the cult of efficiency.* Chicago: The University of Chicago Press.

Catt, C. C. 1924. The cave man complex vs. woman suffrage. *The Woman Citizen* (April 5), p. 16.

Christie, J. 1983. Sarah Christie Stevens: Schoolwoman. *Minnesota History* (Summer), pp. 245-54.

Cooley, W. H. 1904. *The new womanhood.* New York: Broadway Publishing Co.

Driver, L. L. 1922. Report of the committee on the county superintendents' problems. *Addresses and proceedings of the National Education Association.* Washington, D.C.: National Education Association, pp. 293-303.

Eaton, J. 1874. Women as school officers. *Report of the Commissioner of Education, 1873.* Washington, D.C.: Government Printing Office, CXXXIII.

Grenfell, H. L. 1904. The ballot and the schools. Political equality leaflets. Warren, Ohio. National American Woman Suffrage Association.

Gribskov, M. 1980. Feminism and the woman school administrator. In S. K. Biklen and M. Brannigan (eds.), *Women and educational leadership.* Lexington, Mass.: Lexington Books.

Griswold, Mrs. W. S. 1923. The rural school's friend. *The Woman Citizen* (June 16), p. 10.

Larson, T. A. 1980. Wyoming's contribution to the regional and national women's rights movement. *Annals of Wyoming* 52 (1): 2-15.

Maxcy, S. J. 1979. The teacherage in American rural education. *The Journal of General Education* 30 (4): 267-74.

Mead, G. H. 1914. A heckling school board and an educational stateswoman. *Survey* 31: 443-44.

Norton, M. B. 1979. The paradox of "women's sphere." In C. R. Berkin and M. B. Norton (eds.), *Women of America: A history.* Boston: Houghton Mifflin Co.

Noun, L. R. 1993. Carrie Lane Chapman Catt and her Mason City experience. *Palimpsest* (fall), pp. 130-44.

Phelps, E. M. (ed.). 1912. *Selected articles on woman suffrage.* (Second and revised edition). Minneapolis: The H.W. Wilson Company.

Price, E. H. E. 1898. School suffrage and other limited suffragists in the United States. *Hearing on House Joint Resolution 68, House Judiciary Committee,* February 15, pp. 3-5.

Scott, A. F. 1979. The ever widening circle: The diffusion of feminist values from the Troy Female Seminary, 1822-1872. *History of Education Quarterly* 19 (spring), pp. 3-25.

Sewall, M. W. 1885. Woman's work in education. *Proceedings of the National Educational Association.* Boston: J. E. Farwell & Co.

———. 1887. Debate on woman suffrage in the Senate of the United States, 2nd session, 49th Congress, January 25, 1887.

Sicherman, B., C. H. Green, I. Kantrov, and H. Walker (eds.). 1980. Betsey Mix Cowles. In *Notable American women.* Cambridge: Belknap Press, pp. 393-94.

Smith, J. 1979. *Ella Flagg Young: Portrait of a leader.* Ames, Iowa: Educational Studies Press and the Iowa State University Research Foundation.

Stanton, E. C., S. B. Anthony, and M. J. Gage (eds.). 1881. *History of woman suffrage.* Vol. 1. New York: Fowler & Wells (Reprint Salem, N.H.: Ayer Co., 1985).

Todd, J. 1887. *Woman's rights.* Boston: Lee and Shepard.

U.S. Government, Office of Education. 1921. *Biennial survey of education 1916-1918.* Washington, D.C.: Office of Education.

Woodbury, H. L. S. 1909. *Equal suffrage.* New York: Collegiate Equal Suffrage League.

Woody, T. 1929. *History of women's education.* Vols. 1 and 2. New York: The Science Press.

CHAPTER TWO

Women and the Superintendency

What Do We Really Know?

MARILYN TALLERICO

M y goal for this chapter is to acquaint readers with salient research and to provide a brief overview of literature relevant to women and the superintendency in the United States. I focus on published work, unless specifically noted otherwise. My hope is to (1) present a summary both accessible and interesting to a broad professional audience, and (2) inspire other investigations into this growing field of study.

After general comments on the historical context of research on the superintendency, I follow with a more specific summary of studies related to women superintendents. I conclude with suggestions for future research.

THE BIG PICTURE

Of the approximately seventy-five years worth of extant scholarship relevant to the superintendency, most studies have either relied primarily on white, male samples, or have made no mention of the gender, racial, or ethnic backgrounds of their subjects. Only within the past twenty years has attention been directed specifically to female superintendents or superintendents of color. When persons other than white males have been included in research, they have most often been studied in aggregates, for example, in studies of African-American school administrators or of female administrators, including principals, central office staff, and other administrative roles along with superintendents. Moreover, even in some of the most recent and largest-scale national surveys specific to the superintendency (Glass 1992; National School Boards Association 1992), data have only intermittently been disaggregated by sex, race, or ethnicity, and have almost

never been analyzed by sex *and* race/ethnicity. Such variables are important for
a more complete understanding of leadership dynamics for superintendents,
given that educational administration is so highly stratified by race, gender, and
ethnicity (Bell and Chase 1993; Shakeshaft 1989; Ortiz 1982; Ortiz and Marshall 1988).

In general, research on women and the superintendency may be conceptu-
alized in terms of three interrelated and overlapping domains: profiles, patterns,
and practice. Explanations of each follow.

The first, "profiles," refers to studies that help us understand demographic
characteristics and superintendents' attitudes, opinions, or perceptions of
selected issues. For example, this research seeks answers to questions such as:
How many male and female superintendents are there, and how do current
counts compare to previous years'? (Bell and Chase 1993; Blount 1995; Glass
1992). Who are the black women superintendents, and where are they located?
(Jackson 1996). What are women superintendents' perceptions of the benefits of
their position? (Grady, Ourada-Sieb, and Wesson 1994). What is the average age
of women superintendents, and do they view discriminatory hiring practices as
a major or minor problem? (Glass 1992).

A second domain, "patterns," refers to research that examines career paths
to the superintendency, mobility from one incumbency to another, and other
issues related to access, mentoring, sponsorship, selection, retention, or exit.
Such studies ask questions like: What career patterns exist for women, men, and
minorities? (Ortiz 1982). What influences or shapes those patterns? How do gatekeepers talk about hiring, working with, and observing women school superintendents? (Chase and Bell, 1990). Why have some women exited the superintendency? (see Beekley in this book; Tallerico and Burstyn 1996).

A third domain, "practice," encompasses a wide range of inquiry that seeks
to understand the nature of superintendents' work—what superintendents do,
how they experience the superintendency, how they exercise leadership, and how
superintendents' experiences are shaped by context. Often included here are the
various educational, managerial, and political roles enacted by superintendents,
the latter of which draw attention to issues of power, visibility, collaboration, conflict, and governance shared with school boards. Since much of the research
summarized in this chapter falls into the domain of experience, I will cite more
specific issues in the section titled "Practice."

PROFILES

Profile data on educational administrators contribute to our understanding of the
broader sociopolitical environment within which women superintendents work.
The white, male dominance of that environment has existed since the position

of superintendent was first created by school boards in the late nineteenth century (Crowson 1987; Tyack and Hansot 1982). However, accurate counts of superintendents (and other school administrators) by gender have been difficult to come by (Shakeshaft 1989; Wheatley 1981; Yeakey, Johnston, and Adkison 1986). And specific counts by both gender and race are largely nonexistent; that is, "in most reports available on the public school superintendency, data are reported by gender only, or race only" (Bell 1992, 24).

What *do* we know? The most recent national studies tell us that 6.6 percent (Glass 1992) or 7.1 percent (Montenegro 1993) of all superintendencies are occupied by women. Bell and Chase (1993) report that, specific to K-12 school districts, 5.6 percent have women superintendents. Montenegro's (1993) research found that, including Washington, D.C., and the thirty-seven states that reported counts of racial minorities in the superintendency, 1.4 percent are black, 1.5 percent are Hispanic, 0.5 percent are American Indian, and 0.1 percent are Asian or Pacific Islanders, for an aggregate total of approximately 3.5 percent racial minority superintendents. Bell and Chase (1993) were the first to provide numerical profiles of grades K-12 women superintendents by race and ethnicity. They found that in the thirty-nine states reporting data for the period 1991–1992, there were a total of 460 women superintendents, 424 of whom were white, nineteen black, nine Hispanic, four Asian, three American Indian, and one woman of unknown race/ethnicity.

Not surprisingly, a theme common to the conclusions of all of these researchers is that women and persons of color continue to be woefully underrepresented in the superintendency. Banks (1995) notes that

> Justification for increasing the number of women in educational administration is frequently based on the disproportionate number of women who are classroom teachers compared to the number of women who hold administrative positions [whereas] increasing the number of minorities in educational administration is frequently justified on the basis of the growing number of students of color in the public schools. (p. 70)

But documenting scarcity is not the only outcome of research profiling women superintendents. Grady et al. (1994) interviewed fifty-one female superintendents from urban and rural areas across the United States to examine their perceptions of the positive aspects of the superintendency. They identified multiple sources of job satisfaction, including making a difference, creating change, providing direction, meeting children's needs, having control, and working with people. They found that most women felt quite fulfilled in their roles and that the benefits of superintending include the variety of work involved and the many opportunities to increase skills and grow on the job.

Other sources of profile data are the decennial surveys of superintendents by the American Association of School Administrators (see Cunningham and Hentges 1982; Glass 1992). These provide a broad range of information about the personal characteristics of superintendents, their career patterns, their opinions on key issues in education, the characteristics of their communities and districts, and their relationships with board members. Their most recent data (Glass 1992) are disaggregated by sex and minority status for some of the information reported by their 1,734 respondents. For example, Glass (1992) found that women and minority superintendents have more academic degrees, are more liberal politically, and accord a higher priority to curriculum and instructional activities than do white, male superintendents. Female, male, and ethnic minority superintendents all identified finances as being the highest-ranked problem facing their school boards. Glass (1992) concludes that, overall, "the differences between women and minority superintendents compared to their white male counterparts are not great" (p. xii).

Other investigations that enrich our understanding of the profiles of this key leadership role ask, "Where are the superintendencies of women and persons of color?" Jackson's (1996) presentation at the annual meeting of the American Educational Research Association is one of very few empirical works (other than dissertation studies) focused on African-American women superintendents. She identified a total of thirty-two black women superintendents in the United States during the period 1993-94. She found that the majority had doctorates and were in their fifties or sixties. Jackson also found that a disproportionate number of black women serve in major cities. This is consistent with Kowalski's (1995) report that "women and minorities had a greater presence in the superintendencies of urban school districts than they did in public school districts in general" (p. 7): females made up approximately 15 to 18 percent of urban school superintendencies; minorities made up 51 to 65 percent of urban superintendencies. Such findings echo earlier research which, although not focused exclusively on superintendents, suggests that women and minorities gain access to administrative leadership positions in buildings or districts characterized by difficulties or extraordinary challenges (Ortiz 1982; Valverde 1974; Valverde and Brown 1988; Yeakey et al. 1986). Jackson and Cibulka (1992) found that "cities with racially representative school boards are more likely to have an African-American superintendent than those which do not have representative boards" (p. 75). And previous studies of black superintendents, though not focused on women, suggest that opportunities for African Americans are often limited to those districts with large concentrations of students of color (Jones 1983; Moody 1973, 1983; Scott 1980; Sizemore 1986).

Prior reviews of research (Banks 1995; Ortiz and Marshall 1988; Sizemore 1986; Yeakey et al. 1986) have noted that increases in the number of women superintendents have occurred primarily in very small districts (for whites) and in troubled urban districts (for persons of color). Bell (1988) concludes that the overall "picture [is] one of a hierarchy of districts, arranged according to their desirability" (p. 38), with women and persons of color occupying the superintendency in those settings lowest in this unwritten but widely recognized hierarchy. A much higher proportion of women superintendents (28 percent) than men superintendents (14 percent) occupies superintendencies in districts with fewer than 300 students (Glass 1992, 9). The only other enrollment size category wherein the proportion of women in the superintendency (11 percent) is higher than men (8 percent) is in districts with more than 25,000 students. This may be explained by the fact that African-American women, in particular, have become superintendents in urban areas in the past several decades.

In sum, studies related to superintendent profiles help us answer questions about who, how many, and where women are located. They also provide information about women superintendents' points of view on various educational issues and on their roles. Sometimes women's profiles are studied in and of themselves; other times they are compared to the profiles of male superintendents.

CAREER PATTERNS

Research on career patterns often aims, either directly or indirectly, to help explain why women administrators are where they are (and are not). I focus on selected studies that lend insights into the question of why there are relatively few women in the superintendency. These studies relate to job aspirations and opportunity structures, access to and exits from the superintendency, gatekeepers' roles, and career mobility.

Aspirations

Edson's (1981, 1988, 1995) longitudinal study of 142 female aspirants to the principalship may be important to consider, since most superintendents' careers include experience as principals. Edson described her original respondents as persistent, hopeful, and determined to "push the limits" of school administration to gain entry into leadership positions and make a difference for children. Her five- and ten-year career follow-ups found that, although initial optimism had been tempered somewhat, about 60 percent had met or exceeded their goals of becoming principals, and maintained their commitment and determination. The participants in her study had greater success obtaining elementary, rather than secondary, principalships. She also found that, of those who had mentors early in their careers, 42 percent became principals or beyond by the end of ten years, whereas only 17 percent who did not have mentors were able to advance" (Edson 1995, 42).

Grogan's (1996) research included twenty-seven female aspirants to the super-intendency and two consultants experienced in running superintendent searches for school boards. Like Edson, she too arrived at largely hopeful conclusions about how her study's participants successfully negotiated potential obstacles, held on to their aspirations, and resisted discouragement. Grogan found gender to be a pre-dominant factor in these women's preparation for the superintendency. She describes some of the conditions under which women aspire to the superinten-dency, including: the white, gendered nature of educational administration; long-standing structures of sponsorship and gatekeeping in the profession; and tensions involved in balancing personal and professional lives.

Sherr (1995) studied thirteen female central office administrators (assistant superintendents and directors) considered to be a "potential pool for future superintendents" (p. 313). She found that six did and seven did not intend to become superintendents. She also found that aspirants and nonaspirants viewed the superintendency in essentially similar ways: that is, as a powerful role, in which politics, high visibility, and public scrutiny predominate. Sherr's respon-dents defined power in traditional ways, underscoring authority, control, and autonomy. They tended to focus on the negative in the public and political nature of the role, emphasizing potential board conflict, vulnerability of the superintendent, and pressures from multiple stakeholder groups. Sherr con-cludes that these perceptions of the role: (1) were largely drawn from her respon-dents' experiences working with male superintendents; (2) may not be congru-ent with women's views of themselves, nor their preferred ways of leading; and (3) may explain why some women do not aspire to the superintendency.

Career Mobility

Beyond individual aspirations, the societal context and sex-differentiated opportunity structures within educational organizations also help explain the scarcity of women and persons of color in the superintendency. Gaertner (1981) analyzed the five-year job histories of public school employees in Michigan's 520 school districts to identify three mobility paths in school administration, two of which led to the superintendency. One path to the superintendency is from cur-ricular or instructional supervisor to administrator of instruction to assistant superintendent to superintendent. The other path to the superintendency is from curricular or instructional supervisor to assistant secondary principal to sec-ondary principal to superintendent. The third mobility pattern is from assistant elementary principal to elementary principal; this is where women are more likely to be found, and it is the path that rarely leads to the superintendency.

Paddock (1981) found that for superintendents and other high-level educa-tional administrators, the career paths of men and women incumbents look essentially the same. Glass (1992) found some differences in the career patterns of men, women, and ethnic minority superintendents. One difference is that higher proportions of women and minority superintendents than men superintendents begin their administrative careers in elementary, rather than secondary, positions (Glass 1992). Sixty percent of ethnic minority superintendents, 39 percent of women superintendents, and 38 percent of men superintendents follow a path from teacher to principal to central office position to the superintendency. Fourteen percent of ethnic minority superintendents and 22 percent of women superintendents attain the superintendency after serving as teacher and principal, whereas 38 percent of male superintendents follow that path (Glass 1992). Thus, it seems that male superintendents are equally likely to have attained that position from a principalship or from a principalship and a central office position. Women and ethnic minorities are likely to attain a superintendency only if they have "covered more bases"; that is, a principalship and central office position. This may be explained by the fact that women and minorities have greater opportunities for principalships at the elementary level.

Ortiz's (1982) work explicates where the majority of women and minority administrators are located in the leadership hierarchies of schools, noting that "there is a difference between male and female [administrators] in the way their careers develop" (p. 54). She studied 350 educators with administrative certificates in California and found that women and minorities were not socialized as teachers to enter administrative positions as white men were. Administrative opportunities for minorities were likely to be limited to elementary principalships and special projects positions focused on working with other minorities; for women, elementary principalships and staff positions (such as reading or special education specialists, coordinators, directors, and assistant administrators); and for white men, line positions (including secondary principalships and assistant superintendencies). The latter have historically provided the visibility, socialization, and other opportunities necessary for career advancement to the superintendency.

Ortiz's (1982) research supported Kanter's (1977) conclusions drawn from the study of a large, multinational corporation: structures of power, position, social composition of peer groups, opportunities, and resources create barriers to success for those who are different from the traditionally homogenous upper management groups. Wheatley (1981) drew from Kanter's (1977) work to examine the particular features of school organizations that serve to distribute opportunities in ways that discriminate against women. She uncovered powerful informal social systems that constrain the selection of administrators by allowing personally held stereotypes to greatly influence hiring decisions that continue sex-role stratification in schools.

All of this work on career patterns sheds light on the enduring sameness in the demographic profile of superintendents in this century. I turn now to additional research related to access to the superintendency.

Access

As Wheatley (1981) points out: "Statistics on the number of women admin-istrators in the school systems bear eloquent testimony to the strengths of the patterns of sponsorship and peer alliances within schools and communities that act to sustain male school leadership" (p. 266). Hudson's (1991, 1994) work illu-minates some of these informal systems. She studied 281 superintendents, including black and white women and men. She found that minority superin-tendents (that is, women and blacks) were more likely than majority superinten-dents (white males) to use informal sources to learn about jobs, whereas white males use formal and informal contacts in relatively equal proportions. Formal job sources include college placement offices, newspapers, and position vacancy pamphlets/flyers; informal sources include other superintendents, school board members, professional acquaintances, and college professors. Hudson (1994) concludes that, "White males may be trusted even if they apply through formal job routes, while blacks and women must first prove themselves and be known before they are considered for superintendencies" (p. 390). Hudson also con-firms what she terms "territorial discrimination," wherein job contacts "operate within [limited] race- and gender-defined employment territories," with "black school districts for blacks, or, for white women, small, less-sought-after school districts" (Hudson 1991, 96).

Maienza (1986) also examined access to the superintendency, with ten men and ten women superintendents participating in her study. She found that all who gain access are highly skilled in and assertive about "using the resources and sponsorship of important others in their environment" (p. 69). She also found that men were more likely to be sponsored by professors of educational admin-istration and state-level professional associations, women, by "consultants to whom they have become visible by virtue of extraordinary activity within their own districts and across districts" (p. 70).

Both Maienza's (1986) and Hudson's (1991, 1994) conclusions about the significance of sponsorship specific to superintendents confirms Ortiz's and Marshall's (1988) analysis that, in the entire field of educational administration, "sponsored mobility provides differential access" for women, minorities, and white men (p. 127).

Gatekeeping

School boards and the consultants they hire to run superintendent searches also play key roles in determining access to the superintendency. Marietti and Stout (1994) collected data from 114 school board presidents in nineteen West-ern states. They found that higher proportions of female-majority boards hired female superintendents than did male-majority boards. They also found that, compared to boards that hire males, boards that hire female superintendents are more likely to govern in grades K-8 districts, have high numbers of females in administrative positions in their district, and have a greater number of higher social status members, as reflected in higher levels of education and household income, and in greater percentages holding management or professional positions.

Grogan and Henry (1995) also studied the relationship between school boards and women superintendent candidates. They found that "the superintendency continues to be constructed as a male arena" (p. 172), with emphasis placed on prior experience: with budget and finance, with discipline and control, in a sizable district, and with advocacy by powerful others. They conclude that "warrior, military, or business mentality" (p. 172) predominates in conceptions of the superintendency. Such androcentric perceptions disadvantage women superintendent candidates.

Chase and Bell (1990) investigated how fifty gatekeepers (forty-four school board members and six search consultants) talk about hiring, working with, and observing women school superintendents. They found considerable diversity in that discourse. Some gatekeepers' talk focuses on the problematic features of the context within which women superintendents work, for example, norms that constrain females and collective (rather than individual) responsibility for contributing to or eliminating obstacles that women confront. Frequently, however, gatekeepers' discourse focuses instead on "individual achievement and gender neutrality" (p. 163). This focus shifts attention away from the problematic social and organizational environment, emphasizes the women superintendent's individual responsibility for overcoming barriers, and obscures "the relation of those obstacles to a system of structures and ideologies" (p. 174). This research points to subtle forms of sex discrimination by showing how school board members and superintendent search consultants "may be helpful to individual women and at the same time participate in processes that reproduce men's dominance" (Chase and Bell 1990, 174).

Exiting

Some research has pointed out that, while focus on issues of access, selection, career paths, and entry is crucial, attention to women's retention in the superintendency is equally important to improving women's numerical representation and integration into that role (Tallerico and Burstyn 1996; Tallerico, Burstyn, and Poole 1993). This concern has led to studies of the reasons some women exit the superintendency and seek subsequent nonsuperintendent positions.

Beekley (1996) conducted five case studies of Midwestern school districts whose female superintendents had exited. She uncovered evidence of marginalization and isolation as women in a male-dominated role, overt and covert forms of gender discrimination, and diminished personal quality of life for the women superintendents in her study. These experiences influenced their decisions to leave. Beekley's research is consistent with some of Tallerico et al.' (1993, 1996) conclusions that gender politics exacerbate the challenges of an already complex and difficult leadership role for its women occupants (see Beekley's chapter in this book for additional details).

Tallerico et al. studied twenty women who had exited superintendencies in nine different states. Their analyses suggest that proportionately more than men, women continue to occupy superintendencies in the smallest and least cosmopolitan districts, with the fewest central office administrators, declining student enrollments, more reported stress in the job, less satisfaction, and the greatest vulnerability to significant school board conflict. Tallerico and Burstyn (1996) argue that such unpromising contexts contribute to the premature exit of qualified women superintendents, reflect an ingrained system of gender stratification, and reinforce the continued disproportionate formal power of men in the superintendency. Their research also echoes Sherr's (1995) findings regarding potential superintendent aspirants and Marshall's (1985) conclusions about women in male sex-typed careers in general: some women may be "rejecting a patriarchal, political, manipulative model of school leadership . . . seeing [such models] as disconnected to the core technology of schooling" (Marshall 1985, 150).

In sum, studies related to women superintendents' career patterns encompass a wide gamut of specific subtopics, including aspirations, access, opportunity structures, gatekeeping, retention, and exit. While some results of this work are hopeful (reminding us of the persistence, resilience, and determination of current and prospective women superintendents), much draws attention to the considerable barriers that endure even today.

PRACTICE

I introduced this chapter by suggesting three broad domains of research relevant to women superintendents: demographic profiles, career patterns, and the nature of the superintendency, as practiced and experienced by women. As in the previous two domains, there is a rich and growing body of literature about practice in the 1980s and 1990s.

Pitner (1981) observed the on-the-job behavior of three female and three male superintendents to examine the nature of their work. She found that, regardless of sex, superintending is characterized by brief, fragmented activities and frequent oral communication with varied individuals and groups. She also found that, compared to men, women superintendents "were less formal in personal style, more directly involved in the instructional program, and established peer relationships predominantly with their female counterparts" (p. 291).

Ortiz and Marshall (1988) urge caution in interpreting comparative studies of men and women administrators' work and suggest that prior experience, rather than gender, may explain observed or reported differences. Yeakey et al. (1986) and Gray (1996) underscore a parallel caveat: What is experienced by white women administrators may have little to do with the unique situations of other racial or ethnic minority groups. Each occupies different relative positions of power and status in the larger social system. Moreover, within each group, there is tremendous variation. Accordingly, some researchers have emphasized nonandrocentric (e.g., Bell 1988) and non-Eurocentric (e.g., Banks 1995) approaches to the study of women superintendents.

Persons of Color

Sizemore's (1986) literature review on black superintendents reveals that, as with early published studies of the superintendency in general, male samples predominated. Overall, this literature demonstrates the constraints on the black superintendency, including lack of financial support, resistance to redistribution of resources by others, racism, and the historical context of blacks' struggle for equity and education. In addition to published work, Sizemore's review included relevant dissertations. Of the fifteen dissertations related to black superintendents, two included specific focus on black females (Chambers 1979; Revere 1985).

Jackson and Cibulka (1992) reported findings from historical case studies of four urban school districts, three with African-American male superintendents and one headed by an African-American female. This recent work confirms conclusions summarized earlier: African-American superintendents face extraordinary performance pressures for reform of school districts operating under very difficult conditions and with numerous political demands (see Jackson in this book for one of the few published studies of the experiences of black women superintendents in and of themselves, rather than subsumed within or compared to men's experiences).

What do we know about the practice of women superintendents of color other than African Americans? Flora Ida Ortiz has pioneered efforts to study Hispanic female superintendents (Ortiz 1991; Ortiz and Ortiz 1993, 1995). Her 1991 single case study demonstrates the critical role superintendents can play in educational reform. The Hispanic female studied re-shaped the destructive culture of a large, diverse school district, bringing order, stability, and hope by systematically attending to every level of the organization and keeping the focus on students' educational achievement (Ortiz 1991).

Ortiz and Ortiz (1993, 1995) added a second case to the original study, to explore how Hispanic female superintendents developed leadership strategies within the context of a culture biased toward white male leadership. They found that these superintendents pay careful attention to the symbols they project. They

also found that even commonplace executive actions can become highly politi-
cized for Hispanic female superintendents, because the interpretation of those
actions by others "can be conveniently placed in the context of gender and ethnicity" (Ortiz and Ortiz 1993, 165). These women's work involves confronting
assumptions due to bilinguality, that is, assumptions that difficulties are a result
of communication problems. Ortiz and Ortiz's (1995) work reveals that the Hispanic female superintendent is an outsider in the superintendency on two
counts—gender and ethnicity—and that this outsider status prompts suspicion of
favoritism toward members of her own group, skepticism of her abilities, and
increased need for support from her school board when implementing changes.
These cases reveal how gender and ethnicity interact in the superintendency.

"Feminine" Leadership Practice

Some studies of women's experience in the superintendency echo findings
from noneducational settings regarding a leadership style of positive feminine
qualities, including nurturance, supportiveness, caring, cooperation, and atten-
tiveness to relationships (Brunner, in press; Helgesen 1990; Rosener 1990). For
example, Sherman and Repa (1994) conducted case studies of two female superintendents at work. They concluded that their findings corroborated Gilligan's
(1982) conceptualization of an "ethic of care" guiding women's decisions. The
participants in their study viewed themselves as healers and nurturers, rather
than "movers and shakers," contributing to a more "humanized" school district
culture (Sherman and Repa 1994, 61, 62).

Wesson and Grady (1994, 1995) and Grady et al. (1994) studied fifty-one
women superintendents and found that female superintendents rely on collegial
and collaborative leadership practices. These researchers conclude that this style
represents a new leadership paradigm that values relationships and connectedness over bureaucracy and is different from more prevalent enacted models of
educational administration as command and control of hierarchy.

In a similar vein, Brunner's (1995) case study of an educational community
with a female superintendent found that women and men define power differently. The male definition emphasizes "power over," whereas the female definition ("power to") emphasizes the ability to get things done through collaboration
and consensus building. Brunner found that successful women superintendents
are not necessarily co-opted into adopting the male use and definition of power
in their work. Brunner's (1997b) further work with twenty-five men and twenty-
two women superintendents found that most often the men studied defined
power as "power over," while the women studied more often defined power as
"power to."

Brunner also (1997a) studied the experiences of twelve successful European-
American women superintendents, triangulating her data with interviews of

twenty-four informants who knew these superintendents' work. This research revealed that the practices used by these women to be successful in the superintendency paralleled Castaneda's (1981) seven "principles of power governing the riddle of the heart": (1) knowing their surroundings, (2) focusing their work and lives, (3) keeping things simple by choosing battles carefully, (4) taking risks and being fearless, (5) retreating periodically to regain strength, (6) compressing time so as not to waste precious moments, and (7) exercising power with, rather than over, others. The latter confirmed findings from her earlier study (Brunner 1995).

Diversity of Practice

Colleen Bell and Susan Chase (1990, 1993, 1995, 1996) coinvestigated the experiences of twenty-seven women superintendents of K–12 school districts in six different states. In addition to document analysis and field observation, these researchers interviewed some ninety-two persons: the twenty-seven racially and ethnically diverse women superintendents, forty-four of their school board members, eight state-level officials and search consultants, nine husbands or partners of the superintendents, and four staff members who worked with the superintendents. All of their studies summarized later are drawn from that same rich database, which they continue to mine for important insights on women and the superintendency.

Bell (1988) explored how contextual features shape the negotiation of authority between women superintendents and school board members. She found that sex ratios, male dominance of power structures, and stereotyped gender-related expectations exacerbate problems of authority in this governance relationship. Since "usually, trustworthiness and predictability are signified by social homogeneity" (p. 56), " the woman superintendent's gender is interpreted as a symbol of overriding difference and risk" (p. 55). This influences the superintendent's hiring as well as ongoing interactions. It means that the woman superintendent must make extra efforts to assure the school board of her loyalty and predictability.

Bell and Chase (1995) critiqued dominant theories of educational leadership that rely on gendered distinctions between task-centered and follower-centered styles. They pointed out that most leadership theory "has either ignored or simplified the significance of gender" (p. 219). The women superintendents Bell and Chase studied understood and practiced leadership in integrated ways, "defy[ing] the idea that women are more likely to be interpersonally oriented than task oriented" (1995, 201). They found that women's leadership strategies are shaped by a work context of bureaucracy, stratification, and segregation by sex, and male dominance as both a structural and ideological feature.

Bell and Chase (1996) also explored women superintendents' professional

relationships, including colleagues, mentors, informal networks, and professional organizations. Again, their conclusions underscore the importance of
understanding the broader social context of leaders' work. They found that
women superintendents' positive professional connections to white men held
promise for being integrated into the power structures and support networks of
educational administration. Such connections to other women often meant giving or seeking personal support. However, the latter could be risky: while
"groups of men are not criticized for choosing to affiliate with men" (p. 129),
women who choose affiliations with women's groups may raise suspicion. Bell
(1995) found that some women superintendents deliberately distance themselves
from other women (to defeminize themselves, in Hochschild's (1974) terms),
because our culture defines "professional" and "woman" as contradictory identities. In male-dominated professions, "pressure to disaffiliate from other women
arises from women's need to prove themselves different from a negative stereotype of others like them" (Bell 1995, 308). Bell and Chase (1996) found that
women's relationships with male colleagues included evidence of mentors and
supporters as well as detractors and discriminators. Bell (1995) points out that
women superintendents hold contrary statuses as outsider and insider, belonging and not belonging.

Themes of diversity in women's experiences and the influential role played
by the inequitable context of male dominance are more fully elaborated in
Chase's (1995) book. Here she focuses on the narratives of four women superintendents from the larger study to develop the concept of "ambiguous empowerment": women's "contradictory experiences of power and subjection" (p. xi).
She found that their narratives "bring together two kinds of talk that generally
do not belong together in American culture: talk about professional achievement
and talk about subjection to gender and racial inequalities" (p. 10). The individual is the focus of the former; persons as members of some race, class, or gender group are the focus of the latter. Chase (1995) concludes that, in this male-
dominated profession, "isolated struggle against inequality is the requirement
and cost of professional success" (p. 33). Unfortunately, as she and Bell pointed
out in earlier work, "Individuals often do resist the constraints they face, but
individual actions do not change the systems that produce the constraints"
(Chase and Bell 1990, 172).

CONCLUSIONS

There is a small and growing research base specific to women and the superintendency, published largely in the 1980s and 1990s. While I have chosen to discuss this knowledge base in terms of three broad domains of inquiry (profiles,
patterns, and practice), many individual studies focus on and inform several of

these categories simultaneously. Taken together, these studies remind us that research on one gender, ethnic, or racial group should not be generalized as truth to both genders or all ethnicities and races. Some of this research additionally reminds us that attention to intragroup variation leads to a fuller view of the superintendency.

In many cases, women superintendents' perspectives and experiences are being studied on their own terms, and, in some cases, androcentric theories are being challenged. In virtually all cases, it is women and persons of color who are studying women superintendents and superintendents of color. Overall, attention has been dedicated to documenting the meager distribution of women and persons of color in the superintendency, to developing explanations for why this is so, and to describing and analyzing women superintendents' experiences and leadership practices.

FUTURE RESEARCH

In every category mentioned previously in this chapter, additional research is needed. For example, even for "simple" counts, we still do not have an accurate, reliable, longitudinal, and comparable-across-states database on superintendents, including information on gender, race, and ethnicity. Bell and Chase (1993) point out that multiple definitions of superintendency exist across studies, often with all manner and types mixed together (e.g., county, vocational school districts, K–8 systems, K–12 systems, intermediate units).

With respect to career patterns, many unanswered questions remain. For example, in states with higher proportions of women superintendents, do historic patterns of incumbency in the lowest-status districts still hold? What is the search process like for today's superintendencies? What can we find out about the applicant pools for superintendencies, including the variables of race and gender? How widespread is the phenomenon of some women exiting the superintendency prior to normal retirement?

Regarding leadership practice, Shakeshaft (1989) lamented the dearth of individual accounts, biographies, histories, case studies, or ethnographies "centered on women in administration" (p. 56). Since then, Bell, Brunner, Chase, and Ortiz have published case and ethnographic studies of the experiences and perspectives of women superintendents. However, we need more than just a handful of researchers working toward this end in the future. Moreover, while several have contributed to our understanding of women superintendents of color (e.g., Ortiz for Hispanics; B. Jackson for African Americans; and see also Alston and Méndez-Morse in this book—two researchers recently focusing on African Americans and Hispanics), I could find no studies relevant to women superintendents of other racial or ethnic backgrounds. Additional studies of nondominant group members' experience and leadership practice can contribute new perspectives on organizational life and the superintendency. We need to understand more about how organizational structures shape the experiences of women superintendents, as well as how women and persons of color do, or could, reshape the superintendency itself. Also, Bell and Chase (1995) wisely point out that little attention has been devoted to "differences within individual women's strategic thinking and action across situations and over time" (p. 209).

Schmuck (1987) underscored that "the inclusion of women within the domain of inquiry must change the nature of the inquiry" (p. 9). In this volume, Brunner, Grogan, and D. Jackson collaboratively experiment with new ways of authenticating studies of women superintendents by using feminist poststructuralist analytic lenses and asking practitioners to examine the worth of their research. There is a need for more such creative approaches in the future.

In sum, these are exciting times for students of the superintendency. The researchers whose work has been cited in this review provide abundant inspiration for learning all that we can about the profiles, career patterns, and practice of women superintendents. I urge others to build on these scholars' fine, foundational work.

REFERENCES

Banks, C. M. 1995. Gender and race as factors in educational leadership and administration. In J. A. Banks and C. A. McGee Banks (eds.), *Handbook of research on multicultural education*. New York: Macmillan.

Beekley, C. 1996. *Gender, expectations, and job satisfaction: Why women exit the public school superintendency*. Paper presented at the annual meeting of the American Educational Research Association, New York.

Bell, C. 1988. Organizational influences on women's experience in the superintendency. *Peabody Journal of Education*, 65 (4): 31-59.

———. 1992. Resisting genderalities in education. *The Hamline Review*. Vol. 16. St. Paul, Minn.: Hamline University.

———. 1995. "If I weren't involved with schools, I might be radical": Gender consciousness in context. In D. Dunlap and P. Schmuck (eds.), *Women leading in education*. Albany, N.Y.: State University of New York Press.

Bell, C., and S. Chase. 1993. The underrepresentation of women in school leadership. In C. Marshall (ed.), *The new politics of race and gender: Yearbook of the Politics of Education Association*. Washington, D.C.: Falmer.

———. 1995. Gender in the theory and practice of educational leadership. *Journal for a Just and Caring Education* 1 (2): 220-22.

———. 1996. The gendered character of women superintendents' professional relationships. In K. Arnold, K. Noble, and R. Subotnick (eds.), *Remarkable women: Perspectives on female talent development*. Cresskill, N.J.: Hampton Press.

Blount, J. 1995. The politics of sex as a category of analysis in the history of educational administration. In B. Irby and G. Brown (eds.), *Women as school executives: Voices and visions.* Austin, Tex.: Texas Council for Women School Executives.

Brunner, C. 1995. By power defined: Women in the superintendency. *Educational Considerations* 22 (2): 21-26.

———. 1997a. Working through the riddle of the heart: Perspectives of women superintendents. *Journal of School Leadership* 7 (1): 138-64.

———. 1997b. Exercising power. *The School Administrator* 6 (54): 6-10.

———. 1998a. Can power support an "ethic of care?" An examination of the professional practices of women superintendents. *Journal for a Just and Caring Education* 4 (2): 142-75.

———. 1998b. Women superintendents: Strategies for success. *Journal of Educational Administration* 36 (2): 160-82.

Castaneda, C. 1981. *The eagle's gift.* New York: Washington Square Press.

Chambers, R. 1979. An identification and comparison of problems encountered by black and women superintendents. Unpublished dissertation, University of Iowa, Ames.

Chase, S. 1995. *Ambiguous empowerment: The work narratives of women school superintendents.* Amherst, Mass.: University of Massachusetts Press.

Chase, S., and C. Bell. 1990. Ideology, discourse, and gender: How gatekeepers talk about women school superintendents. *Social Problems* 37 (2): 163-77.

Crowson, R. 1987. The local school district superintendency: A puzzling administrative role. *Educational Administration Quarterly* 23 (3): 49-69.

Cunningham, L., and J. Hentges. 1982. *The American school superintendency, 1982: A summary report.* Arlington, Va.: The American Association of School Administrators.

Edson, S. 1981. "If they can, I can": Women aspirants to administrative positions in public schools. In P. Schmuck, W. Charters, and R. Carlson (eds.), *Educational policy and management: Sex differentials.* New York: Academic Press.

———. 1988. *Pushing the limits: The female administrative aspirant.* Albany, N.Y.: State University of New York Press.

———. 1995. Ten years later: Too little, too late? In D. Dunlap and P. Schmuck (eds.), *Women leading in education.* Albany, N.Y.: State University of New York Press.

Gaertner, K. 1981. Administrative careers in public school organizations. In P. Schmuck, W. Charters, and R. Carlson (eds.), *Educational policy and management: Sex differentials.* New York: Academic Press.

Gilligan, C. 1982. *In a different voice.* Cambridge: Harvard University Press.

Glass, T. 1992. *The 1992 study of the American school superintendency.* Arlington, Va.: American Association of School Administrators.

Grady, M., T. Ourada-Sieb, and L. Wesson. 1994. Women's perceptions of the superintendency. *Journal of School Leadership* 4 (2): 156-70.

Gray, L. 1996. Keynoter questions the connection between race and gender. *Eastern Researcher Newsletter* 1.

Grogan, M. 1996. *Voices of women aspiring to the superintendency.* Albany, N.Y.: State University of New York Press.

Grogan, M., and M. Henry. 1995. Women candidates for the superintendency: Board perspectives. In B. Irby and G. Brown (eds.), *Women as school executives: Voices and visions*. Austin, Tex.: Texas Council for Women School Executives.

Helgesen, S. 1990. *The female advantage: Women's ways of leadership*. Garden City, N.Y.: Doubleday.

Hochschild, A. 1974. Making it: Marginality and obstacles to minority consciousness. In R. B. Kundsin (ed.), *Women and success: The anatomy of achievement*. New York: William Morrow & Co.

Hudson, M. 1991. *How educators get top jobs: Understanding race and sex differences in the 'old boy network'*. Lanham, Md.: University Press of America.

———. 1994. Women and minorities in school administration: R-examining the role of informal job contact systems. *Urban Education*, 8 (4): 386-97.

Jackson, B. 1996. *The voices of African American women public school superintendents: A preliminary report*. Paper presented at the annual meeting of the American Educational Research Association, New York.

Jackson, B., and J. Cibulka. 1992. Leadership turnover and business mobilization: The changing political ecology of urban school systems. In J. Cibulka, R. Reed, and K. Wong (eds.), *The politics of urban education in the United States*. Washington, D.C.: Falmer.

Jones, E. 1983. *Black school administrators: A review of their early history, trends, problems in recruitment*. Arlington, Va.: American Association of School Administrators.

Kanter, R. M. 1977. *Men and women of the corporation*. New York: Basic.

Kowalski, T. 1995. *Keepers of the flame: Contemporary urban superintendents*. Thousand Oaks, Calif.: Corwin.

Maienza, J. 1986. The superintendency: Characteristics of access for men and women. *Educational Administration Quarterly* 22 (4): 59-79.

Marietti, M., and R. Stout. 1994. School boards that hire female superintendents. *Urban Education* 8 (4): 373-85.

Marshall, C. 1985. The stigmatized woman: The professional woman in a male sex-typed career. *The Journal of Educational Administration* 23 (2): 131-52.

Montenegro, X. 1993. *Women and racial minority representation in school administration*. Arlington, Va.: American Association of School Administrators.

Moody, C. 1973. The black superintendent. *School Review* 81 (3): 375-82.

———. 1983. On becoming a superintendent: Contest or sponsored mobility? *Journal of Negro Education* 52: 383-97.

National School Boards Association. 1992. *Urban dynamics: Lessons in leadership from urban school boards and superintendents*. Alexandria, Va.: Author.

Ortiz, F. I. 1982. *Career patterns in education: Women, men, and minorities in educational administration*. New York: Praeger.

———. 1991. A Hispanic female superintendent's leadership and school district culture. In N. Wyner (ed.), *Current perspectives on the culture of school*. Cambridge: Brookline Books.

Ortiz, F. I., and C. Marshall. 1988. Women in educational administration. In N. Boyan (ed.), Handbook of research on educational administration. New York: Longman.

Ortiz, F. I., and D. J. Oritz. 1993. Politicizing executive action: The case of Hispanic female superintendents. In C. Marshall (ed.), The new politics of race and gender: Yearbook of the Politics of Education Association. Washington, D.C.: Falmer.

————. 1995. How gender and ethnicity interact in the practice of educational administration: The case of Hispanic female superintendents. In R. Donmoyer, M. Imber, and J. Scheurich (eds.), The knowledge base in educational administration: Multiple perspectives. Albany, N.Y.: State University of New York Press.

Paddock, S. 1981. Male and female career paths in school administration. In P. Schmuck, W. Charters, and R. Carlson (eds.), Educational policy and management: Sex differentials. New York: Academic Press.

Pitner, N. 1981. Hormones and harems: Are the activities of superintending different for a woman? In P. Schmuck, W. Charters, and R. Carlson (eds.), Educational policy and management: Sex differentials. New York: Academic Press.

Revere, A. 1985. A description of black female school superintendents. Unpublished dissertation, Miami University, Ohio.

Rosener, J. 1990. Ways women lead. Harvard Business Review 68 (6): 119-25.

Schmuck, P. 1987. Introduction. In P.A. Schmuck (ed.), Women educators. Albany, N.Y.: State University of New York Press.

Scott, H. 1980. The black school superintendent: Messiah or scapegoat? Washington, D.C.: Howard University Press.

Shakeshaft, C. 1989. Women in educational administration. Newbury Park, Calif.: Corwin.

Sherman, D., and T. Repa. 1994. Women at the top: The experiences of two superintendents. Equity and Choice 10 (2): 59-64.

Sherr, M. 1995. The glass ceiling reconsidered: View from below. In D. Dunlap and P. Schmuck (eds.), Women leading in education. Albany, N.Y.: State University of New York Press.

Sizemore, B. 1986. The limits of the black superintendency: A review of the literature. Journal of Educational Equity and Leadership 6 (3): 180-208.

Tallerico, M., and J. N. Burstyn. 1996. Retaining women in the superintendency: The location matters. Educational Administration Quarterly 32: 642-64.

Tallerico, M., J. N. Burstyn, and W. Poole. 1993. Gender and politics at work: Why women exit the superintendency. Fairfax, Va.: National Policy Board for Educational Administration.

Tyack, D., and E. Hansot. 1982. Managers of virtue: Public school leadership in America: 1820-1980. New York: Basic Books.

Valverde, L. 1974. Succession socialization: Its influences on school administration candidates and its implications for the exclusion of minorities from administration (Project 3-0813). Washington, D.C.: National Institute for Education.

Valverde, L., and F. Brown. 1988. Influences in leadership development among racial and ethnic minorities. In N. Boyan (ed.), Handbook of research on educational administration. New York: Longman.

Wesson, L, and M. Grady. 1994. An analysis of women urban superintendents: A national study. *Urban Education* 8 (4): 412-24.

———. 1995. A leadership perspective from women superintendents. In B. Irby and G. Brown (eds.), *Women as school executives: Voices and visions.* Austin, Tex.: Texas Council for Women School Executives.

Wheatley, M. 1981. The impact of organizational structures on issues of sex equity. In P. Schmuck, W. Charters, R. Carlson (eds.), *Educational policy and management: Sex differentials.* New York: Academic Press.

Yeakey, C., G. Johnston, and J. Adkison. 1986. In pursuit of equity: A review of research on women and minorities in educational administration. *Educational Administration Quarterly* 22 (3): 110-49.

PART TWO

"Do It Anyway"

Gaining Access

C. CRYSS BRUNNER

> Although some might really prefer you behave yourself and not climb
> all over the furniture in joy or all over people in welcome, do it any-
> way.
>
> —Clarissa Pinkola Estés, *Women Who Run With the Wolves*

Funny things happen when people are free. They are joyful and lose their self-consciousness—they become themselves. In this section, we encourage women to be themselves even when social norms have worked against such behavior. We assert, "Even if you think that wanting to be a superintendent is outlandish, do it anyway!"

The research in this section represents the actuality that women, across race, are out there getting jobs. And in places—if one looks carefully—the research provides "toe-holds" and "secret passwords" for those willing to "do it anyway."

CHAPTER THREE

The Role of Search Consultants in the Career Paths of Women Superintendents

ESTELLE KAMLER and
CHAROL SHAKESHAFT

I n recent years, women have made significant gains in some administrative positions in schools. Montenegro (1993) reports that women have a representation of 34.2 percent in the principalship and 24.3 percent in the assistant superintendency. However, the superintendency has seen the slightest gains, as compared to other positions. In 1992, when this study was initiated, on the national level, 10.5 percent of the superintendents nationwide were women, compared to 17.2 percent in New York state. In comparison, during the period 1996-97, the percentage of women superintendents in New York state declined to 15.9 percent. In 1992-93, the percentage of women superintendents in the 129 school districts on Long Island, where this study was done, was 10 percent, and in 1996-97, the percentage was 16 percent.

Recently, search consultants have been used more frequently by boards of education to assist them in the selection of a superintendent. Search consultants, by definition, are gatekeepers (Castro 1992). Studies have shown that search consultants rely heavily on a network of friends, professional associates, and associations to develop a field of candidates to present to boards of education for consideration. With the limited number of women securing superintendencies in comparison to the percentage of women in other administrative positions, and with the increase in the engagement of search consultants by school districts to conduct searches for superintendents, we questioned the relationship between the role of the search consultant and the small percentage of women appointed to the superintendency. Can search consultants be considered an extension of the "old boy" network? Who are these consultants? What are their connections, affiliations, and procedures for identifying candidates? What is their process for limiting the field? What proactive activities do they engage in that may promote women? What conscious or unconscious prejudices or concerns influence the decision making of the search consultant? Does the search consultant serve as a barrier to women seeking the superintendency?

The purpose of this study was to examine the role of the search consultant as the gatekeeper in promoting or preventing women from attaining a superintendency. The researchers conducted a regional study concentrating on Long Island, a small geographical area, in an effort to explore in depth the web of network connections as a way to better understand the search consultant's method of operation, his or her sponsorship position, and the factors that influence the final selection of candidates presented to the boards of education.

POOL OF SEARCH CONSULTANTS

This study was focused on the search consultants who conducted searches that resulted in the placement in the period 1992-93 of superintendents in the 129 school districts on Long Island in New York state. To identify the search consultants, a mail survey was sent to superintendents to determine how many had been placed by a search consultant; of the 81 percent who responded, 70 percent, or seventy-five, reported having been involved in a search that used a search consultant. Nineteen search consultants were reported to have conducted these seventy-five searches. Of these searchers, 46 percent were directed by a New York Regional Service Unit, 31 percent by retired superintendents, 21 percent by consultants who also were college professors, and 2 percent by other firms. All but one university team included a former superintendent turned professor.

Out of the field of nineteen search consultants/search consultant firms, fifteen (79 percent) consultants were interviewed; eight of the nine consultants who conducted the most searches were in the group of consultants interviewed.

REPRESENTATION OF WOMEN AMONG CANDIDATES

Consultants who had been conducting searches for at least a decade spoke about the women who applied for superintendencies approximately ten years ago. They noted that the number of women were very few, and the number of qualified women were even less. Two consultants specifically described women who applied for the superintendency; however, they did not articulate the same reasons for disqualifying them from the field of finalists. One consultant said,

> The women who applied, by and large, were totally unqualified. We eliminated them without interview. We had a woman who, by extreme example but not atypical, was in charge of advertising in the cattle industry in Canada somewhere. She saw this ad and saw no

reason why she couldn't become a superintendent of schools. Women who thought it was now women's turn, and therefore, nothing else mattered, and they were going to see that they could do it. Teachers applied directly for the superintendency. They had never been anything else—classroom teacher! We had no women finalists in those first three years.

One of the female consultants commented, "I don't remember more than two women [who applied for the position]. They were very brittle, very businesslike, very aggressive, not soft and charming and attractive. . . . But women were not competing much for the superintendency."

All of the consultants spoke of the increased number of women applicants for the superintendency, although some noted that the ratio of male to female candidates was still high.

In examining the number of women applicants reported by the consultants, there appeared to be a significant difference between the number of women applicants vying for elementary superintendencies (K-6) and K-12 superintendencies; approximately 50 percent of the candidates for K-6 superintendencies were women versus 10 to 15 percent for K-12 superintendencies. In explaining the number of women candidates, search consultants hypothesized that women were more place bound than men because of their spouses' positions. They also cited family or responsibility for children as a consideration, which may cause a woman not to want to take on the commitment required of the superintendency.

Although the consultants were aware of the number of women who had moved into highly visible and responsible administrative positions, such as assistant superintendents for curriculum and instruction, some thought that women viewed service in this capacity as being more satisfying than the superintendency. One consultant also spoke of what she categorized as the myth that she believed some women have about being loyal and remaining an assistant superintendent with the thought that when the superintendent leaves or dies, they will inherit the position. She said,

> They wait and wait and wait, and the likelihood is that when that guy goes, they never look inside. They say, 'Thank God! Now we can get a new breath of air.' That woman has waited out her career there in this kind of second nurturing position, expecting to inherit, and of course, she doesn't—when she could have moved at a time when she was much more saleable and marketable.

Another factor consultants voiced as being a detriment was the rarity of women as high school principals. The consultants viewed the rise to the superintendency from this position as being easier and still quite prevalent. One consultant noted, "It's much more difficult, even for a male, to go from the elementary school [principalship] to a superintendency than it is from a secondary [school]."

Because many of the districts studied would only hire candidates who had previously been superintendents, women were at a disadvantage. Given the small number of women superintendents initially, women who would be eligible to compete in a field of experienced superintendents are limited. In the search, which was conducted by a retired male and female superintendent, utilizing only outreach to current superintendents, out of the initial twelve candidates, there was only one woman who had been enticed to apply by the female consultant. This candidate survived the first cut because of the lobbying efforts of the female search consultant, but she was not presented in the final field of three outside candidates to the board for interview.

RECRUITMENT OF WOMEN

While nine of the fifteen consultants studied indicated that they used outreach as one approach to secure candidates, only six of them (40 percent) reported that they placed great emphasis on outreach to women. They recalled contacting specific women for a particular superintendency. They spoke of knowing these women through their work in professional organizations, or being referred to them by friends and/or associates who may have nominated them for a superintendency.

One member of a national search consultant firm told of his conversation with the dean of education at a prominent university, who herself was a promoter of women, and who connected him with several potential women candidates. He also told of his phone call to a female superintendent from another state, who had informed him that she was seeking an opportunity to relocate to the New York area. He encouraged her to apply, and she was selected by the board as the new superintendent for this district.

Another national consultant, an avid supporter of women candidates for the superintendency, sent brochures and invitations for applications to all of the professional women's organizations in the United States. In addition, he and his female partner attended all major functions of these organizations to become acquainted with women who aspired to the superintendency. They also nominated women candidates for each superintendency in which they served as the search consultants. Both of these consultants believed that when a school board hired them to find a superintendent, the board was relaying the message that a woman superintendent was not only okay but desirable. The male consultant in this partnership said, "They wouldn't hire us in the first place if they did not want a woman or a minority." These consultants were adamant about the need to reach out to women as well as minorities. They described calling women from all over the country who they thought would be interested or who would be able to connect them to other women candidates. Their dialogue included the following questions: (1) Are you interested? (2) Do you have an assistant? and (3)

Is there somebody you're working with who you think is ready? They noted that most of the women they encouraged to apply for particular superintendencies did not "sit down and apply" on their own.

The reasons consultants gave for not being able to encourage women included lack of interest by women in the superintendency and avoidance of failure. For instance, one response from a woman was, "I don't want to do that. I watch what the superintendent does, and I just don't want to do that seven nights a week."

Another consultant had a slightly different experience with a female candidate whom he met when she applied for her first superintendency, and whom he placed in the field of finalists to be interviewed by the board. She was not hired, and when the consultant tried to convince the candidate to apply for subsequent superintendencies, she declined. The consultant said, "One of the things she told me was that she was in the district adjoining the one she applied to; she knew all about it. If she couldn't get that one, she wasn't interested in going further in her field."

Not all women stopped competing. For instance, one female candidate who was hired as a superintendent had previously held a variety of positions, including two assistant superintendencies in districts. She also had been active in local professional organizations. The consultants who placed her indicated that they had known this woman for years. "We had been expecting her to become a superintendent . . . she was a finalist with us for the last four years."

Although the percentage of female applicants ranged from a high of 50 percent to a low of 10 percent in a given search, every consultant indicated that in the final field of candidates presented to the board, whether there were five or fifteen, women candidates were always on the slate. There would be one or two, and one consultant reported that in some searches he conducted there were more women finalists than men. Most of the consultants noted that there was a higher percentage of women presented as finalists in comparison to the percentage of women who were in the original field of applicants. One consultant, who has conducted numerous searches and has been in the business for many years, commented,

> I think, today, almost every board that I work with, in terms of, if
> there isn't a female . . . or a number of females in that group of fif-
> teen or twenty, would raise questions and say, 'Why not?'

One member of a national consultant team indicated that in the last K-12 superintendent search his group completed, there were two women out of the eight finalists who were presented to the board—one was a superintendent and the other a State Education Department senior administrator. Another consultant noted that he had at least two women in each finalists' group of six or seven candidates in the last three years.

As one search consultant reported, "I've never had a full slate of women, but I've had many slates where the women were the majority recommended to the board. . . . What the board does with it later is based on its own vision of the world and the schools." Although women were reported as finalists in all of the seventy-five searches, 12 percent (or nine superintendencies) was actually filled by women.

Thus, the search consultants report that women candidates are in the final pool in a superintendent search. This is a change from a decade ago, when women were not presented as finalists. Nevertheless, national statistics confirm that although women have made it into the candidate pool, they are still not being hired in proportion to their numbers in the profession or their skills as administrators.

BIAS AGAINST WOMEN

Many of the consultants talked freely and in detail about their perceptions of the way board members and other members of the school community view women candidates. Many of these perceptions were generated by comments and questions from board and community members to the consultants during informal discussions.

One consultant summarized:

> My sense is that there are myths about women . . . women are too emotional and can't see things rationally and so that affects their decision making. The other thing is that women are nurturers to a greater extent than men are. That doesn't sit well in the superintendency; we [superintendents] have to make these tough decisions . . . women are not as strong in dealing with the major issues as men would be.

He continued to talk about what he considered the dichotomy between the perceived weaknesses of women by boards and what defines the current thought about effective leadership, which emphasizes the need for "more considerate, more caring, more nurturing administrators who are able to be a participatory leader rather than the old boss kind of thing."

One consultant said that he has worked with boards of education who have specifically talked about gender concerns. He lamented, "The most difficulty women have is that they almost can't win." He continued to explain:

> If a woman exhibits certain characteristics, and this is not too different than the certain characteristics the board would in a male consider an indication of strong leadership, she will be too male and unsympathetic and uncaring. On the other hand, if she is a woman and shows too much femininity, she is too weak, too soft. How is she going to

negotiate with the union? How is she going to handle serious discipline problems? Women are always walking this fine line of trying to be both formulas. It's wrong if they are not too feminine because they are too male, and that's no good, but they can't show weakness. They have to be tough. They have to be able to do what men can do.

Another consultant said, "I personally feel the biggest obstacle to women's promotion are women." He spoke of women PTA members who left a community input session by saying, "Hire a man!" This point also was emphasized by a second consultant, who noted, "If a woman is president of a board of education, or if there are a number of women on the board, a woman candidate is not going to be selected—you're wasting your time." These consultants believed the myth that women are their own worst enemy, and reported that women board members preferred male candidates. In contrast, research on board member preferences indicates that in districts where women are hired, there is a greater proportion of women board members, and that women are more likely to support women than are men (Fairbairne 1989). It remains important to understand why—despite evidence to the contrary—the woman-against-woman stereotype persists.

Other consultants also referred to negative attitudes that some men have about women. One consultant spoke of a particular board member in a district who blatantly told him, "Don't, whatever you do, bring any 'broads' to us in the finals." A different consultant commented that the person most opposed to women candidates is the male high school principal.

One of the consultants commented on the level of experience that may hamper women in actually securing superintendency. He said,

> Women and minorities, in general, may be at a disadvantage in some respects in that they may not have had the length of experience at certain levels along the way that men have had. A board may find that they want to hire someone who has been at a job longer than someone else, and I would say that at the secondary level the men probably have had longer experience at principal's jobs and assistant superintendent's jobs because women haven't had the opportunity until recently to begin to take those jobs in any meaningful numbers.

Last, a well-established regional consultant raised the following issue:

> Many of the females had been teaching fifteen, twenty, twenty-five years, so they were very experienced teachers—senior-type persons. At fifty-five or sixty, they're out looking for a superintendency when the males were retiring at fifty-five, and so it was difficult for them to get jobs. The board's looking [to replace] somebody who is retiring at fifty-five and the women who were applying for the job were fifty-eight and had never been a superintendent. Board members were saying, 'Well, wait a minute.'

FUTURE PROSPECTS

Although the consultants addressed what they considered to be bias against women candidates for the superintendency, many of the consultants spoke optimistically about the prospects of women candidates moving into the superintendency if they so desired. One of the professors noted that more women were attaining administrative posts such as principalships and central office positions, including business administrator. He saw females coming down the "pipeline." A consultant who has exclusively worked on Long Island also indicated that in the last three years, almost universally, women who applied for the superintendency had a doctorate or were assistant superintendents and were well qualified. The university professors confirmed that the number of women in advanced degree courses outweighed the men seeking those degrees. One professor noted, "Today, . . . 55 to 60 percent of our admissions are female."

One consultant also spoke about his perceptions of the change he was seeing in boards of education. He explained,

> Their readiness to accept women is much greater than the last six years have been. As a matter of fact, one board started out the search looking for a woman. . . . They thought a woman would be more sympathetic to students and would understand students better than a man could.

SUMMARY

With 70 percent of the responding superintendents indicating that search consultants were used to search for superintendents, it is clear that search consultants played a major role in hiring superintendents. Given that the consultants reported that in most searches the percentage of women that they included in the field of finalists for the board to interview was greater than the percentage of the women who applied, the consultant's influence *may* account for the limited but growing number of women who are interviewed for the superintendency.

Although we were prepared to find that consultants had subtly and not so subtly helped keep women out of the superintendency, we found more advocacy and gender equity than we expected—and than had been evident in consultant's behavior, even a decade ago (Chase and Bell 1994). Nevertheless, fewer than half (40 percent) of the consultants spoke about their outreach to women and their involvement with women's organizations to encourage women to apply for the superintendency.

Several of the consultants told us why women should be hired as administrators. They talked about the research on female styles and the success that women are believed to have in building teams and creating a supportive climate. The consultants reported that they shared this information with boards. Thus, women may begin to benefit from this change of thinking when boards begin to have a different vision of leadership. If collaboration is applauded as the predominant mode of operation, women may not only be more interested in the superintendency but be viewed in a more desirable light for the position.

As a way to summarize our findings and to present the flavor of the interviews we did, we have included a vignette that we hope captures how search consultants, at the time we did this study, were thinking and talking about women candidates for the superintendency.

> Setting: The Concord Hotel—a mid-sized conference room clearly marked at the entrance with a sign, "The Consultant's Hour." Entering the dimly lit quarters, one sees round tables strewn with resumes, brochures advertising available superintendencies, water glasses, and coffee cups. A long service table on the side of the room has large pitchers of water and urns for coffee and tea. Exiting the side door are the last of the interested applicants—two women dressed in suits and a man in a jogging outfit. At a corner table sit three men—one 70ish, one 60ish, and one 50ish, all in jackets and ties, and all speaking in low tones—each nodding in agreement as the other speaks.

Marv: More and more. Each year, there are more and more. For the last two searches I have conducted for elementary districts in the last year, I got at least 50 percent of the applications from women.

Joe: In the search I did just three years ago for an elementary district, there were twelve women applicants out of the fifty-five candidates, but two out of the six candidates I presented to the board were women.

Al: I remember when I was a superintendent and I was hiring principals, women were not candidates; women never applied. Women wanted to be home when the kids were home from school. Then women started to apply. I recall an elementary principalship opening in the '70s, I had 100 candidates. The six finalists turned out to be women, which surprised the hell out of me. I didn't have any idea what would happen when I finished, and my God, all the choices were women. All those women were divorced women; they had all the time in the world. In a way, they were replacements for the women who, in my time, when I was a student, never married.

Joe: You're not serious about divorced women having all the time in the world? I had an intern years ago, you know, Beth. She's a superintendent now on the east end. What a dynamo! I don't know how she did it; doing the job she did and raising those teenagers! I've recommended her for several superintendencies. She's top flight!

Al: Well, I will say that the women who are applying today are at least qualified. When I first started doing these superintendent searches seven years ago, I would eliminate the women without even interviewing them. I mean, we had a woman who was in charge of advertising in the cattle industry in Canada somewhere; she saw the ad and saw no reason why she couldn't become a superintendent of schools. Teachers applied directly for the superintendency. They had never been anything else. Classroom teachers! We had no women finalists in those first three years.

Marv: Look, women are as well prepared, if not more prepared, these days for administrative jobs as men. That isn't the problem. Women are winning appointments to superintendencies at a much greater clip than they have. I think that in the last two years, 20 percent of the superintendencies in New York state went to women. It took so long to get from 1 percent to 4 percent, but to get from 4 percent to 15 to 20 percent took much less time, and frankly, I think it will continue in that direction.

Joe: I know so many more women now through my professional contacts with the university and with the different associations. I can really get some solid information about women candidates, not only through my women friends. I don't mean personal friends—you know, professional friends, then I did before. Now that so many of the assistant's jobs have gone to women, I can also get the lowdown through their superintendents. Hey, I'm real comfortable recommending a woman if she's got the right credentials and, in my gut, I think she's got the stuff that the district is looking for. There are some women that I've backed many times over.

Al: We had the same experience. There were two women who were appointed superintendents this year who had been finalists with us for the last four years. The board that picked Joan was so impressed with her that there was no contest. They thought she was clearly ahead of the class.

Marv: There is no doubt on the elementary level on Long Island, women are doing much better than they have for some time, but their lack of experience at the secondary level holds them back. Sometimes boards want to hire someone who has been at a job longer than someone else, and at the secondary level, the men have had longer experience at principal's jobs and assistant's jobs because women haven't had the opportunity until recently to begin to take those jobs in any meaningful numbers. Still there really are very few women in high school principalships.

Al: Come on Marv, do boards really know what they want? Everyone wants someone who walks on water. They want people skills; they want academics;

they want business skills; they want people to listen—who think through things; someone who stands up for what he or she believes in and fights for it, and at the same time, he or she should do what everyone wants done.

Marv: Well, I can agree boards seem to be stuck with some hide-bound traditions. Often, whether it's a woman or a minority candidate, a board will say, "They're not ready for it!" I think it's not true. I think many of the communities are ahead of their boards in being able to accept a woman or minority superintendent. But boards are so sensitive about making the wrong decision because of what they see as the consequences on their budget and on their longevity on the board. They create many of these taboos themselves. Maybe that's the way it was for many years until women and minorities began to break some of these taboos. Boards are very slow in readjusting to the real world.

Al: If I've seen it once, I've seen it a hundred times. If a women exhibits certain characteristics the board would consider in a male to be an indication of strong leadership, they will think she is too male and unsympathetic and uncaring. On the other hand, if a women shows too much femininity, they think she's too weak, too soft! How is she going to negotiate with the union? How is she going to handle serious discipline problems? Women are always walking this fine line of trying to be both formulas.

Joe: Boards are just going to have to wake up and smell the coffee. Women and minorities have enormous talent waiting to get tapped, and boards have to deal with that. By the way, we do too. You know Jeanne Blanchard is getting a lot more business than I am lately. I think I'd better add a woman to my search team if I want to stay in business.

Marv: Yeah, me too. Well, we'll see how well the women we interviewed today fare in their quest for a superintendency.

Joe: It's getting late, I've got a tennis game. Beth is meeting me at the courts with her assistant, Janet. I've asked Rick to join us. I wonder if mixed doubles will replace golf up here?

REFERENCES

Castro, M. M. 1992. *Career paths of female school superintendents in Illinois.* Doctoral dissertation, Southern Illinois University at Carbondale.

Chase, S. E., and C. S. Bell. 1994. How search consultants talk about female superintendents. *The School Administrator* 51 (2): 36–42.

Fairbairne, L. 1989. *A survey of board of education/superintendent relationships: Does sex of the superintendent make a difference.* Doctoral dissertation, Hofstra University.

Montenegro, X. 1993. *Women and racial minority representation in school administration.* Arlington, Va.: American Association of School Administrators.

Radich, P. A. 1992. *Access and entry to the public school superintendency in the state of Washington: A comparison between men and women.* Doctoral dissertation, Washington State University.

CHAPTER FOUR

Power, Gender, and Superintendent Selection

C. CRYSS BRUNNER

Clearly, the processes for selecting a superintendent of schools are important for anyone wanting to be one. For women, these processes are even more critical, since in large part women do not get selected for the position (Arnez 1981; Blount 1993; Edson 1988; Grogan 1996; Montenegro 1993; Ortiz 1982; Shakeshaft 1989). The purpose of this chapter is to share the results of a study designed to examine and explain—using an important but neglected theoretical perspective—what happened during a particular selection process when a woman was selected as superintendent of schools.

The theoretical perspective used in this single-case ethnographic study suggests that the hiring of women as superintendents can be explained by exploring the regularities in what is said and done (Cherryholmes 1988) by the community power network relative to power (Clegg 1989). Cherryholmes (1988) stated that "professions are constituted by what is said and done in their name" (p. 1). He asserted that consistencies in what is said (definitions) and done (practices, use) are based on shared beliefs and values. These shared beliefs and values become the basis for decision making that is grounded in the following questions: How was this done before? What definitions and practices related to power drove decisions in the past? What definitions and uses of power were expected of superintendents in the past? Clearly, using these question as the basis for making decisions creates a consistency or sameness in decisions. What happened in the past dictates what happens in the future.

Specifically, I suggest that since the male power wielders in a given community are a dominant force, and the position of superintendent is viewed as a powerful and masculine position, then a woman wishing to be a superintendent must define and use power in the same ways as the community's male power wielders. She must define and use power in the same way that male superintendents before her have.

RESEARCH METHODS

This single-case ethnographic study was designed to examine the question: What is it about the definitions and uses of power in a given community that would allow a woman to be selected as superintendent of schools?

My hypothesis is the following: A woman wishing to be a superintendent of schools must adopt the same definitions and uses of power as the male power wielders in a given community in order to be selected for a position of power most often filled by a man.

To begin an examination of this hypothesis, I undertook a single-case ethnographic study (1992–94) of a Midwestern community, "New View" (pseudonym), which hired a woman as its superintendent of schools in 1989. New View, a rapidly growing "bedroom community" near the largest city in the state, had a relatively well-educated and affluent population of 15,000. New View was selected as the site for this study because it had appointed a woman superintendent three years before the study started. The fact that the woman superintendent had been in her position for three years was considered optimal for the study, since this period seemed long enough for others to be familiar with her administrative practices and short enough for them to accurately recall the circumstances surrounding her selection.

In the discussion that follows, the woman superintendent is given the pseudonym of "Dr. Osburn." All other names used in the story are pseudonyms as well.

Research Design

Because this study was concerned with discovery and understanding rather than with verification, ethnographic methods were employed. Documents and records concerning the hiring of Dr. Osburn and the major policy issues in the school district preceding and following her selection were reviewed and analyzed. In addition, nonparticipant and participant observation data collection procedures were employed. However, the data collected by these methods proved useful largely to corroborate the findings from the primary data collection strategy: nonstandardized interviews with two groups of power wielders in New View and with Dr. Osburn and her associates. Multiple interviews were conducted with Dr. Osburn, enabling her to react to interpretations of previous interviews, elaborate on existing understandings, and correct misunderstandings that had emerged. At least two interviews also were conducted with each of thirty members of Dr. Osburn's immediate circle of employers and employees: the preceding superintendent, the board of education, key coworkers, other central office administrators, principals, and teachers.

The two groups of power wielders in New View were developed using procedures drawn from Floyd Hunter's (1953) "reputational method" for identifying influential members in the community of Atlanta. To identify power wielders, Hunter made lists of leaders occupying positions of prominence in civic organizations, business establishments, and government, as well as persons prominent socially because of their wealth. After compiling lists, he asked persons who had lived in the community for some years and who had a knowledge of community affairs to select and rank people on the lists in a way that identified the most influential leaders. Not surprisingly, the resulting lists contained only the names of men.

I followed a similar but modified procedure in New View. My modifications were made primarily to create lists that included the names of women. When constructing the original lists, I purposely sought names of women as well as men. I kept the names of women on one list and the names of men on another and asked people to rank the two lists separately. The resulting lists were comprised of eight women participants and eleven men participants, all of whom were judged to be most active and influential in the New View community.

All individuals on the lists, associates of Dr. Osburn, and Dr. Osburn were interviewed in a nonstandardized format on at least two occasions to discuss three things: (1) their perspectives on the events surrounding the hiring of Dr. Osburn; (2) their understandings of the policy issues confronting New View schools at that time, and (3) their conceptions of power. Over 100 interviews were conducted in order to draw from the understanding and perspectives of each participant (Guba and Lincoln 1981; Lather 1991; Patton 1980). In brief, ethnographic methods were useful for understanding each person's definitions and uses of power in his or her own terms.

Background: New View Selects a Woman Superintendent

In 1989, New View's superintendent, Mr. Hamilton, retired. He had been the superintendent in New View for five years, business manager for several years before that, and a prominent figure in New View's power structure. The selection committee, put together by the board of education, had the charge to select five finalists for the superintendent position. The finalists included three men from outside the district—who had impressive experiences in central office administration—the male assistant superintendent of curriculum and personnel in New View (Mr. Robinson), and the female principal of New View High School (Dr. Osburn). For the purposes of this chapter, it is useful to discuss the candidacies of Mr. Robinson and Dr. Osburn, the two inside candidates who were favored in the selection process.

On the one hand, because Mr. Robinson had talent, ambition, and central office experience, many informants expected him to be hired as superintendent. On the other hand, other informants cited a number of factors that worked against him. First, he was not "the teachers' candidate." His role as personnel supervisor put him in the unpopular position of implementing a board decision to abandon collective bargaining with the teachers' union and offer "unilateral contracts" to the teachers. Second, his candidacy was not supported by Mr. Hamilton, the departing superintendent. During the time the two men worked together, Mr. Robinson made his ambitions clear, and Mr. Hamilton struggled to keep Mr. Robinson subordinate. Third, Mr. Robinson was known to be an authoritarian leader rather than one who sought the opinions of others. In the opinion of the participants in the study, Mr. Robinson thought his way was the right and only way.

Dr. Osburn lacked Mr. Robinson's central office experience, but she had a strong record as principal of New View High School. Several factors worked in her behalf. First, she had a reputation for effectively addressing the needs of students, developing the curriculum, establishing teamwork among staff members, developing strong lines of communication throughout the school, and sharing power with others. Briefly, she was viewed as a collaborative leader rather than an authoritarian one. Second, Mr. Hamilton—the departing superintendent—was her mentor and supported her. He encouraged her to seek the superintendency and used his position in the school system and the community to advance her candidacy.

Third, Dr. Osburn was respected as an effective advocate for the building of a new high school, an issue that dominated the educational politics of New View. In two recent past elections, New View voters had rejected bond issues to finance the new school. Most New View power wielders favored passage of the bond election because of overcrowded conditions at the school which, in their view, threatened the growth of the community. Historically, the excellent reputation of the New View school system had attracted affluent and upper-middle income residents from the larger metropolitan area to live in New View, but the mobile classrooms around New View High School disturbed many potential newcomers. Because the decision to build a new school rested in the hands of the voters, they needed to be convinced that the schools were effective, and that passing the bond issue would benefit all children throughout the district.

While the departing superintendent's authoritarian style of leadership had been relatively sufficient during his tenure, it was not appropriate for convincing the voters that the need for a new school was important enough to raise their taxes. The board of education believed that Dr. Osburn's collaborative leadership skills would enable her to effectively address this community problem.

The selection committee included four people: two women (a state legislator and a school board member) and two men (both university professors). According to the respondents in the study, this committee was gender balanced and open to collaborative leadership styles, things not characteristic of selection committees in the past. Interviews with the committee members revealed that they did not believe that including Dr. Osburn as one of their nominees was controversial, even though she would eventually be the first woman superintendent in New View, and, in fact, one of only two women superintendents in the entire state at the time.

When the final decision for selection came before the board of education, its members were responsive to the views of the departing Mr. Hamilton. This was not surprising, as Mr. Hamilton was admired and trusted by the power structure of the community and was leaving office to the regret of most people in the school system and community. In this context, his views were highly regarded.

Mr. Hamilton's opinion may have been given extra credence for another reason. During previous superintendent selection processes, members of the New View power structure had taken a keen interest in the appointment of the superintendent of schools. This was not the case when Dr. Osburn was selected. When asked why they were not as involved, members of the power network indicated that Mr. Hamilton was able to reflect their interests, making it unnecessary for them to attend in the same way. In addition, they were older, their children had graduated from school, and their businesses were strongly established and no longer depended as much on school issues.

Thus, while Mr. Hamilton's opinion—as a recognized member of the power structure—was important to the board of education, other power wielders in the community were not pressuring the board to move in any particular direction when hiring a superintendent. Further, informants reported that the board members themselves had tired somewhat of the authoritarian leadership of Mr. Hamilton and were ready to hire someone whom they believed was less independent and would allow them greater autonomy. As one informant said,

> I think the board wanted to hire someone whom they could control somewhat—to get done what they wanted. I don't think that Mr. Hamilton followed them. He listened to people, but I don't think he asked for input. He felt he knew more than other people.

In principle, the board of education sets educational policy, and the superintendent implements the will of the board. On the one hand, if the board wanted to select someone whom they could control, Dr. Osburn appeared to be a better choice than Mr. Robinson. As stated, Dr. Osburn had a reputation for using power collaboratively, while Mr. Robinson was known for using power in a domineering way. Dr. Osburn had succeeded in a man's world, but as a woman she had been socialized to believe that women should remain subordinate to those with formal authority. On the other hand, the discomfort of the New View Board of Education with its largely oversight role could be interpreted not simply as a desire by board members to replace bureaucratic domination with their own, but as an attempt to further democratize educational policy making.

FINDINGS

Mr. Hamilton and Mr. Robinson and Power

The brief background description of New View's selection of Dr. Osburn as superintendent indicates that the men (Mr. Hamilton and Mr. Robinson) were perceived as using power in domineering and authoritarian ways, while the woman (Dr. Osburn) was perceived as using power in a collaborative way. While Mr. Robinson, when interviewed, stated that he did not use his power to control decision making, Mr. Hamilton was definite in an interview that he used his power in the superintendency to control people and situations. Both men stated that when difficult decisions had to be made, it was necessary at some point to terminate discussion and make the decision themselves. Each had considerable confidence in his ability to make informed judgments.

Mr. Hamilton and Mr. Robinson were considered authoritarian and domineering decision makers by every educator and community member whom I interviewed. Both men defined power as the "ability to influence people." People who worked with these men stated that they made decisions and then delegated subordinates to carry out actions that supported those decisions. Some participants talked about methods of intimidation used by these men. Others said that Mr. Hamilton and Mr. Robinson talked over their ideas informally with a few people, but in the end made the decisions themselves.

Dr. Osburn and Power

In contrast, Dr. Osburn defined power as the "ability to achieve desired outcomes." When asked to elaborate on how she achieved desired outcomes, she said,

> I have the ability to organize people in a manner that achieves desired goals—that manner being the ability to lead people to consensus. I bring together the people who will be affected by the decision and say, 'Here is the perceived problem. Is this really the problem?' You may find that it is not the real problem, so you come to consensus about what the real problem is. Then you discuss many solutions to come up with a solution which benefits the most people—especially who is affected by it. It needs to be for the greatest good.

Dr. Osburn also stressed the importance of collaboration:

> I've always believed that we win when we quit worrying about who gets the credit. I want the project complete. If it happens by a coalition, then great. I am not interested in claiming that I did such and such. I think, as women, we have always known that we have to work with people to accomplish anything. A mother who runs a household doesn't always get the credit for what the children accomplish, but her preparing and planning helps these accomplishments to happen. I

always think of myself as the vehicle in the snowstorm who goes out and moves the snow so that other people can operate. I think that is it important that we do that. I don't want to be seen in the position of supervisor. You must give people the tools to do the job, but you can get out of the picture if you train people and give them the tools.

Perhaps most revealing of Dr. Osburn's commitment to collaborative power and rejection of controlling power is the following statement:

One of the harder things to do is to support a decision that you wouldn't have made yourself. Having given someone else the opportunity to make it, you need to support them. I think that the decision I make is to make decisions collaboratively. Then, I give up the right to the final decision. I must support whatever is decided.

Clearly, Dr. Osburn believed that power was defined as collaboration.

Observations and interviews with other participants indicated that Dr. Osburn did in fact practice her beliefs about power when she was a high school principal and continued the same practices as superintendent. Every respondent interviewed, male and female—from the community and from the school system—referred to Dr. Osburn as a collaborator/consensus builder. They claimed, for example, that "Dr. Osburn wields power through other people," that "she is less than direct . . . not confrontational not frontal," that "she listens, collaborates, gets the best out of the people," that "she builds consensus . . . and delegates authority," that "she operates with one vote," that "she shares authority and empowers others," and that "she defines power differently than men."

The Male Power Wielders and Power

The male power wielders of New View most often defined power as the capacity to influence decisions, and they tended to stress the resources that one needs to exercise influence: "You must have a position." "You need political connections." One man said,

Knowledge is power. You influence because you work hard and know more than other people. Information is power, too. If I have information and you don't, I have power in that particular area.

The men in the power network did not define power as the ability to get things done, as Dr. Osburn had. Some talked about the desirability of consensus, but were more willing to invoke a command-and-control use of power because they thought consensus building hindered actual accomplishment.

One man asserted, "If you cannot persuade people to do what you want, then you use chain of command and make them do it." Another man stressed that he relied on others trusting him. "I must be accepted and trusted. They look to me as someone they can trust. They have reason to believe that I know how to get it done, so they trust my decision." Since others trusted him, he believed that he had the right to make decisions for them.

One man talked about the need to work with others to get things done, and admitted that "things aren't completely in my control. But," he said, " I push in that direction. I don't accept 'no'." In general, what emerges from the men in the power network of New View is that power is defined as the ability to get done what they want done. They believed that to gain compliance from others, power wielders must rely on what were considered legitimate resources—office, allies, knowledge, ability to persuade, money. I noted that although legitimate resources were relied upon, they were used to implement the ideas or wishes of one person rather than a collective body of people.

In general, the men in the male network of power in New View defined and used power the way in which Mr. Hamilton and Mr. Robinson did. They believed that power was the ability to influence others to agree with the decisions made by those in powerful positions or roles.

The Female Power Wielders and Power

The women power wielders in New View most often defined power as the ability to get things done with others. They elaborated that such ability involved consensus building, empowering others, enlisting the help of others, motivating others, and being a servant. Compared to the men in the male power network of New View, the women in the female power network did not define power as being a quality of particular persons—especially themselves. Rather, they considered it collective action taken as a result of a collaboratively made decision. Most in fact expressed surprise that their names were provided by informants as being among New View's top influentials. One typical comment was, "I think more of the responsibility than the power of it." Another woman claimed that power "is teamwork." The women claimed that important aspects of exercising power included "letting people know that they are important," "communication with others," "caring . . . by letting others know that their experiences are valued," "listening," "giving rather than taking," and "seeking multiple inputs."

Overwhelmingly, the women in the female power network of New View defined and used power as Dr. Osburn did. They believed that power is the ability to get things done with others. They believed that what was to be done should be agreed upon by all of the people involved.

DISCUSSION AND ANALYSIS

Discussion and analysis of the findings fall under two major themes: Dr. Osburn's definition and use of power as it relates to power theory; and, New View comes to value a different definition and use of power.

Dr. Osburn and Power Theory

The findings made evident that the New View's male power network had different definitions and uses of power than New View's female power network. Further, Mr. Hamilton's and Mr. Robinson's definitions and uses of power matched those of the men in the male power network, and Dr. Osburn's definitions and uses of power matched those of the women in the female network of power. While I was surprised to find this dramatic division along gender lines, a similar division can be found in the philosophical literature on power.

Theoretical analyses of the concept of power generally occur along two primary trajectories (Clegg 1989, 21-38; Hartsock 1981, 3-19; Pitkin 1972, 276-77; Stone 1989, 219-33; Wartenberg 1990, 9-50). The dominant trajectory in the history of political thought and in contemporary political science defines power as control, command, and domination over others (Clegg 1989; Hartsock 1981). The subordinate (less emphasized, analyzed, and appreciated) trajectory defines power as a capacity to accomplish certain social goals through cooperation and collaboration among people with various interests and concerns (Follett 1942; Sarason 1990).

According to John Stuart Mill (1869, 208), "A man's power is the readiness of other men to obey him." Wartenberg (1990), Clegg (1989), Hartsock (1981), and others have shown that contemporary political scientists and sociologists have largely conceived and analyzed power as command, control, and domination (Bachrach and Baratz 1962; Dahl 1961; Lukes 1974; Lasswell and Kaplan 1950; Nagel 1975; Polsby 1980; Russell 1938; Simon 1953; Schumaker 1991; Weber 1924).

However, while (mostly) male political theorists and scientists were proposing and analyzing these various aspects of the dominant conception of power, the most prominent female political theorist of the twentieth century, Hannah Arendt, sought to reestablish the subordinate trajectory of power that had been largely abandoned by contemporary analysts. According to Arendt (1972), "[P]ower corresponds to the human ability not just to act but to act in concert. Power is never the property of an individual; it belongs to a group and remains in existence only so long as the group keeps together" (p. 143).

Arendt's approach to the concept of power was emphasized and elaborated by Nancy Hartsock (1981, 1983), who clearly differentiated a masculine emphasis on power as domination from an alternative feminine tradition. According to Hartsock (1983), "Theories of power put forward by women rather than men differ systematically from the understanding of power as domination. While few women have theorized about power, their theories bear a striking similarity both to one another and to theories of power recently characterized as feminist understandings of power" (p. 210).

Hartsock did not propose a fixed alternative conception to power as domination, but found intriguing possibilities in the writings of such women as Arendt, Dorothy Emmet, and Hannah Pitkin. In Arendt, she saw a model in which the heroic person finds her power not through dominating others in competitive situations but through "action in connection with others with whom one shares a common life and common concerns" (Hartsock 1983, 217). In Emmet (1953-1954), she saw a useful distinction between coercive power and coactive power, and found a hopeful attempt to redefine power as "any kind of effectiveness in performance" (Hartsock 1983, 223). In Pitkin (1972, 275), she saw an attempt to connect power to community and the capacity of the community to act toward common ends.

Nancy Hartsock (1987, 276-77) agrees with other theorists that the idea of power as dominance, authority, and control is significantly different than power as collective, shared, and collaborative, and she takes this division further by calling for a theory of power for women—a theory that begins from the experience and point of view of the dominated. She points out, "Such theories would give attention not only to the ways women are dominated, but also to their capacities, abilities, and strengths. . . . [Said] theories would use these capacities as guides for a potential transformation of power relationships—that is, for the empowerment of women" (p.158).

These feminine notions about power are in evidence in a recent essay on "Women and Power" by Jean Baker Miller (1993). Miller claimed that women have been powerful in ways that are transparent next to the masculine perspective of power as domination. According to Miller, "[W]omen use power all the time, but generally must see it as used for the benefit of others"; a woman's identity demands that her power be regarded as neither destructive nor selfish for fear that she will be abandoned, and thus women are encouraged to use their capacities in collaborative ways that serve the needs of broader communities.

In short, an impressive number of women have written about power in a way that distinguishes authoritarian power from collective power. This is not to say that collective power is an exclusively feminist idea and has been ignored by men (see, for example, Ball 1993; Habermas 1981; Issac 1993; Stone 1989). Women and men have begun to reconceptualize power in ways that emphasize its cooperative and collaborative aspects and have recognized that the achievement of collective power serves the goals of a community and does not simply subordinate some people to the will of others.

Thus, the collaborative model of power is not only a feminist idea that represents the experiences of women; it may also be an increasingly emergent paradigm of power. In other words, feminists view orthodox conceptions of power as incorporating masculine preoccupations with how people control one another to secure their personal wants, and they suggest that such conceptions must be complemented with more feminine concerns about how people can effectively organize themselves to solve social problems and transform their environments.

In the case of Dr. Osburn and the women in the female power network, their definitions and uses of power matched descriptions of the subordinate, sometimes called "feminine," trajectory of power. Rather than adopt the dominant, "masculine," definitions and uses of power like those of the male power network, as I had hypothesized, Dr. Osburn's definitions and uses of power remained "feminine."

New View Comes to Value a Different Kind of Power

At the time Mr. Hamilton was selected to be superintendent, New View valued power defined and used as authority and control. With the selection of Dr. Osburn, it was evident that those values had changed. I came to understand that there were at least six possible reasons for this change: (1) The need for a collaborative leader arose because of the bond election and teacher contract issues; (2) The board of education desired autonomy; (3) The male power network showed little interest in the selection of Dr. Osburn; (4) The membership of the selection committee was representative; (5) New View had changed from an elite community power structure to a more pluralistic one; and (6) Dr. Osburn's candidacy was supported by the respected departing male superintendent. In the paragraphs that follow, I briefly discuss each of these reasons.

The need for a collaborative leader. To begin, the key issues confronting New View schools at the time of Dr. Osburn's appointment seemed more amenable to collective rather than coercive power and leadership. The most important issue in New View during the period of this study was public approval of a bond to finance a new high school. As discussed earlier, superintendents cannot command and control the public to finance their projects. The process of getting the public to approve bonds involves building a large enough coalition so that the requisite votes are attained. Leaders must attend to what various segments of the voting public want and will support. They need to incorporate various interests and constituencies in developing a proposal that will succeed with a majority of voters.

In New View, previous bond proposals that failed were neither developed nor promoted in this manner, leading board members to understand the need for a new approach. As one part of that approach, they sought to repackage their bond proposal so that "there was something in it for everyone." As a second part of that approach, they sought a superintendent who would build public confidence in the schools by serving as a bridge between the public and the board, communicating public concerns to the board and explaining to the public how the board's proposal served the vital needs of the students.

The second most important issue in New View at the time of Dr. Osburn's appointment was lingering teacher discontent over the board's decision to impose unilateral contracts. Such an approach to dealing with teachers' salaries was deemed necessary by the school board to demonstrate that they, and not the teachers' unions, controlled the schools. Whatever the merits of this policy—which had been implemented at the end of Mr. Hamilton's tenure—it had negatively affected teacher morale throughout the district. Rebuilding teacher morale was clearly not a problem that could be addressed by a domineering superintendent. Again, the collaborative approach that Dr. Osburn brought to school matters, which involved consulting extensively with teachers, actively affirming their importance, and seeking to empower them in various ways, offered hope for alleviating this problem.

By means of a collaborative model of decision making within the schools, morale among New View teachers improved. Both men and women in the study, in both the educational and community-wide power structures, praised Dr. Osburn's leadership style. Dr. Osburn was strongly supported by the community and the public education system, and this support seemed to stem largely from her definition of power and her effective use of it.

The Board of Education's desire for autonomy. The school board wanted to increase its policy making role. While school boards have extensive formal authority over educational policy, they are notorious for deferring to the professionalism and expertise of the administrative staff. At the time of Dr. Osburn's selection, the board of education was strongly led by Mr. Hamilton. Not only did he and his staff play a major role in determining the agendas of board meetings, control most of the information that was brought to bear on that agenda, and present their recommendations in a relatively unequivocal manner, but Mr. Hamilton also played an active role in soliciting board members to run for election.

Policy making procedures that stress mere formal authorization and accountability of governmental officials are clearly less democratic than those in which effective policy makers are elected representatives who encourage citizens' participation and are responsive to citizens' concerns (Schumaker 1991, 23-29). As noted earlier, the discomfort of the New View Board of Education with its largely oversight role can be seen not simply as a desire by board members to replace bureaucratic domination with their own, but rather as an attempt to further democratize educational policy making. If the board and the broader public were to play a larger role in policy making, it made sense to hire a superintendent who sought multiple perspectives on educational problems, who maintained open channels of communication with everyone involved, and who had the ability to support proposals that differed from those that she preferred.

The male power network and the selection of Dr. Osburn. In the past, members of the New View power structure (particularly the men) had taken a keen interest in the appointment of the superintendent of schools, but they were little involved in the selection of Dr. Osburn. In part, their inactivity indicated trust in Mr. Hamilton's ability to reflect their interests, but it also indicated their declining interest in the position. Their children were grown, and their businesses were established in ways that reduced their dependency on school issues.

Membership of the selection committee. The selection committee was relatively representative and open minded. The "old boy network" had been abandoned as a method for hiring top administrative personnel. Procedures involving the aggressive recruitment of highly qualified candidates were in place. Formal qualifications were established that emphasized qualities predicting effectiveness on the job rather than "paper credentials." The appointed selection committee—a school board member and a state legislator (two women) and two university professors (both men)—was composed of representatives of the various constituencies that the superintendent would serve (Walzer 1983, 129–54). The fact that women comprised half of the selection committee illustrates its representative nature.

The power structure of New View changes. The power structure of New View had become relatively pluralistic, dispersed, and indeed fragmented by the time of Dr. Osburn's appointment. During the early years of its development, New View had an elitist or a centralized power structure; an "old boy network" controlled most issues and the appointment of most administrative positions. Community power theorists have shown that as communities grow and age, they become more heterogeneous in the demographic composition of their citizens, in the diversity of their interests, and in the emergence of a complex and diversified set of groups that become politically active (Trounstine and Christensen 1982). The resulting loss of homogeneity challenges social control by a unified and an active power structure (Tilly 1984).

Such processes were at work in New View during the 1970s and 1980s. New residents arrived who were unwilling to defer to "the old elite." Many of these residents commuted to the metropolitan center, and were less interested in supporting the economic interests of the old elite than in maintaining the aesthetic and environmental amenities of a "bedroom community." Most new residents also were relatively affluent and highly educated, and held many social values that challenged the parochialism and traditionalism of the old elites of small towns (McClosky and Brill 1983). In this context, the power structure of New View became less a unified, active, and like-minded group that "ran the city" and more a diverse group of individuals who had access to various power resources, who were generally informed about community (and school) issues, and whose cooperation helped accomplish various community goals when that cooperation could be secured. The previous "old boy network" would surely have taken an interest in the school superintendency and sought to influence the appointment, but that network had more or less dissipated by the late 1980s. Those listed as being influential in the current power structure comprised a more diverse group whose members seldom interacted with one another; most had limited interest in the appointment, and the issue was such that their involvement was not required to secure an acceptable person. Thus, a traditional and parochial power structure did not stand in the way of Dr. Osburn's appointment.

Mr. Hamilton supports Dr. Osburn's candidacy. Dr. Osburn had a mentor in Mr. Hamilton. He supported her in her role as principal of New View High School; he encouraged her to apply for the superintendency; and he became her advocate before the selection committee and the board of education.

CONCLUSION

In conclusion, I have come to understand that it was, in large part, Dr. Osburn's definition and use of power that made her selection as superintendent possible. Clearly, she did not adopt the dominant definitions and uses of power in order to be selected as I had hypothesized. Not only were her definitions and uses of power gender appropriate, but they also were coincidentally important to the New View community and school district at the time of her candidacy.

Several characteristics of New View played an important part in Dr. Osburn's selection, and I suggest that they may be important for other women superintendent candidates whose definitions and uses of power are ones that support collaboration and shared decision making. Those characteristics include: (1) a rapidly growing community that has become more pluralistic due, in part, to the decline of the power elite; (2) a school district that needs a collaborative leader because of issues that require consensus building; (3) a board of education that wishes to play a greater role in policy making; and, (4) a district where a prominent, respected male insider will support the woman's candidacy as superintendent.

As our nation matures and becomes more pluralistic, the ability to work among and with various interest groups becomes essential. Perhaps this need will open doors to the superintendency for women whose "feminine" definitions and uses of power have become valued in a new way.

REFERENCES

Arendt, H. 1972. *Crises of the republic: Lying in politics, civil disobedience on violence, thoughts on politics, and revolution.* New York: Teachers College Press.

Arnez, N. 1981. *The besieged school superintendent: A case study of school superintendent-school board relations in Washington, D. C., 1973-75.* Washington: University Press of America, Inc.

Bachrach, P., and M. S. Baratz. 1962. Two faces of power. *American Political Science Review* (57): 947-52.

Ball, T. 1993. New faces of power. In T. Wartenberg (ed.), *Rethinking power*. Albany, N.Y.: State University of New York Press.

Blount, J. 1993. The genderization of the superintendency: A statistical portrait. Paper presented at the annual meeting of the American Educational Research Association, Atlanta, Ga.

Cherryholmes, C. H. 1988. *Power and criticism: Poststructural investigations in education*. New York: Teachers College Press.

Clegg, S. R. 1989. *Frameworks of power*. London: Sage Publications.

Dahl, R. A. 1961. *Who governs?* New Haven: Yale University Press.

Edson, S. K. 1988. *Pushing the limits: The female administrative aspirant*. Albany, N.Y.: State University of New York Press.

Emmet, D. 1953-1954. The concept of power. *Proceedings of the Aristotelian Society* (54), London.

Follett, M. P. 1942. *Creative experience*. New York: Longmans, Green, and Co.

Grogan, M. 1996. *Voices of women aspiring to the superintendency*. Albany, N.Y.: State University of New York Press.

Guba, E., and Y. Lincoln. 1981. *Effective evaluation*. San Francisco: Jossey-Bass.

Habermas, J. 1981. Hannah Arendt's communications concept of power. In S. Lukes (ed.), *Power*. New York: New York University Press.

Hartsock, N. C. M. 1981. Political change: Two perspectives on power. In C. Bunch (ed.), *Building feminist theory: Essays from Quest*. New York: Longman.

———. 1983. *Money, sex, and power: Toward a feminist historical materialism*. New York: Longman.

———. 1987. Foucault on power: A theory for women? In L. Nicholson (ed.), *Feminism/postmodernism*. London: Routledge Press.

Hunter, F. 1953. *Community power structure: A study of decision makers*. Chapel Hill, N.C.: University of North Carolina Press.

Issac, J. 1993. Beyond the three faces of power: A realist critique. In T. Wartenberg (ed.), *Rethinking power*. Albany, N.Y.: State University of New York Press.

Lasswell, H. D., and A. Kaplan. 1950. *Power and society*. New Haven: Yale University Press.

Lather, P. 1991. *Getting smart: Feminist research and pedagogy with/in the postmodern*. New York and London: Routledge.

Lukes, S. 1974. *Power: A radical view*. London: The MacMillian Press Ltd.

McClosky, H., and A. Brill. 1983. *Dimensions of tolerance*. New York: Russell Sage.

Mill, J. S. 1869. *Human mind*. Referenced by T. Wartenberg, *The forms of power*. (Philadelphia: Temple University Press, 1990), p. 18.

Miller, J. B. 1993. Women and power. In T. Wartenberg (ed.), *Rethinking power*. Albany, N.Y.: State University of New York Press.

Montenegro, X. 1993. *Women and racial minority representation in school administration.* Arlington, Va.: American Association of School Administrators.

Nagel, J. 1975. *The descriptive analysis of power.* New Haven: Yale University Press.

Ortiz, F. I. 1982. *Career patterns in education: Women, men and minorities in public school administration.* New York: Praeger.

Patton, M. Q. 1980. *Qualitative evaluation methods.* Beverly Hills, Calif.: Sage Publications.

Pitkin, H. 1972. *Wittgenstein and justice.* Berkeley: University of California Press.

Polsby, N. W. 1980. *Community power and political theory.* New Haven: Yale University Press.

Russell, B. 1938. *Power: A new social analysis.* London: Allen and Unwin.

Sarason, D. B. 1990. *The predictable failure of educational reform: Can we change course before it's too late?* San Francisco: Jossey-Bass Publications.

Schumaker, P. 1991. *Critical pluralism.* Lawrence: University Press of Kansas.

Shakeshaft, C. 1989. *Women in educational administration.* Newbury Park, Calif.: Sage Publications.

Simon, H. A. 1953. Notes on the observation and measurement of power. *Journal of Politics* (15): 978-90.

Stone, C. 1989. *Regime politics.* Lawrence, Kans.: University Press of Kansas.

Tilly, C. 1984. *Big structures, large processes, huge comparisons.* New York: Russell Sage.

Trounstine, P. J., and T. Christensen. 1982. *Movers and shakers.* New York: St. Martin's Press.

Walzer, M. 1983. *Spheres of justice.* New York: Basic.

Wartenberg, T. E. 1990. *The forms of power: From domination to transformation.* Philadelphia: Temple University Press.

Weber, M. (1924, 1947). The theory of social and economic organizations. Edited by A. H. Henderson, and T. Parsons. Glencoe Ill.: Free Press.

Whitaker, K. S., and K. Lane. (February, 1990). Is a woman's place in school administration? Women slowly open the door to educational leadership. *The School Administrator*, pp. 8-12.

Yeakey, C. C., G. S. Johnston, and J. A. Adkison. 1986. In pursuit of equity: A review of research on minorities and women in educational administration. *Educational Administration Quarterly*, 22 (3): 110-49.

CHAPTER FIVE

Climbing Hills and Mountains

Black Females Making It
to the Superintendency

JUDY A. ALSTON

Given the obstacles that exist for black women in America, those who obtain visible top leadership positions must be exceptional (Reid-Merritt 1996). Despite the barriers of race and gender, hard work and endurance have always been the foundation upon which black women have made great strides. Life for these women has never been a "crystal stair" (Hughes 1954). For black women seeking leadership positions in education, it is a continual cycle of "climbin' on, reachin' landin's, turnin' corners, and sometimes goin' in the dark" (Hughes 1954). The use of the extended metaphor, the "crystal stair," seems to refer to an image of a "bed of roses," an easier life. The staircase in Hughes's poem, however, is a metaphor for a battered and bruised life, yet a life filled with courage and determination (*African-American Literature*, TM 1992). Today's black female school superintendents are those women who have coupled courage and determination in order to become some of the most successful women in educational leadership.

During the 1995–96 school year, Moody and Moody (1995) identified forty-five black female superintendents across the United States. Black women constituted less than 2 percent of the total population of superintendents in the country. Seeking to determine the reasons for the low numbers, I did a study to determine the constraints and facilitators that black females encountered as they continued to climb the "stairs" to the superintendency.

Despite increased support from people and policy, women, in general, represent a minority in administrative positions; black females make up an even smaller minority. Traditionally, women, especially black women, are underrepresented in the superintendency in public education. The underrepresentation of black women could be related to many things. For example, a review of the literature (Moody 1983, 1995; Jackson 1995) reveals that the position is becoming increasingly more challenging for blacks, particularly black women. When they do succeed in attaining the position, black women are more than likely to be located in difficult urban centers or older suburban communities (Venable 1995).

Research on women in educational administration leaves little doubt about difficulties that all women face in seeking administrative careers (Edson 1988). The universality of the male experience has long been the norm, and women are continuously held up to a male-centered paradigm of management and leadership (Smyth 1989). Robertson (1992) suggested that low representation of women in administration confirmed that women's exclusion from leadership positions is more entrenched in the field of education than in other professions. However, because of black women's work, family experience, and grounding in African-American culture, it is suggested that black women as a group experience a world different from those who are not black or female (Collins 1990). Black women inhabit a "micro" world living simultaneously within the larger macroculture, and theirs is a harder climb when compared to white men and women.

WOMEN AND LEADERSHIP: A BRIEF REVIEW OF THE LITERATURE

Career Paths/Barriers

The typical woman administrator not only does not look like the typical male administrator, but the path she takes to achieve her position differs as well. The literature on careers and career paths in administration does not fit the experience of women administrators (more specifically black women), primarily because the experiences used to define career and document career routes have come from men.

Women have attained positions of every type in the administrative hierarchy. Women in public schools have a better chance of being top-level administrators in small districts or in elementary school districts. The minority woman principal is most often working in schools with 20 percent or more minority population in a Southern state. As leaders in these predominantly minority schools and as superintendents in these school districts, they are perceived and treated differently from other principals and school administrators (Ortiz 1982). Also, women begin their careers committed to education; nearly half major in education or in the humanities with an education specialization. In their thirties, women tend to turn toward administration, and for both the typical and atypical woman in administration, the three most common ways for women to enter school administration are through specialist positions, elementary principalships, and supervisory posts (Shakeshaft 1989).

In many cases, the perceptions and images of women and work are still those perceptions and images of the nineteenth century. This general stereotype about working women, and women in general, is the notion that the women's place is in the home (Smith and Piele 1989). This image creates barriers for women who are seeking to enter management positions. Fox and Hesse-Biber (cited in Smith and Piele 1989) have noted that this stereotype has remained in female-dominated fields such as nursing, social work, and teaching, because of the following:

- weakly developed theoretical bases of knowledge;
- lack of authority and autonomy;
- less intensive training; and
- emphasis on hierarchical ranking and differential duties in these fields.

These stereotypes have remained and continue to influence the socialization process of women, causing them to accept subordinate roles and limit their aspirations (Smith and Piele 1989).

Not setting administrative career goals created a barrier for women in the past, but it also appears that there are still definite barriers women must challenge (Green and Manera 1995). Barriers that women face have been categorized as internal, external, and androcentric. Internal barriers that have been identified are those historical and societal assumptions that pressure women to conform to roles and behaviors traditionally associated with women. External barriers are those societal stereotypes and organizational structures that perpetuate discrimination against women, while androcentrism presupposes that women function as men and, therefore, should view the world from a male perspective (Green and Manera, 1995). Barriers faced by women leaders in education are more clearly articulated through the questions raised, such as, Is it not a societal expectation that women solve other people's problems rather than define problems for others to solve? How is an individual woman's communication pattern interpreted, given a commonly held stereotype of women as caretaker? (Green and Manera 1995).

In the business world, the concept of the glass ceiling (women as a group are kept from advancing higher because of their gender) dominates studies about why there are so few women in leadership positions (Morrison, White, and Van Velsor 1987). In a study conducted by the Center for Creative Leadership over a three-year period, results coincided with those of educational studies and found few women in top leadership positions.

The results of this study proposed that there are two parts to the glass ceiling that constitute barriers for women. The first barrier occurs at the general management level, which represents added responsibility, admittance to "the club," and sharing perks. In order for women to break through the ceiling, they must possess credibility and prestige, strong advocacy of at least one influential person higher in the company, and pure luck. The second barrier is a wall of tradition and stereotype that keeps women out of senior executive levels by placing even more obstacles in their path. Top jobs are more restrictive to women because of more scrutinized acceptability and increased unrealistic expectations based on the assumption that women have different leadership styles and, therefore, are different and outsiders (Morrison et al. 1987).

In a study of women and the structure of organizations, Kanter (1975) pointed out that the lack of women in executive jobs is not just division of labor between men and women, but one of sex stratification by class. Women are rewarded for routine service associated with a secondary job market class, while men are rewarded for decision making and leadership, a primary job market class.

In the same vein, Smith and Piele (1989) noted that few women work as school administrators, that the positions women get are the lowest ranking ones, that the women who get the jobs are older than men working at comparable levels, and that the situation is getting worse all the time. Those women who succeed in entering the realms of educational decision making and leadership are expected to meet higher expectations in administrative ranks because of the devalued status of women in society and education as well.

Using sociocultural and structural explanations of why women are absent from leadership positions and why their experiences have not been significantly addressed, Bell (1988) analyzed women in administrative roles. She used sociocultural explanations such as sex role stereotyping, career socialization, and women's culture to explain the gender differences between women's and men's ambition, access to opportunity, career patterns, and work styles. She used structural explanations, including Kanter's (1977) theory of organizational behavior to contrast the differences between women and men related to ambition, mobility, work style and efficacy. In these analyses, the focus was on organizational arrangements, and gender was downplayed as a way to explain people's experiences.

Relationship between Blacks and Women and the Superintendency

Blacks who aspire to the superintendency could probably learn much from the plight of women who presently hold the same position, since they both, as minorities, face similar problems and obstacles (Williams 1984). McDade and Drake (1982) identified special problems that women encountered en route to the superintendency. The top five special problems were:

- Women usually must be better than their male competitors to be considered for administrative appointment.
- Successful women usually are viewed as the exception.

- Aggressiveness usually is viewed as a negative trait in women.
- Women frequently do not receive salary, title, and status to match their responsibilities.
- Women usually are not willing to compete for top level jobs. (p. 210)

These issues directly apply to the variable of race. Many times, however, the gender/race issue becomes so intertwined that it is difficult to determine which one is actually taking precedence. Also, while black women and white women may face some of the same barriers in their advancement to positions of leadership, their experiences do differ. Pigford and Tonnsen (1993) noted that since society socializes black women to be second-class citizens because of both race and gender, overcoming internal barriers might present a more formidable challenge. As a result, black women are systemically oppressed in their quest to become administrators.

In addition to the barriers listed, when black women are hired as superintendents, they often are presented with the chance to be "messiahs, scapegoats, or sacrificial lambs" (Yeakey et al. 1986). They are given the poorly maintained and badly managed urban school districts with high minority populations. Despite these conditions, black women continue to climb the stairs to success.

Feminism, Educational Administration, and Leadership

Often in research on women in administration, there is an absence of feminist scholarship. This absence and silence of women in leadership is perpetuated by the contention that women are trying to be leaders inside of hierarchical organizations that promote gender stratification by roles and maintain values and beliefs based on men's experiences. This incongruence creates social tension for women in administration (Hart 1995). By analyzing gender as an invisible social construct in stratified roles, Hart argued that organizations apply deliberate and unconscious tactics to the socialization of new members that result in different types of responses.

Shakeshaft (1989) developed several theoretical framework approaches for studying female administrators. They include the symbolic interaction framework that addresses how schools appear to the women who administer them; a feminist framework that focuses on female leadership as community building; and a revisionist approach that addresses rethinking organizational theory by adding women's experiences. In addressing these approaches and relating them to women in superintendencies, Bell (1988) raised the following questions:

> How do women in the superintendency think about what it means to be one of a few women in a male-dominated occupation? What part does this gender consciousness play in the ability to examine and understand problematic work situations? How do women think

about and relate to female colleagues? How do characteristics of the position interact with gender? Are there situations in which traditional meanings and implications (i.e., for male superintendents) do not hold for women? (p. 35)

These questions have implications for this study on black female superintendents because of the underrepresentation of the selected population, the lack of research on the selected population, and the importance of the answers pertaining to black females in educational administration. These issues are pertinent for changing thoughts and practices in preparation and placement programs and educational networks.

While much of the literature on educational management and theories of management and organization ignores women, either by making the assumption that managers are male or by assuming a "gender-free" position, the literature also ignores the issue of race, specifically the black female manager/leader. Collins (1990) noted that black women have long occupied marginal positions in academic settings. She argued that many black female intellectuals have made use of their marginality, that is, their "outsider within" status, to produce black feminist thought that reflects a special standpoint on self, family, and society (Glazer, Bensimon, and Townsend 1993, 45).

Feminist methodology begins with the view that women are oppressed (Adler, Laney, and Packer 1993). Klein (1983) argued that a fair amount of feminist scholarship has not contributed to women's visibility in a feminist frame of reference, but instead continues to perpetuate the dominant androcentric one. Therefore, it is research "on" women rather than research "for" women. Research "for" women is that which tries to take women's needs, interests, and experiences into account and aims at being instrumental in improving women's lives in one way or another . . . (p. 90).

Black women do not neatly fit into the various models of feminist theory. In the early days of the women's movement in this country, black women were largely ignored and marginalized. But feminism now empowers black women and women in general to address the problems in American society that make cavalier attitudes toward women acceptable. Black women have been addressing the concerns of white male domination and hegemony from the very beginning. Sojourner Truth's question "Ain't I a Woman?" still rings true. And as bell hooks (1989) stated resoundingly, "We can and do speak for ourselves. And our struggle today is to be heard."

METHOD OF STUDY

Based on a survey of black female superintendents, the purpose of this study was to identify constraints and facilitators that black female school superintendents encountered en route to the superintendency. The study used a four-part questionnaire. The first section of the questionnaire solicited data pertaining to personal characteristics (age, degree, marital status, etc.) and career data (prior experience, classroom experience, administrative experience, etc.). The second section listed, in alphabetical order, fourteen issues affecting superintendents that were identified by the American Association of School Administrators (AASA). The respondents were asked to prioritize the issues on a scale of 1 (most important) to 14 (least important). The third section of the instrument, a Likert-type scale, provided the respondents with opportunities to address those factors (constraints and facilitators) that they may have encountered en route to the superintendency (Williams 1984). Finally, the last section of the instrument listed five open-ended essay questions about the respondents' perceptions of the superintendency.

The total population of black female superintendents (N = 45) during the 1995–96 school year was surveyed. The rate of response was 51 percent. An initial mailing yielded 20 responses; a second mailing yielded three more responses (total returned was 23). The mailings were done two weeks apart from one another.

OVERVIEW OF THE FINDINGS

This section analyzes the findings of the study and focuses on the following: personal and professional background, and job performance factors (constraints and facilitators) encountered en route to the superintendency.

Personal and Professional Background

The majority of the black female superintendents revealed that they were in the 50–54 age range and came from urban or rural community backgrounds. The majority of the respondents held a doctorate and began their careers as elementary teachers. An analysis of their professional educational experiences revealed an interesting contrast to the research on male administrators' career paths. These women averaged more years in the classroom in contrast to their male counterparts. This finding agrees with previous research on women in the superintendency and suggests that women have more educational experience than their male counterparts before becoming superintendents.

Another finding revealed that while some of the women began their administrative careers at the building level, a large percentage of them followed the classic pattern for women superintendents: classroom, central office, and the superintendency. The women were most often steered in the direction of becoming specialists.

Participants' responses to questions about tenure and the superintendency revealed that the majority held only one superintendency for an average of four years. Further, these women were usually appointed from within the district. This may suggest that after many years in their district's "proving ground," they were then given the green light to become the head of the district.

Finally, the majority (30 percent) of the black female superintendents headed urban school districts. This, too, was congruent with previous research on minorities—minorities often head urban districts with high populations of minority students. Those respondents holding superintendencies in suburban school districts comprised 22 percent of the sample.

Job Performance Factors

The women in the study were asked to identify constraints and facilitators encountered en route to the superintendency. Sixteen constraints and six facilitators were listed—for respondents to check—under "job performance factors" on the survey instrument. Also, an open-ended question asked respondents to list "who or what were some of their facilitators" en route to the superintendency.

Black female school superintendents ranked the following five factors as being either moderately or greatly constraining their "stalking" (Brunner 1995) the superintendency:

1. absence of "old boy network," support systems, or sponsorship
2. lack of awareness of the political maneuvers
3. lack of role models
4. societal attitudes that blacks lack competency in leadership positions
5. no formal or informal method for identifying black aspirants to administrative positions

These results mirror those of previous research on barriers that women face in educational leadership. Black female superintendents, in general, did not report any other constraints that kept them from the superintendency. Overwhelmingly the respondents agreed that racism and sexism were not major obstacles for them.

The six facilitators that were listed under "job performance factors" were ranked in the following way:

1. positive working relations with the school board
2. solid teamwork with experienced qualified staff and faculty
3. acceptance by nonblack employers
4. confidence in personal and professional capabilities
5. provision of mentor or sponsor
6. acceptance by black administrators and teachers

From the responses to the open-ended questions emerged two distinct categories of facilitators: (1) those associated with the school and school system, and (2) those that were personal and intrinsic motivators. Most of the facilitators listed by the respondents were found in the school or within the school system. Facilitators such as former and other superintendents, board members, teachers, and staff were listed. In addition, personal and intrinsic facilitators such as religious beliefs, self-confidence, sense of mission, and good communication skills were cited. Resoundingly, the respondents agreed that family and friends played a major role in their success as superintendents.

CONCLUSION

Mainstream literature surrounding secondary school leadership has historically been grounded in masculine "scientific" theories of motivation and management (Hertzberg 1968; McGregor 1960; Sergiovanni 1967), with little emphasis on sociocultural or feminist theories of leadership (Dillard 1995). In contrast, the power of a feminist lens makes it possible to focus on the gaps and blank spaces in male-dominant culture, knowledge, and behavior (Gosetti and Rusch 1995). More specifically, the feminist lens is useful to identify the struggles of black female superintendents, but not enough. I believe a feminist lens of a particular quality is required—a lens that might be called a black feminist lens.

Because of the small number of black female school superintendents, the move from the "outsider within" status to beyond the glass ceilings and then up the "crystal stairs" is an almost impossible one. Such a move requires that black women be treated as a group unto itself and that black women be viewed as a group unto itself through a black feminist lens. Evidence of the need for this lens can be found in the writing of bell hooks (1989), when she noted that, "In much of the literature written by [w]hite women on the 'woman question' from the nineteenth century to the present day, authors will refer to '[w]hite men' but use the word 'woman' when they really mean '[w]hite woman.' Concurrently, the term '[b]lacks' is often made synonymous with [b]lack men" (p. 140). Black women superintendents in the literature, then, become invisible, leaving no trail for other black women to follow. This is a loss for the educational culture and for the black culture. Black women superintendents bring to educational leadership a strong commitment to and high expectation for improved student outcomes (Venable 1995), and their collective and individual voices are significant.

Thus, there is a great need for research focused directly on black women in the superintendency. Just "adding [black] women [to the generic research] and stirring" results in the adoption of androcentric frameworks, and experiences become misconstrued (Bell 1988). When black women are not an identified part of educational thought and research, policy suffers; the society's devaluation of black women's lives, works, and experiences is reinforced; and the field of educational thought itself is diminished (Martin 1984).

Zora Neale Hurston (1969) noted that black women have been thought of and treated as "'de mules uh 'de world." This reference stirs up the image of a race of women who, despite constant mistreatment, are hard working and spiritually unconquerable. As a collective, black women have made and continue to make great strides in this country. They have climbed and continue to climb the "crystal" stairs of educational administration in districts across the country. Sadly, however, while strides have been made, statistics show that the overall number of black women superintendents is dropping at a time even when the enrollment of minority children is rising (Venable 1995). Thus, it is with a sense of urgency that this particular study on black female school superintendents is offered as a foundation of support for a much needed change in educational administration in the next millennium.

REFERENCES

Adler, S., J. Laney, and M. Packer. 1993. *Managing women: Feminism and power in educational management.* Philadelphia: Open University Press.

African-American literature: Voices in a tradition (Teacher's Manual). 1992. Austin, Tex.: Harcourt Brace Jovanovich, Inc.

Bell, C. S. 1988. Organizational influences on women's experience in the superintendency. *Peabody Journal of Education* 65 (4): 31-59.

Brunner, C. C. 1995. *Gathering cultural wisdom: Principles for women "stalking" the superintendency.* Paper presented at The University Council for Educational Administration Annual Conference, Salt Lake City, Utah. ERIC Document (EAO27681).

Collins, P. H. 1990. *Black feminist thought.* Cambridge, Mass.: Unwin Hyman Inc.

Dillard, C. B. 1995. Leading with her life: An African-American feminist (re) interpretation of leadership for an urban high school principal. *Educational Administration Quarterly* 31 (4): 539-63.

Edson, S. K. 1988. *Pushing the limits: The female administrative aspirant.* Albany, N.Y.: State University of New York Press.

Glazer, J. S., E. M. Bensimon, and B. K. Townsend (eds.) 1993.*Women in higher education: A feminist perspective.* Needham Heights, Mass.: Ginn Press.

Gosetti, P.P., and E. Rusch. 1995. Reexamining educational leadership: Challenging assumptions. In D. Dunlap, D. and P. Schmuck (eds.),*Women Leading in Education.* Albany, N.Y.: State University of New York Press.

Green, V. A., and E. Manera. 1995. Educational leadership: The practice of successful women administrators in the USA and Canada. *International Studies in Educational Administration* 23 (2): 10-15.

Hart, A. W. 1995. Women ascending to leadership: The organizational socialization of principals. In D. Dunlap and P. Schmuck (eds.),*Women Leading in Education.* Albany, N.Y.: State University of New York Press.

Hertzberg, F. 1968. One more time: How do you motivate employees? *Harvard Business Review* 46: 53.

hooks, b. 1989. *Talking back: Thinking feminist, thinking black.* Boston: South End Press.

Hughes, L. 1954. Mother to son. *Selected poems of Langston Hughes.* New York: Alfred A. Knopf.

Hurston, Z. N. 1969. *Their eyes were watching God.* Greenwich, Conn.: Fawcett.

Jackson, B. L. 1995. *The voices of African-American women public school superintendents: A preliminary report.* Seminar: National Alliance of Black School Educators, Dallas, Texas.

Kanter, R. M. 1975. Women and the structure of organizations: Explorations in theory and behavior. In M. Millman and R. M. Kanter (eds.) *Another voice,* Garden City, N.J.

———. 1977. *Men and women of the corporation.* New York: Basic Books.

Klein, R. D. 1983. In G. Bowles and R. D. Klein, *Theories of women's studies.* Boston: Routledge and Kegan Paul.

Martin, J. R. 1984. Bringing women into educational thought. *Educational Theory* 34 (4): 341–53.

McDade, T., and J. M. Drake. 1982. Career path models for women superintendents. *Journal of Educational Research* 75: 210.

McGregor, D. 1960. *The human side of enterprise.* New York: McGraw-Hill.

Moody, C. D., Sr. 1983. On becoming a superintendent: Contest or sponsored mobility? *Journal of Negro Education* 52 (4): 383–97.

Moody, C. D., Sr., and C. Moody. 1995. *Survey results of African-American superintendents.* Pre-conference seminar presented at the National Alliance of Black School Educators National Convention, Dallas, Tex.

Morrison, A. M., R. P. White, and E. Van Velsor. 1987. *Breaking the glass ceiling.* Reading, Mass.: Addison-Wesley Publishing Company, Inc.

Ortiz, F. I. 1982. *Career patterns in education: Women, men, and minorities in public school administration.* New York: Praeger.

Pigford, A. B., and S. Tonnsen. 1993. *Women in school leadership.* Lancaster, Pa.: Technomic.

Reid-Merritt, P. 1996. *Sister power: How phenomenal black women are rising to the top.* New York: John Wiley & Sons.

Robertson, H. J. 1992. *Gender and school restructuring: Thoughts on the presence of absence.* Paper presented at the International Conference Linking Research and Practice, Toronto.

Sergiovanni, T. J. 1967. Factors which affect satisfaction and dissatisfaction of teachers. *Journal of Educational Administration* 5: 66–82.

Shakeshaft, C. 1989. *Women in educational administration.* Newbury Park, Calif.: Sage Publications.

Smith, S. C., and P. K. Piele (eds.). 1989. *School leadership: Handbook for excellence.* Eric Clearinghouse on Educational Management: University of Oregon.

Smyth, J. (ed.) 1989. *Critical perspectives on educational leadership.* Philadelphia: The Falmer Press.

Venable, B. P. 1995. *Issues on survival of African-American women superintendents: Empowering through networking.* Panel presentation at the National Alliance of Black School Educators Annual Conference, Dallas, Tex.

Williams, T. L. 1984. *A study of black superintendents' perceptions regarding crucial issues, personal characteristics, and factors related to success.* Unpublished doctoral dissertation. University of the Pacific.

Yeakey, C. C., G. S. Johnston, and J. A. Adkison. 1986. In pursuit of equity: A review of research on minorities and women in educational administration. *Educational Administration Quarterly* 22 (3): 110-49.

CHAPTER SIX

Seeking and Selecting Hispanic Female Superintendents

FLORA IDA ORTIZ

This chapter is about the way Hispanic females are sought and selected for the superintendency. The report is based on data collected from twelve Hispanic female superintendents located in a number of Southwestern school districts. The women differ in their educational and work experiences and in the type of districts they have led. Most, however, were sought and selected in a similar manner.

Wanous (1980) claims that "organizational entry includes the wide variety of events occurring when new members join organizations. By its very nature, the entry process must be considered from the perspective of both the individual and the organization. Individuals choose organizations, and organizations select newcomers from among applicants" (p. 1). This means that the Hispanic females must choose to be school district superintendents, and school board members must select them from among other applicants to be their district's superintendent. All indications show that this is problematic. Women, and specifically Hispanic women, are not appointed to the superintendency very often. Grogan (1996) reports in her study that in 1990, women superintendents had increased from 4 percent to 5.5 percent, increasing to 7.1 percent in 1993. (Blount 1993 and Montenegro 1993). Glass (1992), likewise, reports that "of the more than 4 million professional educators in the United States, fewer than 1,000 women guide the 15,000 school districts in executive leadership positions" (Grogan 1996, 12). Within this group of executive women, there are about twenty-five to thirty Hispanic females. Although Hispanic females are increasingly found in a number of U. S. school districts, most of them are located in the Southwestern states.

Several explanations have been forwarded. First, men are more likely to aspire to the superintendency than are women, and women are more likely to consider the principalship as the ultimate position to hold. Thus, more men than women are likely to apply or be available for the position. Second, since advancement in educational administration requires sponsorship, females, less likely to have sponsors, are also less likely to advance. Women, therefore, would not hold positions that propel them to the superintendency, nor would individuals exist who would nominate them for the superintendency. Third, women's educational and work experiences may not include the areas most likely to appeal to search committees and school board members. Women would be more likely to be in curriculum and instruction, and Hispanic females in ethnic-related areas, thus they would be perceived to be less capable in personnel and finance matters. Fourth, the organization consisting of a larger number of males in the executive ranks and possibly in the district's school boards may not have access to information regarding capable women, and Hispanic women, in particular. Finally, since the search and selection process focuses on *matching* the candidate to the district, and the final decision for the superintendent tends to be personal rather than professional, the likelihood of a Hispanic female being personally preferred is remote at best. Nevertheless, some Hispanic females are appointed to the superintendency. How can this be explained?

Wanous (1980) writes that there are "two different types of matching [in selection processes]: (1) between abilities (and/or potential abilities) and organizational job requirements, and (2) between individual needs *and* organizational climates." Most organizations have put their strongest efforts toward the ability and job requirements match, rather than toward the individual needs and organizational climates match. This practice influences how Hispanic females are appointed to the superintendency.

Carter, Glass, and Hord (1993) report that there "appear to be two well-represented procedures that culminate in superintendent selection: one is the screening process, the other is a search for appropriate candidates" (p. 78).

In the screening process, a call to fill the position is advertised in the media. Criteria are presented, and applications are solicited. Individuals apply, and from this pool, the board and possibly community representatives select a group to be interviewed. Based on the interviews, a final selection is made, and a new superintendent is appointed.

The search procedure is more comprehensive, focused, and complex. It may be conducted by a consulting firm or by a specially constituted board or citizen's committee. A common practice is to hire a professional consulting firm. The board and other interested parties meet with the consultant to prepare a statement of qualifications for prospective candidates that serves as the basis for the search and for the screening and interviewing of applicants. The consultant seeks and contacts qualified candidates to encourage them to apply. The submitted applications are screened to determine matches between the district's needs and the applicants' qualifications. The search team then identifies those candidates who appear to be appropriate. Interviews are conducted, and a new superintendent is appointed.

The appointment of a superintendent is preceded by a search and selection process that is largely in the hands of the districts' school board members. The quality and character of that process is heavily dependent on the district's history, the community, and the organization of the school system (Carter et al. 1993; Johnson 1996; Miklos 1988). The search and selection process is usually explained by the school board members and others as a process that seeks to *match* the individual to the district, or to find the person who best *fits* the school district's need (Carter et al. 1993; Johnson 1996; Wanous 1980). This match or fit is meant to be between the superintendent and a particular place and the superintendent and a particular time (Johnson 1996). How are Hispanic female superintendents matched with the districts they lead?

HISPANIC FEMALES' PREPARATION FOR THE SUPERINTENDENCY

Hispanic females prepare themselves for the superintendency in a number of ways. They tend to be highly educated. Of the twelve women in this sample, six have doctoral degrees from prestigious universities, three have doctoral degrees from their state universities, and three have master's degrees from their state universities. They also tend to have experience in school administration, ranging from site administration to central office administration. The women in this sample who obtained their graduate degrees in the 1970s are more likely to have traditional school administration careers. That is, they taught in the secondary schools, were principals of secondary schools, had a number of positions in the central office, and were advanced from associate superintendents to superintendents in different school districts. The exceptions to this profile are two women superintendents of small, rural, primarily Hispanic school districts. They have spent their entire careers in the same district, moving from teacher to principal to superintendent. One of them described her career.

> I was born in this area, educated in the local schools, and went to the state university for the undergraduate degree. I returned here to teach. While teaching I obtained the administrative certificate, the master's degree and slowly moved up to the superintendency. Today, I can say I know everybody in the area. I am older and know the history of this district better than most. This district hasn't changed much. It is natural I should be the superintendent now and for a few more years. The school board members wouldn't feel right replacing me. In very real terms, it is quite hard to sell this place.

These women have expressed with intensity their commitment to administration and the superintendency. As Carter et al. (1993, 74) found, "Females with greater intentions and readiness to seek the superintendency seemed to position themselves in the right place at the right time." The Hispanic females in this sample likewise positioned themselves for advancement. One put it in the following way: "Once I became a teacher, I began to think that if I were to have a good income, help lots of children, and enjoy my work for a lifetime, I had to be a school administrator and eventually a superintendent."

Another expressed the same sentiment this way: "My experiences in schools included some administration, and I found out I liked the challenge. It was fun to manage and to deal with adults in the school and outside, but most of all, I could claim I could manage resources in a way to improve all of the schools in my district." From the perspective of the Hispanic female, the attainment of the superintendency is lodged in a personal need to be a superintendent and the willingness to prepare for it.

Compared to the women presented here, younger women educated in the 1980s have prepared and obtained the superintendency in a shorter time. Their careers tend to deviate from the most common pattern. For example, two women, doctoral degree graduates of prestigious universities, spent short periods of time in the classroom, accepted administrative positions besides the principalship, and were appointed to the superintendency several times, remaining in each position less than three years. An example of this type of career is illustrated by Dr. Zagala. Her teaching career was brief, followed by experience as a school board member, where she not only participated locally but also was actively involved at the state level. She then accepted a superintendency in a small elementary school district. After two years, she accepted the superintendency position, which she occupied when these data were collected. She is currently in her fourth superintendency position.

Another example is Dr. Duran, who

> breezed through high school and undergraduate programs, looking for a job at twenty. My parents said, 'Teach.' I went to the local university, got a teaching credential while teaching under a provisional credential. I liked working in schools, decided I wanted to advance, applied for graduate programs, left the state for a graduate program, stayed until I received the Ph.D. From there I applied for a principalship in the high school. I stayed there three years before I became a superintendent of this school district. I have been in schools eight years. I doubt many can claim such a career. But then, this superintendency has its problems.

Dr. Duran is in her third superintendency position now.

The rest of the women represent a first superintendency appointment. Two are in their third year, one in her fourth year, and the remaining one retired after three years.

The four most successful superintendents from this sample had traditional career patterns with support from sponsors. They moved between school districts, obtaining school site and central office administrative experience, but they retained their appointments as superintendents seven years and beyond. The tenure of the exemplary superintendents identified by the American Association of School Administrators (AASA) and the National School Boards Association (NSBA) is reported to be 8.5 years, contrasted with the national figure of 6.2 years (Carter et al. 1993).

THE SCHOOL DISTRICT SEARCHES FOR THE SUPERINTENDENT

The selection of a superintendent can easily be considered the most important decision that the board makes. However, because most board members do not expect the appointment of a superintendent to lead to a permanent relationship, the immediate context determines to a great extent how the search and selection process is conducted and who the likely appointee is (Johnson 1996). Nonetheless, criteria are usually cited when the search for a superintendent is initiated. As Miklos (1988) notes, since administrative work is perceived as multidimensional, multiple selection criteria are employed. The criteria include areas such as understanding how the school board operates, how the board and superintendent relate, management of the budget and financial resources, and developing relationships with parent and community groups (Carter et al. 1993; Powell 1984; Robertson 1984).

Pringle (1989) found that school board members preferred superintendents with competencies in managing finances, facilities, operations, personnel, and board and community relations. Researchers also have reported that there is a difference in the emphasis placed on these criteria. For example, Sclafani (1987) found that the smaller the district, the more managerial the emphasis, while the increase in size called for greater emphasis on executive skills. He also reported that there were regularities among school districts, such as those seen in the typical suburban districts that emphasized curriculum and instructional skills as well as performance goals.

The establishment of the criteria and the search and selection decisions are ultimately made at the board level, but these boards may have assistance from search committees.

Johnson (1996) found that search committees paid attention to social class, race, ethnicity, and values. They considered whether the new superintendent could become "one of us"; could the presence of the new superintendent contribute to "feelings of comfort" for all? Search committees are reported to favor candidates who are quick, clever, and experienced in a broad range of administrative responsibilities.

Nine of these superintendents' appointments involved a search committee in the search for a new superintendent. The exceptions include the two, small, rural superintendents presented earlier and one appointed to a small elementary school district with suburban characteristics. At the time she was appointed, the district was moving toward consolidation. She led the district for three years while it consolidated into a unified school district. She subsequently retired. Without exception, however, the nine women who were appointed in school districts with search committees admitted that the search committees served to find them and legitimate their applications, but their appointment was linked to someone who knew them personally.

As stated before, the call to fill a superintendency position is usually advertised in the media. For example, the call for the position filled by Dr. Zagala's second superintendency was featured in the local newspaper as "The Arena Unified School District is looking for a bilingual superintendent, someone able to mix comfortably at a service-club meeting in a predominantly Anglo arena and a Cinco-de-Mayo celebration in Plaza Alegre. We want someone who not only lives in the district full time, but is involved in the community." Dr. Zagala, fully qualified as bilingual, answered the call.

The match and best fit between the Hispanic female and the school district is one in which the superintendent serves to *represent* the Hispanic groups who may be sources, or perceived as sources, of conflict or unrest in the school district. One school board member described how they searched and selected their superintendent. "We specifically advertised as desirable in our superintendent bilinguality in the Spanish language and a willingness to live and be involved in local affairs. . . . We wanted someone who could address those populations identified as 'getting short shrift.'"

Hispanic females are matched to specific contexts. For example, in one school district, the community perceived the school district as stable; however, the increasing proportion (55 percent) of Hispanic children in the district called for some attention. The two aspects of the context that determine the search for Hispanic females are the "increasing proportion of Hispanic children" and the "call for some attention." The fact that the community perceived the school district as being stable means that the appointment is not meant to "change" or "disrupt" the district. The appointment is to attend to the increasing Hispanic presence without fundamental disruption to the district's organization. This also means that it is not expected that this appointment is permanent or long lasting.

Dr. Valencia's case illustrates how these searches are enacted. One of the school board members said, "This district has been in disarray for several years. We need a superintendent who can calm the Hispanic community, represent it to the rest of the community, and move the district forward."

Dr. Valencia described her appointment:

This district has had several superintendents appointed. From a distance, it looks like a desirable district, but its financial and personnel troubles have been so serious, no one could clean them up. I was hired as the last resort. First, it seemed that maybe, because I don't look very Hispanic, the non-Hispanics wouldn't be too suspicious of me and second, because I am Hispanic, maybe I can represent the group and thereby calm that section of the community. The school board members really like that. My real capabilities are in balancing budgets and dealing with unions and personnel issues, but the descriptors for my appointment, my job, and my success have been and continue to be that I represent the Hispanic community. I have been here for seven years now, the district is thriving, but the school board president and other community influentials are now saying that possibly the Hispanic representation in the district is balanced, meaning that the superintendent as a Hispanic is no longer necessary for the district.

The data for this report show that Hispanic females are more likely to be sought when school districts are in trouble. The *match* between nine out of the twelve women was with districts undergoing difficulties.

THE SELECTION OF HISPANIC FEMALES TO THE SUPERINTENDENCY

Stott (1991) reported that the exemplary superintendent group "obtained their superintendency positions in districts more often where boards had utilized the services of a professional search firm." His analysis also showed that "most of the professional search firms are staffed by former and retired superintendents" (Carter et al. 1993, 62).

Because the final decision for appointment is lodged in the school board, it is important to understand the factors that play a part in the selection process. Personal attributes including judgment, personality, character, open-mindedness, physical and mental health, poise, intelligence, sense of humor, voice, and cultural background are important when considering the candidates. Carter et al. (1993) go so far as to state that "there is little chance for school board members to select superintendents who have not essentially had the same type of background and professional experiences compared with their predecessors. Some variability in personality traits and leadership styles may occur, but for the most part, the 'men' who fill the superintendency appear to be more alike in personal characteristics and life histories than they are different" (p. 44; see also Feistritzer 1988). The conclusion is drawn that both the search committees and district school boards tend to assess the candidate as a person rather than as a professional (Carter et al. 1993; Grady and Bryant 1991; Johnson 1996).

The Interview

Search committees and school board members seek information regarding the candidate by examining the candidate's personal and work history, education, training, and experience through the interview process. Most studies of interviews indicate that the order in which information is presented to the interviewer is a highly significant factor. The "information presented *first* has a more significant impact on the decision to hire than that gathered later in the interview" (Wanous 1980, 108). Springbett (1958) referred to this as the "primacy effect." In the same report, he claimed that a *single* piece of negative information led to a 90 percent chance of rejection (as reported in Springbett 1958).

The interview is the event where the "match" or "fit" between the candidate and the school district is first concretely tested. The school district has released information regarding itself and the list of interviewees. As one community leader later explained,

> If the interview list includes a Spanish surname, you can be sure this district has some problems. The criteria including facility in Spanish, spelled out before, serves to alert that the school district is having difficulties with its changes. The more serious the school district is about hiring a Hispanic, the surer you can be that there is trouble.

Thus, true or not, the presence of a Spanish surname in the interview process is perceived as the school district not being as desirable as others.

Conversely, Hispanic females must provide information that highlights their accomplishments, capabilities, and talents. They also must ensure that negative information does not precede them or is not presented at the interview. Dr. Castillo explained, "For me, the interview was frightening because I have only been in the field for a short time, especially compared to most who are appointed superintendent."

The Appointment

Unlike the appointment of white males to the superintendency, the appointment of Hispanic females has both symbolic and political overtones. The appointment is problematic for both, because the position of the superintendent is affected in two major ways when it is assumed by a Hispanic female. First, it serves as a symbol for the school board and community, and second, it challenges the existing school organization structure.

These sentiments are supported in various ways. For example, Dr. Zagala raised expectations and mobilized the Hispanic community at the same time that it increased suspicion and apprehension in the non-Hispanic community. Having a Hispanic male, Mr. Martinez, as the board president did not abate doubts. The presence of two Hispanics in the top ranks raised suspicions within the organization and the non-Hispanic community. One of the principals expressed these notions in this way, "Her Hispanic background and the fact that she speaks another language certainly helps the Hispanics here."

The local newspaper reported the appointment by highlighting Dr. Zagala's salary. It also emphasized the fact that she had served as both principal and superintendent of a tiny, unionized elementary school district of 15,000 students. She was described as the first woman and the first Hispanic to be hired in the twenty-six-year history of the district. The paper's description of her first public appearance was that she was unflappable and addressed the audience in both Spanish and English.

The appointment of a Hispanic female to the superintendency creates an underlying tension for the organization and the individual. Due to perceptions regarding gender and ethnicity, the appointment is accompanied by skepticism with regard to the superintendent's abilities, as well as the suspicion that she will act to favor members of her own group. Hispanic females face the dilemma created when the justification for appointment is a symbolic gesture, rather than a quest for organizational leadership.

Dr. Zagala described how this is displayed in her work:

> From my perspective, ideally, the situation would be being hired with something specific in mind and being supported throughout the process. It is probably the ideal way. I think what happens not only in Arena, but in many other organizations, is being hired with the understanding of the specific purpose, but people go about their business and forget about the reason why somebody was brought in and then you do something. In the meantime, you cannot change values, and there are still people who know, but are saying, 'What the hell are we doing with a Hispanic superintendent here? She doesn't know what she's talking about.' People look for any slipping of decisions or error and I think that is where there has to be consistency.

CONCLUSIONS

When we examine the school districts where Hispanic women are appointed, several characteristics are pronounced. For example, the two women in the small, rural school districts appear to hold the position because no one else is likely to want it. Since they are part of the community, they are qualified for the position; because they have always been there, their match is, as one stated, "natural."

The remaining ten women were appointed to the superintendency in school districts undergoing dramatic changes of one form or another. Some school districts were bankrupt. Other school districts had a constant turnover of school administrators. Some school districts had dramatic demographic and economic changes. Still others were urban school districts undergoing all of the typical urban problems. Two districts consisted of areas of severe poverty and enormous wealth. The two sections were in constant conflict over the area the school superintendent should represent. All of these districts had a large proportion of Hispanic students and families.

Carter et al. (1993) reported that most superintendents are small-town people, but the recent dramatic demographic changes are producing candidates from suburban and urban areas. In this sample, with the exception of two, Hispanic females seeking the superintendency were women from suburban and urban areas. Their social and political skills were, therefore, lodged in suburban and urban values and norms. These factors, many times, were not fully appreciated by school board members or search committees. This means that these women were capable of handling the technical as well as the political aspects of the job. The superintendents who were successful were those who developed the *personal* connections necessary for support, who understood the interdependence between symbolic and professional expectations, and who enacted a subtle political profile. The younger women, moving through the hierarchy too fast without adequate *personal* support, and who did not have enough experiences to integrate symbolic, professional, and political skills, were the most vulnerable.

REFERENCES

Blount, J. 1993. The genderization of the superintendency: A statistical portrait. Paper presented at the Annual Meeting of the American Educational Research Association. Atlanta, Ga.

Carter, D., T. Glass, and S. Hord (eds.). 1993. *Selecting, preparing, and developing the school district superintendent.* Washington, D.C.: Falmer Press.

Feistritzer, C. E. 1988. *Profile of school administrators in the U.S.* Washington, D.C.: National Center for Education Information.

Glass, T. E. 1992. *The study of the American school superintendency: America's education leaders in a time of reform.* American Association of School Administrators. Arlington, Va.

Grady, M., and M. Bryant. 1991. School board turmoil and superintendent turnover: What pushes them to the brink? *The School Administrator* 28 (2): 19–25.

Grogan, M. 1996. *Voices of women aspiring to the superintendency.* Albany, N.Y.: State University of New York Press.

Johnson, S. M. 1996. *Leading for change: The challenge of the new superintendency.* San Francisco: Jossey Bass.

Miklos, E. 1988. Administrator selection, career patterns, succession, and socialization. In N. J. Boyan (ed.), *Handbook of research on educational administration.* New York: Longman.

Montenegro, X. 1993. *Women and racial minority representation in school administration.* Arlington, Va.: American Association of School Administrators.

Powell, R. E. 1984. A comparison of selection criteria and performance evaluation criteria for Missouri school superintendents. Unpublished doctoral dissertation, University of Missouri, Columbia.

Pringle, P. G. 1989. Relationship of general administrative leadership skills to superintendent selection and contract renewal. Unpublished doctoral dissertation, University of Texas, Austin.

Robertson, M. C. 1984. A survey of the selection of school superintendents in Massachusetts. Unpublished doctoral dissertation, Boston University, Boston.

Sclafani, S. 1987. AASA Guidelines for preparation of school administrators: Do they represent the important job behaviors of superintendents? Unpublished doctoral dissertation, University of Texas, Austin.

Springbett, B. M. 1958. Factors affecting the final decision in the employment interview. *Canadian Journal of Psychology* 12: 13–22.

Stott, J. D. 1991. An analysis of personal and professional characteristics of superintendents selected as being exemplary. Unpublished doctoral dissertation, Northern Illinois University, DeKalb.

Wanous, J. P. 1980. *Organizational entry: Recruitment, selection, and socialization of newcomers.* Reading, Mass.: Addison-Wesley.

PART THREE

"Small but Brilliant"

Living the Life

C. CRYSS BRUNNER

A desert is a place where life is very condensed. The roots of living things hold on to that last tear of water and the flower hoards its moisture by only appearing in early morning and late afternoon. Life in the desert is small but brilliant and most of what occurs goes on underground. This is like the lives of many women.

—Clarissa Pinkola Estés, *Women Who Run With the Wolves*

There are women who have chosen to become superintendents and succeeded. But, because there are not many women superintendents in a given region, they sometimes forget what other women look like. They are so small in number, in fact, that often their work settings take on the characteristics of a desert. They look across the terrain and see nothing familiar, so they live part of their lives underground to survive, to remain female. This does not mean, however, that they fail at the work in the desert. They may be "small" in number, but they often are "brilliant." This section reflects their ways of "living the life," even to the point of their departure from it.

CHAPTER SEVEN

The First Years

What Should a Female Superintendent Know Beforehand?

BARBARA NELSON PAVAN

T he statistics on gender percentages in the superintendency and some previous reports on beginning superintendents provided the context for this
study of four female superintendents—recounting the experiences of their early
years.

THE CONTEXT

The percentage of school superintendents who are women creeps up only slowly,
despite affirmative action efforts such as the 1972 passage of Title IX and the
1991 Glass Ceiling Act. This is puzzling, since by 1990, women earned 59 percent of the master's degrees and 51 percent of the doctoral degrees granted in the
United States in educational administration (Snyder 1993). Between 1970 and
1980, less than 1 percent of the superintendents in Pennsylvania were women,
and by 1985 (Pavan 1985), 3.6 percent were women, a figure slightly higher than
the national level (Shakeshaft, 1989). National data compiled by Glass (1992),
including K-8 districts not found in Pennsylvania, revealed that 6.4 percent of
the superintendents were women, while in Pennsylvania, twenty-eight women
held 5.6 percent of the positions (Pavan, Winkler, and Dovey 1995). This number was increased to thirty-four (6.8 percent) in the 1993-94 year, when the
women participants in this study assumed the role of superintendent. As the
result of a retirement incentive bill, and possibly a changed public attitude, there
were fifty female superintendents in Pennsylvania in the 1994-95 school year, an
astounding jump to 10 percent. As delightful as this change is to contemplate,
there exists in this state a sufficient number of certified and experienced women

to more than double this number. The lack of female school administrators cannot be blamed on women's low aspirations, unwillingness to get the needed credentials, or make extensive job search efforts (Pavan 1987b, 1988b, 1989).

Tallerico and Burstyn (1994) noted that female superintendents are found in
higher proportions in very small, rural districts with under 300 students. In such
districts, the superintendent wears many hats and has no other administrator to
delegate the myriad job-related tasks. Relations with the school board and the
community are quite close, leading to high levels of stress for superintendents and
to a short tenure. The authors concluded that these "starter districts" are
extremely unfavorable places for a woman to begin her superintendency.

Scherr's (1994) case studies of two entry-level female superintendents found
both the outsider and the insider spending the majority of their time building relations, but the insider could more comfortably delegate communication responsibilities to her deputies. Only the outsider noted gender as a barrier, but the
insider worked in a district where 50 percent of the principals and of her cabinet
were women. Female administrators have reported more barriers in both corpo-
rate and educational workplaces than their male peers (Kanter 1977; Pavan 1986.)

After following four (two men and two women) superintendents during
their first year in office, Keedy (1995) noted that all four had agendas focusing
on improving services for children, but only three utilized strategies that board
members perceived as a good fit with district needs. In another case, even with
7 to 2 school board support after her work to get a school bond issue passed,
Superintendent Connors decided to resign. Her social change agenda did not fit
the context of the stable community that she headed. This district of 60,000 students did not provide a deputy, an assistant, or even a full-time secretary to assist
her with the needed work (Bogotch 1995).

THIS STUDY

The purpose of this study was to determine the major issues faced by four female
entry-level superintendents, how they handled these situations, and the strategies
they used in their early years as superintendents. Further, the study gathered
from the women information that they felt should be shared with all women
before assuming a superintendency.

During the summer and fall of 1993, four women to whom I served as doctoral advisor, assumed their first contracted superintendencies in Pennsylvania.
While these women shared a common doctoral program, they rarely shared
classes, so even their educational experiences were somewhat diverse. Their personal backgrounds and their school districts had both similarities and differences. At the end of their first year as superintendents, we met together as a
group so that they could explore their experiences.

The four women had known me since the beginning of their doctoral study (one for over twenty years), and they had kept in contact often, using me as a sounding board for job-related issues. It is common practice for aspiring female administrators to use their professors as mentors (Pavan 1987c). Two women had worked together in the same school district, thus there was a comfortable level of familiarity among the group, making communication free and open.

Unlike my previous research, this study was not a series of individual interviews, but a sharing of experiences in a group. While the interviews were structured by questions posed by me (the interviewer), they were augmented by the responses given. The order of the questions was altered to enable the dialogue to flow naturally and to allow time to develop thoughtful responses. Listening in a group to the others triggered remembrances in each participant that might not otherwise have been uncovered. Commonalties and differences became readily apparent as the women talked together. At times, the discussion became a problem-solving session where the women traded stories and helped each other determine strategies for action. The women were open and supportive of each other, yet would present differing opinions reflecting their individual beliefs. They preferred the group format over individual interviews, because it enabled them to learn from hearing the experiences, strategies, and rationales of the other superintendents.

The conversation was audiotaped and transcribed, resulting in a single-spaced, sixty-three-page transcript. My task was to find themes that were common to all of the participants and those that were unique to only one of the superintendents. With the exception of district documents given to me by the participants, unsolicited comments from school administrators whom I encountered for other reasons, and newspaper articles, this research was based on the self-reports of the four superintendents.

To maintain authenticity, the language used by the participants and the free-flowing, somewhat unorganized quality of the sessions have not been revised for this chapter. While some readers may be concerned about the validity of the participants' remarks, the dialogue was considered valid by the group as a way to resolve their own issues. Time was not needed for me, as the interviewer, to gain the trust of the participants, because these women already knew and trusted me. In any case, their perceptions, as presented in this chapter, represented reality as the participants experienced it.

A second session was held about thirty months into the participants' superintendencies. This was after a paper had been prepared (Pavan 1995) utilizing data from the initial meeting about their first year. Once again, the session was audiotaped and a notated script was made. A last-minute family emergency prevented one of the women from attending this second session. She listened to the recorded tape and taped her comments to be included in the analysis. Even though it had been difficult to schedule the first two sessions, afterward the women asked when they would meet again.

Both papers were sent to the women for their comments and revisions. Contacts were made with the women while this chapter was being prepared to get their perspectives after forty-two months. This research benefited the participants by providing a vehicle for support, information seeking, and self-analysis, even beyond the focus on women seeking their first superintendencies.

THE WOMEN AND THEIR DISTRICTS

Dr. Smith, '80, in her mid-forties, is the youngest of the group, but received her doctorate first. Her career path through six districts, unlike those of the other women and most men (Pavan and McKee 1988), was directly from staff to line positions, with titles including the word "superintendent." She is white, her husband is a physician, they have two school-aged children, and the family resides in another school district. She is employed in a rural district with 3,300 students in five schools; the district is experiencing rapid growth and becoming suburban. She told the board before being hired that her strengths were in personnel, staff development, and curriculum and instruction, not in finance and construction. Dr. Smith found that the board went along completely (9 to 0 beginning contract vote) with her hiring "wish list" and continues to work cooperatively with her as long as she provides them with the data and rationale for a given decision and as long as she focuses on a solid educational program. At the time of her appointment, she was the only female superintendent in her county, but now she has three peers. Her beginning contract was for a five-year period. The budget process was her first major hurdle and demanded much time and energy.

Dr. Jones, '87, spent most of her career in the largest district in the state, then became assistant superintendent of a small urban school district, and beginning in July 1993, led another larger (7,500 students in eleven schools) urban school district with a mostly minority student enrollment. She was the first woman appointed to this position in her county, and while there had been three female superintendents, now there is only one. Her beginning contract was for a three-year period, resulting from a 7 to 2 board vote that was protested by some community members because of a lack of community input into the selection process. This school district is continuously in the newspapers because of political problems in both the school district and the city in which it is located, very low student achievement, and violence in the schools, including more than 300 arrests in the high school during the year preceding her appointment. She accepted this challenging position even after being discouraged by fellow educators. She said, " My whole professional career has been based on having an impact on what happens in the lives of children," and she believed that she could make a difference. In her early fifties, she is African American, a single parent with a daughter in graduate school, and had a partner during the time of the study. She maintained an apartment in the district as a residence during the week.

Dr. *Nells*, '89, spent her entire career in the largest district in the state and left the deputy superintendent position when she was wooed by a suburban district with 6,300 students in nine schools to become the first female African-American superintendent in that county. Since then, two other female superintendents have been hired in her county. Her previous central office instructional responsibilities did not include such close interaction with a school board. She is in her mid-fifties. Her son is grown, and her husband is a teacher in New Jersey. She had an elaborate entry plan, beginning with a document describing her activities for the first four months, which brought her into every school so that early on she could interact with teachers and influence the curriculum and instruction of the school district. The result was a report on the district in January from which a strategic plan was developed and superintendent goals were devised. She has not moved into the district. Her beginning contract for a four-year period resulted from a 7 to 2 board vote, but the 1995 election brought major board changes.

Dr. *Paine*, '94, who completed her dissertation in the early months of her superintendency by interviewing female school superintendents in the state, is married to a retired school superintendent. Their home is outside of her district. They have four children and some grandchildren. She is white, in her mid-fifties, and is the only woman of the four participants who was not an eldest child. When she obtained this superintendency, she became the second female superintendent in the county. Her previous experience included six years as an assistant superintendent and one as an acting superintendent in two different districts. She accepted this position despite rumors that school board members were difficult to work with, because the district staff was caring and worked well together, and because this position enabled her to return home each evening. Her beginning contract was for a three-year period, with a board vote of 9 to 0. After the fall 1995 election, the board changed so that seven of the nine members represented an economy-minded taxpayers group. Her rural district, with just over 2,000 students in three schools, was the smallest district studied.

THE FIRST YEAR

Each woman was driven by her educational vision for her school district with the rallying cry of "What is best for students?" The answers varied, as the districts and the women differed, but all focused on student learning. The fact that each woman valued and felt personally responsible for the cognitive and social learning experience of each individual child dominated the discussion. Dr. Jones talked about receiving pictures and notes from young children after their play-ground had been paved. Administrative visibility in the schools for either them-selves or their administrators was a priority.

Multicultural education was seen not solely as a racial issue, but also as one of class, gender, and religion, with the goal of achieving mutual respect for dif-ferences. A twenty-year-old case in one district of sexual harassment by a teacher that had just surfaced in the media was immediately investigated by the superin-tendent and resulted in a public reading of the school board policy at the next school board meeting. This proactive stance, in strong contrast to the covering-up activities of previous male superintendents, was common to these women.

Much time was spent listening to people in their districts and communities, including service support staff, in such a way that open communication could occur. Dr. Nells spoke directly of modeling behavior, and all of the women were engaged in showing their administrative staffs that confrontation or dictatorial directives were ineffective communication tools.

All went thoughtfully through such routine processes following past prac-tice, while studying them to make revisions for the next year. In the case of the budget, each woman developed a more open process with more information available to more people earlier in the year. These superintendents believed that performance that is monitored is performance that improves. For example, Dr. Smith required monthly reports on the number of teachers observed in their classrooms from each principal. Once the need for quantity was understood, she planned to monitor the quality of writing summative teacher evaluations for improvement.

The superintendents talked to the media to provide their side of the story, hoping that the press would be more positive than negative, although they real-ized that good news does not make news. Dr. Nells writes a local newspaper col-umn that provides a forum for her viewpoint and an opportunity to educate the public. Many positive articles about various school improvement projects in the daily press, along with reports of long-standing district problems based on Dr. Jones' conversations with the media, were shared with the group.

The greatest surprise that these women had was the positive feedback they received for being out in the schools and remaining available. This amused them, since they assumed that knowing what was happening in the schools was an essential part of their job.

Being an Outsider

Because all four women had entered new school districts as superinten-dents, and none had full-time residencies in their districts, they were considered outsiders. They spent three or four nights per week in meetings or functions within the district, creating fourteen-hour workdays, so they tried to preserve weekends as personal or family time. Even with supportive spouses, female superintendents spend more time taking care of household chores than do male superintendents (Pavan 1987b), so the participants' total work week was considerably longer than their male counterparts.

Since all of the women were outsiders, they entered with elaborate entry plans involving interviews with both internal and external stakeholders to learn about their districts. Their entry strategies were markedly similar: the women had been influenced by the same book (Jentz 1982). These plans began with data collection and recording processes if not already available in their districts. Having a process for studying their new school districts enabled the women to indicate during their early months that they could not determine precise goals for the district until this process was completed, and that a goal-oriented plan would be forthcoming based on this input. This process went fairly smoothly in most districts, except for the large urban district, where crisis events such as a drive-by shooting needed immediate responses focused on children's safety, rather than a very measured, "I'm trying to get a complete picture of the district before we develop a strategic plan." One year after Dr. Jones's appointment, the state declared the district financially distressed. A state-appointed control board superseded the local board, which continued to meet. The next day, the teachers, who had been working for a year without a contract, voted for a strike authorization.

Staff evaluation and hiring practices were given strong focus, since they were regarded as most likely to result in improved educational programs for children. The two larger districts had personnel administrators, while in the two smaller districts the superintendents personally interviewed all teachers before hiring.

Since all of the women had previous assistant superintendent experience, they were not new to central office responsibilities, yet they were all dismayed that boards gave more consideration to political issues than to what was best for the children. Even Dr. Paine, a superintendent's wife, still did not anticipate the board's "politicalness" or its lack of respect for the educational level of the person they had hired to be their superintendent. The women understood the financial limitations of the particular communities in which they worked, but putting politics above children remained discouraging to them. They spent considerable time educating school board members to understand that their responsibility was not only to fiscally conservative taxpayers, but also to the education of the district's children. Both Dr. Jones and Dr. Paine knew that their boards had long histories of not working well together, but they assumed that change could be made by a hardworking, caring superintendent willing to provide the needed data for decision making.

The Issue of Gender Surfaces

Even though not an interview question, much conversation ensued regarding the different ways that male and female superintendents handle their jobs. Based on their previous experiences, monthly meetings of the superintendents in four different counties, and the expectations of people in their districts, these woman noted that men seemed more likely not to listen, to bury or ignore or cover up problems, and to issue directives rather than to involve the appropriate people in problem-solving activities. For example, Dr. Nells met "with the guys" (her administrative cabinet) at the beginning of each week, and the cabinet members wanted her to develop an agenda and to issue directives, while she wanted this group to exercise initiative in dealing with problems and solutions.

None of the women felt that their spouses or partners were required to be at the school or school board social events that they attended. Dr. Paine had attended many of her superintendent husband's events prior to her own appointment, since this had been expected of her. However, her school board does not expect her husband to attend. The role of the superintendent's spouse is clearly defined by gender: wives attend, but husbands need not.

Each woman worked incredibly hard and for long hours. While they all struggled for more balance between their personal and professional lives, they knew that especially for the first few years in a new position this would not happen. Most of their partners knew that the job was probably the number one priority for the woman, as for most men. More conflict or guilt can result when there are young children or grandchildren involved, yet the vision of what schools should look like and the desire to get to that point drove the women to try to do all of the things that should be done.

Issues Prominent in the First Year

All four women participants were experienced as assistant superintendents and some also as acting superintendents. They identified—for any woman superintendent regardless of size or type of district or their own personal characteristics—these issues and strategies as being important upon entering a new district: politics, board relations, studying, planning, communication, changing behaviors, and personal and work balance.

INTO THE THIRD YEAR

Board memberships changed for each woman during the November election, with three boards tilting heavily toward representatives from economy-minded taxpayer groups or the dominant local political party. Both Dr. Jones and Dr. Paine did not have their three-year contracts renewed. The nonrenewal of both male and female superintendents' contracts has become quite common in Pennsylvania and nationally (Johnson 1996). The other two contracts for four and five years were not up for renewal, but have since been renewed.

Relating to Dr. Paine's nonrenewal, the board president said, "The district made advancements during [Paine's] term . . . accountability, technology . . . she did a lot of good work, but she and the board didn't get along. There was a personality conflict . . . the board and the superintendent don't mesh. Both sides were at fault here. It isn't just Dr. Paine." He led the 6 to 3 vote not to renew. A local editorial began, "Jeers to the . . . School District board for its vote not to renew the contract of Superintendent [Paine]. . . . Perhaps a [new] contract of one or two years in length [should be extended] with a focus on trying to bridge the personality gaps that the board currently sees between themselves and Paine. . . . Down the road, the upheaval of changing superintendents may prove to be as tumultuous as the personality conflicts the board perceives it cannot solve."

The school board did not follow the superintendent evaluation process that had been accepted in a verbal agreement in the hiring of Dr. Paine. While all board members had provided input for her written evaluation in the third year (no written feedback had been given for the first and second years), they did not see the final written report, which reflected only the viewpoints of those members who opposed her. The yearly written evaluation, agreed upon in the hiring process, was not provided, and salary agreements for a percentage raise and lump sum salary adjustment after the first year were not honored, with the comment that the board "did not remember" these agreements.

The nonrenewal of Dr. Jones appeared to be political. Dr. Jones, while in office, stressed that district hiring processes must allow the most qualified person to be selected for the job (in the event of equal qualifications, she would endorse the local person). This was not the past practice in her district, where the board would write a job description, post it, and hire someone while the superintendent was out of town, even though the state school code required that all candidates be recommended to the board by the superintendent. Because Dr. Jones believed that improvement in children's learning is related to staff quality, she put enormous effort into changing this job patronage system in the district—the same players moved from district to city payrolls and back again. This focus on changing the hiring practices in the district seemed to be the main reason for Dr. Jones's dismissal. The control board did not override the board's decision for nonrenewal of her contract, since they felt nothing positive could happen if the local board would not work with the superintendent.

The area state representative said that the decision was political. Dr. Jones "has worked to turn the schools around; brought in corporations, hospitals, and universities to support education: and put people in place who can work with students. The school board just wants to put someone in place who will be their puppet." With Dr. Jones's nonrenewal counted, there have been five different superintendents in the district since 1991. Dr. Jones was the only one to stay longer than a year. After the vote not to renew her contract, she was put on administrative leave. The district remains in turmoil to the present time.

Sadly, Dr. Jones was nonrenewed, in spite of the fact that she enabled the district to improve, such as the high school being transformed into a clean, safe place for both students and teachers. Further, space for the additional students expected in the fall of 1995 was provided by moving some programs into differ-ent locations and painting a building that had been so troubled that parents had wanted the building closed. Interestingly, Dr. Jones was able to resolve the teach-ers' contract without a strike, no small feat in a district strapped for money and unable to raise taxes. And finally, several building principals who were not per-forming were demoted. While district change appeared slow, there was a total turnaround in many areas.

The school boards, in the districts that did not renew the two women super-intendents, were and had been contentious ones, having many public and pri-vate clashes. Board members had lengthy personal agendas, and finding school district jobs for their constituents was high on their lists. Both boards had his-tories of poor working relations within the boards and with their past superin-tendents. Board members, especially the presidents, appeared to want to be the chief school administrators rather than board members. These people spent long periods of time with the superintendent, attempting to dictate exactly what should be done that particular day.

All four of the participants had interesting thoughts about board members. They reported that some board members spent up to three hours a day with them cutting into time that needed to be spent with students, teachers, and administrators. The women felt that not only is there an ongoing need for gen-eral board orientation sessions and attendance at the Pennsylvania School Boards Association (PSBA) Academy for new members, but that board members need one-on-one sessions on their particular interests. Extensive training seemed a necessity during teacher negotiations, so that board members could understand their appropriate roles. All four of these women decided not to negotiate directly, but to follow the discussions and be available to talk with their teams as needed. Board members required, they said, a great deal of nurturing, even those con-sidered educational advocates.

All of the superintendents provided extensive information to their board members in packets before meetings, and directly to individuals according to their interests, with Dr. Smith honoring a board request to record a daily mes-sage for members to call in and receive. However, the women noted that they could not rely on board members reading even the information they provided. Thus, time was spent before board meetings determining strategies for the method of presentation and how much information to present. Especially for the budget discussions, the most effective procedure seemed to be to present the "short" version and to be prepared with backup materials in the event of questions. Cooper (1996), an educational researcher, learned to tailor his research presentations to his fellow school board members so that the board would understand and use the research in much the same way as these female superintendents found necessary for their school boards. Also, the timing and placement of various items in the board agenda are carefully determined to facilitate the approval of needed curricular programs.

The conversation among the four women participants focused heavily on board members, but other topics came up as well. For example, by the third year, Dr. Nells reported, she had put in long hours with district groups, including community members working on curriculum and instruction initiatives. She found that her continued presence was a signal to the groups that curriculum and instruction efforts were truly sanctioned by the superintendent. The positive attitude her teachers held toward district staff development was probably influenced by her efforts, the district's past practice of six-year curriculum revision cycles, and the involvement of teachers in staff development planning.

At times, the conversation turned to finance and facilities. Finance and building construction were two areas of expertise that all four women thought they lacked. Early on in their superintendencies, they did not question those who had been assigned these functions. When they "felt" something was wrong, they started to ask more and more questions. At first, they were put off, but they soon realized that if the answers did not make sense, the problem was probably with the person asked rather than with themselves. Binney and Williams (1995) confirmed their realizations: "In our experience, managers have a great deal of instinct and intuition about what works and what doesn't. If they feel it is okay to discuss what their instincts tell them, there is a huge well of insights to be drawn from" (p. 49).

After some time in the conversation, Dr. Nells noted that children had not been mentioned. She admitted that during her first year, when one of her objectives had been to visit schools, she probably spent more time with children. However, they all had spent time in child-centered activities, such as reading to first graders, judging spelling bees, joining in women's history celebrations, and explaining to children that in addition to medical doctors there are different kinds of doctors—those who know about other subjects, such as themselves. Yet at the time, providing for children by being able to hire quality personnel using an equitable process (not simply hiring board members' friends), arranging for staff development and curriculum improvement, educating board members, and taking care of the district's finances (an area with which none of them felt comfortable at the beginning) were what consumed their time and dominated this conversation.

Issues Prominent in the Third Year

After thirty months in the superintendency, these issues were prominent in the conversation: nurturing board members, being a superintendent, job-seeking advice, communications, gender differences, and trusting oneself. By then the women realized the need to question anything that was not understandable to themselves, even things asserted by experts in areas such as finance and construction, where they lacked knowledge.

Specific new items noted by the two remaining superintendents one year later were: new school construction; the closing of a military base with housing assigned to military personnel who work outside of the district, resulting in a financial squeeze; superintendent of record for interdistrict vocational school; teachers working without a contract; resurfacing of religious and class differences over the school calendar and school redistricting; provision of annual report on the district; reorganization of district administrative structure and board committees; and death or illness of a parent.

DISCUSSION

While the women were driven to work extremely long hours, as Pavan (1988a) found in her earlier survey of all Pennsylvania female superintendents, their vision of making schools better for children led them to educate their boards, parents, the general public, and the media by using information and modeling appropriate behavior. Each woman came armed with an entry plan to gather data, become informed about the district, and demonstrate an open communication style. Their entry plans proceeded fairly smoothly, except in the urban school district, which was also the largest and clearly the most distressed.

They found that the budget process was their first testing ground, and while modest increases were passed, their procedures were substantially changed for the second year by increasing input, public information, and starting earlier. Personnel hiring and evaluation were considered an important use of their time, since they would most influence the quality of the instruction. Some board members, especially in the larger districts, viewed hiring as a way to help their constituents, and constant vigilance was necessary to preserve a fair process. The superintendents of the smaller districts were quite directly involved in these processes, while the women in the larger districts proposed new positions to handle these functions.

Board Relations

Working with the board and individual members required enormous amounts of time, which continued to be necessary; however, there was some evidence that the emphasis on data, children's needs, and open communication was influencing some board members in this study. Lindle (1990) found that board relations provided the largest source of conflict for both the male and female superintendents in her Pennsylvania study, yet Glass (1992) found that only 16.7 percent of superintendents reported this reason for leaving their last superintendency.

Danzberger (1994) listed ten problems of school boards; six were also indicated by the female superintendents in this study: "micro-managing districts"; responding to special interests or political needs; not devolving decision making to the schools; "exhibiting serious problems in their capacity to develop positive and productive, lasting relationships with superintendents"; "paying little or no attention to their performance and their need for ongoing training"; and responding to the "issue of the day" or maintaining the status quo. The strategies of providing information, training board members about appropriate role behavior and process, increasing community involvement, continuing the dialogue between the superintendent and the board, and keeping the focus on the district strategic plan while maintaining openness and trust, all strategies mentioned by this study's respondents, were noted in the series as being necessary if boards were to be effective.

In their study of women who left the superintendency, Tallerico, Burstyn, and Poole (1993) indicated that thirteen of the twenty left because of nonrenewal of their contracts. These women reported the following "pushes": political factors, school board dysfunction, union influence, noneducational focus on funds and facilities, and ethical clashes due to board insistence on illegal practices. While none saw gender as a primary cause, they thought that they did not act tough enough, that the board felt women should not run things or did not fit "the mold," and that women are held to higher performance standards. The women in this study agreed that the political factors listed in Tallerico et al.s' study were ones they also faced, yet they did not experience undue difficulty with unions. Except for their own beliefs that their performance exceeded that of most male superintendents, they did not mention gender comparisons regarding standards of performance as a chief executive officer.

Some of the difficulty of dealing with school boards, according to Wesson and Grady (1994), may be that boards often hire a superintendent whom they expect will both "introduce and manage change" and "provide stability, structure, and organization for a district." This national study of female superintendents reported that their respondents, like the women in this study, were very high on such personal qualities as "challenging the process, inspiring a shared vision, enabling others to act, modeling the way, and encouraging the heart."

Personal/Work

Finding a balance between a personal life and work demands continued to be an issue that was slowly being resolved, with weekends reserved for family.

Brunner (1997) noted some characteristics of the twelve female superintendents whom she studied that were shared by the women in this study: a strong sense of efficacy, extremely high intelligence, "workaholism," and often being in possession of more skills than their male peers, with the capacity to improvise as needed.

Leadership and Communication

These women all used the "interactive leadership" style defined by Rosener (1990) in her study of managerial women. They "encouraged participation" by involving others in forums such as town meetings, "shared power and information" by having administrators decide on the cabinet agenda and providing data to all, "enhanced the self-worth of others" by insisting that principals who brought them problems also make recommendations for solutions, and "energized others" with their own enthusiasm when talking about the students. This "power to" approach was noted in Brunner's case study (1995) of another female superintendent.

The interactive, open style of these female superintendents stands in stark contrast to the twenty-four male superintendents who, as Blumberg (1985) reported, took a reactive stance to conflict, attempting to defuse it quickly and avoid it if at all possible. They confided in their wives, not in other superintendents, and their greatest dilemma was deciding when to "use one's chips," since their style was the bargaining or bartering style. Berg's case study (1995) of a young male superintendent is an updated version of this political stance. The differences may not be only in gender, for these women noted that some male superintendents new to the job were more likely to be concerned with the students and to be willing to share. Beck (1994) provided additional evidence that caring may be a quality now more respected in the profession, if not by school boards, in the 1990s.

The female superintendents of Western districts studied by Bell and Chase (1989) used bureaucratic policies and hierarchy structure, yet involved others in democratic decision making. These small districts (220 to 2,800 students) would have fewer hierarchical layers and a more informal character than those studied here.

Gender Differences in Superintendents' Contracts

Gender differences surfaced as the women discussed provisions that might be used during their contract negotiations. A long list of known perks in male superintendents' contracts was shared, including a book allowance, car, credit cards, conference and membership fees, medical insurance, both while on the job and until age sixty-five, IRAs or pension plans, additional sick days, not to be used but to be paid at the per diem rate, and salary increases "donated" to a district educational foundation, but counting as salary for retirement. Even with the knowledge that their male counterparts were receiving such perks, the women felt that while they deserved a fair contract, some of these requests were not "fair." As Gilligan (1982) pointed out long ago, boys know the rules and play the game, but girls have a responsibility of caring that does not allow them to take advantage of the system. The women posed these questions: If our contracts are second class to men, do school boards look at us as being second-class superintendents? Could this willingness to be fair be part of the reason why some school board members are disrespectful of their female superintendents? Were we so glad that we got these jobs that we are not able to ask for such contract items?

"IF ONLY WE HAD KNOWN . . ."

Based on the experiences and learning of these four women, the following points are offered to women as they move into their first year of the superintendency:

1. *Job-seeking advice.* Get a four- or five-year contract, find a board that works together, be very clear as to your own strengths and weaknesses so the board understands them, and negotiate as strong a contract as possible, with all agreements in writing. As a candidate, you can learn much about the board by listening to their questions, and you should thoroughly research the district by reading the local newspaper, calling people, and just asking questions wherever you go. Look for a community where businesses are expanding, review the past and projected school district budgets, and investigate the infrastructure to determine if things are "doable." Join a women's administrators group, if available.

2. *Politics.* The reality is that school boards will consider most issues without reference to children. Rather than becoming dismayed, expect to deal with political issues and be aware of all stakeholder groups.

3. *Nurturing board members.* The demands for time from the school board and individual members, especially school board presidents, limit the effectiveness of chief executive officers. The turnover after school board elections requires a continuous effort to train and monitor board members regarding their roles and legal responsibilities. Yet to ignore the care and feeding of school board members leads to total disaster. Remember that the school board position is a stepping-stone to other elected offices.

4. *Studying and planning.* Use the first year to study past practices, such as the budget process, hiring, and evaluation, in order to modify them for the following year. Investigate different procedures for activities, such as collective negotiations, which are not yearly issues. Start with a formal entry plan so that study time is allowed. Provide a written district plan after several months of study, with goals on which district activities may focus. Continue

to refer to this district plan to justify district and budget activities. Put systematic data collection processes in place to provide input for decisions.

5. *Communications.* Start by interviewing all major stakeholder groups and spending considerable time in the schools. The same interviewing process should be the starting point for any planned changes. The superintendent's job is in large part public relations, to interface with the public in an open, honest manner by providing whatever information is needed and to get the positive stories told. Both the staff and the public need to realize the progress made. React to criticism as though it might be helpful rather than in a defensive manner. Investigate issues and report, rather than try to cover up.

6. *Changing behavior.* Rather than using the directive approach, model desired behavior, even pointing out the behavior being used, such as creative problem solving rather than confrontation to educate the staff. Humor and role reversal stories are often more persuasive than confrontation. Administrators not only need to be shown how to generate positive stories but also told how to do them. Set in motion monitoring procedures, such as monthly reports for principals on the number of completed teacher observations.

7. *Gender differences.* Expect differential treatment. In settings with other superintendents, the women noted that they were not "unaccepted," but they were not supported, since the male superintendents tended to interact with their male buddies. Some board members treated male and female superintendents differently.

8. *Personal/work.* Protect your personal or family time. Living outside of the district and not being available on weekends are useful strategies. Strained personal relationships often are the result of this demanding work schedule. Your spouse or partner needs strong personal interests.

9. *Being a superintendent.* The demands of the first two years while learning about the district are exhausting, leaving little personal time. As a result of the knowledge and experience gained, the third year is somewhat more relaxed. All four women in this study loved their work as superintendents and could point to positive school district changes that resulted from their efforts. Two looked forward to continuing work in their present school districts. Of the two women whose contracts were not renewed, one continues to seek a superintendency while working as a consultant/trainer for an educational research lab, and the other is taking a "retirement" year before deciding what to do next.

10. *Trust yourself.* Trust your instincts. Ask many questions. If it does not make sense, there is probably something wrong. Do not assume that the "expert" has the needed expertise. Men are used to playing the game and women do not know the rules.

REFERENCES

Beck, L. G. 1994. *Reclaiming educational administration as a caring profession*. New York: Teachers College Press.

Bell, C. S., and S. E. Chase. 1989. Women as educational leaders: Resistance and conformity. Paper presented at the annual meeting of the American Educational Research Association, San Francisco.

Berg, J. H. 1995. The rashomon of perceptions: Educational leadership and/or politics. Paper presented at the University Council of Educational Administration Convention, Salt Lake City, Utah.

Binney, G., and C. Williams. 1995. *Leaning into the future*. London: Nicholas Brealey.

Blumberg, A. 1985. *The school superintendent: Living with conflict*. New York: Teachers College Press.

Bogotch, I. E. 1995. A case study of a first-year superintendent: The relationship between person and context. Paper presented at the annual meeting of the American Educational Research Association, San Francisco.

Brunner, C. C. 1995. By power defined: Women in the superintendency. *Educational Considerations* 22 (2): 21–26.

———. 1997. Working through the 'riddle of the heart': Perspectives of women superintendents. *Journal of School Leadership* 7 (1): 138–64.

Civil Rights Act of 1964, Title IX, 20 U.S.C. § 1681(a) (1971).

Civil Rights Act of 1991, Title II, The Glass Ceiling Act, 42 U.S.C. § 2000e.

Cooper, H. 1996. Speaking power to truth: Reflections of an educational researcher after four years of school board service. *Educational Researcher* 25 (1): 29–34.

Danzberger, J. P. 1994. Governing the nation's schools: The case for restructuring local school boards. *Phi Delta Kappan* 75 (2): 367–73.

Gilligan, C. 1982. *In a different voice*. Cambridge, Mass.: Harvard University Press.

Glass, T. 1992. *The 1992 study of the American school superintendency*. Arlington, Va.: American Association of School Administrators.

Jentz, B. 1982. *Entry: The hiring, start-up, and supervision of administrators*. New York: McGraw-Hill.

Johnson, S. M. 1996. Turnover in the superintendency: A hazard to leadership and reform. *Education Week* 60 (March 13): 47.

Kanter, R. M. 1977. *Men and women of the corporation*. New York: Basic Books.

Keedy, J. L. 1995. Synopsis of the first-year superintendency: An across case analysis. Paper presented at the annual meeting of the American Educational Research Association, San Francisco.

Lindle, J. C. 1990. Coping in the superintendency: Gender-related perspectives. Paper presented at the University Council of Educational Administration Convention, Pittsburgh, Pa.

Pavan, B. N. 1985. Certified but not hired: Women administrators in Pennsylvania. Paper presented at the annual conference of Research on Women in Education, Boston. ERIC (ED26 686).

———. 1986. Barriers to hiring and promotion experienced by certified aspiring and incumbent female and male public school administrators. Paper presented at the annual meeting of the American Educational Research Association, San Francisco.

———. 1987a. Sex role stereotyping for household chores by aspiring and incumbent female and male public school administrators. Paper presented at the annual meeting of the American Educational Research Association, Washington, D.C. ERIC (ED283303).

———. 1987b. Aspiration levels of certified and incumbent female and male public school administrators. Paper presented at the annual meeting of the American Educational Research Association, Washington, D.C. ERIC (ED284333).

———. 1987c. Mentoring certified aspiring and incumbent female and male public school administrators. *Journal of Educational Equity and Leadership* 7 (4): 318–31.

———. 1988a. Not enough time for body or soul: The experiences of women school superintendents. Paper presented at the annual SIG: Research on Women in Education Conference of the American Educational Research Association, Hempstead, N.Y.

———. 1988b. Job search strategies utilized by certified aspiring and incumbent female and male public school administrators. Paper presented at the annual meeting of the American Educational Research Association, New Orleans. ERIC (ED302879).

———. 1989. Searching for female leaders for America's schools: Are the women to blame? Paper presented at the University Council of Educational Administration Convention, Scottsdale, Ariz. ERIC (ED321392).

———. 1995. First-year district superintendents: Women reflect on contradictions between education and politics. Paper presented at the University Council of Educational Administration Convention, Salt Lake City, Utah. ERIC (ED027186).

Pavan, B. N., and C. C. McKee. 1988. Gender differences in the career paths of educational administrators. Paper presented at the annual meeting of the American Educational Research Association, New Orleans. ERIC (ED302876).

Pavan, B. N., B. A. Winkler, and P. E. Dovey. 1995. Eight years later: Has the superintendency changed for women? Paper presented at the annual meeting of the American Educational Research Association, San Francisco. ERIC (ED 394 962).

Rosener, J. B. 1990. Ways women lead. *Harvard Business Review* 68 (6): 119–25.

Scherr, M. W. 1994. Building community support: Crucial task for new superintendent. Paper presented at the American Educational Research Association Annual Meeting, New Orleans.

Shakeshaft, C. 1989. *Women in educational administration*. Newbury Park, Calif.: Sage Publications.

Snyder, T. D. (ed.). 1993. *120 years of American education: A statistical portrait*. Washington, D.C.: National Center for Education Statistics, Office of Educational Research and Improvement, U. S. Department of Education.

Tallerico, M., and J. N. Burstyn. 1994. Context matters: "Starter" districts and women superintendents. Paper presented at the American Educational Research Association Annual Meeting, New Orleans.

Tallerico, M., J. N. Burstyn, and W. Poole. 1993. *Gender and politics at work: Why women exit the superintendency.* Fairfax, Va.: National Policy Board for Educational Administration.

Tallerico, M., W. Poole, and J. N. Burstyn. 1994. Exits from urban superintendencies: The intersection of politics, race, and gender. *Urban Education* 28 (4): 439–54.

Wesson, L. H., and M. L. Grady. 1994. An analysis of women urban superintendents: A national study. *Urban Education* 28 (4): 412–24.

CHAPTER EIGHT

Redefinition of Self

Mexican-American Women
Becoming Superintendents

SYLVIA E. MÉNDEZ-MORSE

Mexican-American female superintendents are a small, unique, but nonetheless important population. Hispanic females—whether Mexican American or Cuban or Puerto Rican or Central or South American—are severely underrepresented in all educational administrative positions, especially when considering the superintendency. A 1982 American Association of School Administrators national survey found that there were four Hispanic female superintendents (0.1 percent of all superintendents) in the United States (Jones and Montenegro 1982). The number of Hispanic women superintendents, however, has increased slightly since this report. For example, the state education agency of Texas identified eight (.8 percent of all superintendents in Texas) Hispanic female superintendents during the 1992–93 school year (Texas Education Agency 1993). Although this indicates an increase in the number of Hispanic female district leaders, this group of educational administrators remains a unique but neglected population. They are unique simply by having obtained the highest level of administrative responsibility in a public school system and neglected because of their absence in research studies focusing on female superintendents.

Research on women in educational administration has focused primarily on white females. Although this research area is rich with data concerning women, there is limited information on minority female administrators (Adkison 1981; Ortiz 1982a; Valverde 1980; Valverde and Brown 1988; Yeakey, Johnston, and Adkison 1986). Several studies have included Hispanic female administrators (e.g., Valverde 1980), however few focused exclusively on this group (Armendariz-Housen 1995; Colon Gibson 1992; Fernandez 1989; Ortiz 1982b; Ortiz and

125

Venegas 1978). There has been only one case study of a Hispanic female superintendent (Ortiz 1991). Information on Hispanic women superintendents is, in effect, absent from the literature. This lack of research is a serious deficiency.

Perhaps it could be argued that because of the low numbers of Hispanic women in the superintendency, educational administration researchers are justified in neglecting this population. However, it is precisely because of their low, almost invisible, numbers that attention should be afforded to this singular group of women who have become the chief executives of public school systems, especially when those positions are synonymous with white male educational leadership. Negligible presence does not mean insignificance. The presence of Hispanic female superintendents signals an opportunity to explore and examine the larger phenomenon. Furthermore, it is by no means clear that the experiences of Hispanic women superintendents, who are profoundly atypical in their ethnicity and gender from the majority of those who lead public school districts, are either irrelevant or uninformative.

Aside from a few studies documenting the numbers and administrative positions attained by Hispanic females, limited information concerning other aspects of this specific group's experiences in educational administration is available. Several studies specifically focused on the obstacles confronted by Hispanic women as they pursued their administrative careers. Within these, three common barriers this group confronted were found: gender expectations, ethnic stereotyping, and lack of sponsorship (Colon Gibson 1992; Ortiz 1982a; Ortiz and Venegas 1978). Studies that contribute to a reconceptualization of leadership theories using data from a minority educational administrative perspective are few. Two studies (Valverde 1980; Ortiz 1982a), which included Hispanic females in their sample, imply a reconsideration of role conflict theories. Valverde (1980) suggested that role conflict is pervasive in minority administrators owing to a need to demonstrate allegiance to both community and institution expectations. Ortiz (1982a) implied that the same role conflict exists but, in addition, asserted that minority females also contend with both gender and ethnic stereotyping.

The voices of Hispanic female educational administrators are beginning to emerge in recent dissertation studies. Three studies on Hispanic female administrators in a wide range of educational administrative positions provide data from the perspectives of the women themselves (Armendariz-Housen 1995; Colon Gibson 1992; Fernandez 1989). For the Hispanic women studied by these researchers, family support for achieving their educational goals and a strong sense of self were significant ingredients of their success. Learning about the experiences of Hispanic female superintendents contributes to understanding how women, particularly minority women, have managed to become superintendents.

There are various phases in the process of becoming a superintendent, including a stage when the prospective district leader changes her self-perception.

There is a shift from thinking of herself as a person with potential to being strongly convinced that she has the necessary skills and knowledge to lead a public school system. This chapter is based on an in-depth study of what four Mexican-American females experienced while becoming superintendents. Among the experiences found to be common to the four women in this study, the experience of redefining themselves demonstrates an essential component of their process while becoming superintendents. In all cases, this redefinition of self was gradual and began before they actively sought the superintendency position. A slow yet significant transformation occurred during their efforts to secure a district leader position, and their redefinition extended to a brief period during their early experiences as a superintendent. These women redefined themselves; they changed their self-perceptions from persons with the potential to be a superintendent to women with assured confidence in their competence to be a superintendent.

The process of redefinition included three phases. The first was an event in their early administrative careers that acted as an initiation to leadership. During this phase, the women proved themselves capable of accomplishing a self-imposed qualifying task that demonstrated their leadership abilities.

The second phase in the process of redefining themselves was a transformation of self that involved:

1. a conscious and deliberate decision to become a superintendent;
2. a public proclamation of competence to be a district leader; and
3. a validation resulting from being hired as the primary administrator of a public school system.

The final phase in the process of redefining themselves was a metamorphosis to the superintendency, a striking alteration in how they were perceived by others and how the women themselves viewed the district leadership position.

This chapter begins with a brief description of the women participating in this study and proceeds to discuss each of the three phases just outlined. The chapter concludes with remarks about the implications of this study for further research in the area of women—particularly minority women—and the superintendency.

DESCRIPTION OF THE WOMEN

Four Mexican-American women were the participants in this study. These women shared three characteristics: all identified themselves as Mexican American, were employed as superintendents in public school systems, and were married at the time of the study. The women differed in the types of districts they led, the size of the student populations for which they were responsible, and in the number of superintendencies they had held. Two women had held two superintendency positions during their administrative careers. Three women had earned their doctoral degrees. All four women were married; however, three were divorced and had remarried. Two women had children; one woman was a grand-mother. Two women had chosen not to have children in order to pursue their administrative careers. A description of each woman follows:

Antonietta Vidal [pseudonym] was the superintendent of a large, urban school district of more than 20,000 students. The majority of the students were minority members, primarily Hispanic, with a small percentage of African Amer-icans, and a very small percentage of European Americans. Antonietta, at the time of the study, was ending her fourth and beginning her fifth year of her first superintendency. She was married for a second time and had no children. Antonietta had earned a doctoral degree.

Consuelo Perez [pseudonym] was the superintendent of a small, rural school district of approximately 300 students. The student population of this district was composed primarily of European Americans (more than 60 percent), and the remaining percentage represented Hispanic students. Consuelo, at the time of the study, was ending her fourth and final year of her second superintendency and entering retirement. Her first superintendency had been with a large rural school district of about 8,000 students. She served in that position for eight years. She had been married for more than thirty years; she had six children and ten grandchildren. Consuelo's only regret in her life was not having pursued a doctoral degree.

Muñeca Guzman [pseudonym] was the superintendent of a small, rural school district of about 500 students. The student population of this district was composed primarily of European Americans (55 percent) with the remaining per-centage representing Hispanic (25 percent) and Native American (10 percent) students. Muñeca, at the time of the study, was ending the third year of her sec-ond superintendency. Her first superintendency had been with a small rural dis-trict of less than 300 students, all of whom were Hispanic. She served in that position for three and a half years. She had been married to her second husband for more than twenty years, and together they had five children. Muñeca earned a doctoral degree during the duration of this study.

Ventura Luna [pseudonym] was the superintendent of a small city school district of approximately 15,000 students. The student population of this district was about 45 percent Hispanic, 30 percent European American, and 15 percent Native American, with the remaining 10 percent consisting of African and Asian Americans. Ventura, at the time of the study, was in the middle of her second year of her first superintendency. She was married for a second time and had no children. Ventura had earned a doctoral degree.

Despite the differences in the types of districts they led and the number of superintendencies each had held, a redefinition process was common to these four women. They changed their self-perceptions from women as potential super-intendents to women as eventual superintendents. Their redefinition began with an event that served as their personal initiation to leadership. This phase is described in the next section.

INITIATION TO LEADERSHIP

Before the women in this study began contemplating the possibility of becoming a superintendent, they underwent an initiation to leadership, a rite of passage by which the women demonstrated their leadership abilities. A rite of passage is gen-erally considered a ritual associated with a challenge or task that must be per-formed and that will lead to a change in status for an individual. For these women, there was a ritualistic qualifying task, in response to which they exhib-ited a self-imposed standard of ability that allowed them to consider themselves a leader. Although the qualifying task was not identified by the women as an ini-tiation to leadership per se, each woman described in detail an event in their administrative careers that was significant to them. This event is what I have labeled their "initiation to leadership."

The initiation to leadership shared three characteristics. First, the women seized and claimed for themselves an assignment or opportunity as a qualifying task and converted this to a task of more than just completing the assigned responsibility. It became a means by which they could prove to themselves that they were leaders. Although the women's leadership was recognized by others, by accomplishing their self-imposed standard, the women elevated the assigned responsibility to a more significant task for themselves. Second, although their initiation to leadership involved some risk or sacrifice, the women believed them-selves capable of doing the job. They also recognized, in retrospect, that meeting the self-imposed requirement had been a significant event in their administrative careers. Finally, their initiations to leadership led to a change in status in these women's administrative careers.

Two examples of initiations to leadership follow. The first illustrates how Dr. Ventura Luna readily accepted an assigned responsibility that became a qual-ifying task with her self-imposed standard. The second describes how Consuelo Perez seized an opportunity and transformed it into a qualifying task for herself.

Ventura Luna had served as the principal of two middle schools in two dif-ferent urban school districts before her initiation to leadership. She was assigned the principalship of a high school and was specifically given the responsibility of desegregating this school, which was notorious for its biased policies and prac-tices that limited the participation of minority students. Ventura accepted the job and made it her personal crusade to end the discriminatory practices of this high school, which had a large minority student population. Although Hispanic and

African-American students were the majority, student leadership positions throughout the school were held by European-American students who were less than one-third of the student population. In addition, participation of Hispanic and African-American students in extracurricular activities was limited by various traditional practices that excluded or minimized the inclusion of these students.

Dr. Luna described her work in this school with the following words: "The entire school was *totally, totally* segregated. . . . I started to change things in a big way. In fact, I started changing things on the first day when I changed how the extra parking slots in the teachers' parking lot were assigned to students. I changed it to a lottery system; before, only white students had those slots. . . . All the clubs were white and [Hispanic and African-American students] were not allowed into any of the extracurricular activities unless someone sponsored them. . . . We had the first student body president elected by the entire student body; before, it was just done by committee. . . . We had the first Hispanic homecoming queen because the entire student body voted."

Ventura's efforts to dismantle the biased practices and policies of this school were not without ramifications. "I had to integrate each club, and every time I did that I got more people angry at me. There were some white parents who had been running that school like a private school for years. They were very, *very* angry with me." In spite of some parents' harsh and negative reactions, Ventura accomplished her responsibility of changing and ending procedures that discriminated against minority students in this school. She served in this capacity for two years.

While describing this event, she stated, "[It] has been my cross to bear. It has been the toughest job I've ever had." When describing the process of desegregating the school, Dr. Luna stated that, "It was about the privileged ranks all of a sudden not being so privileged . . . I felt like I was back in the sixties in the civil rights era in the South . . . and I wouldn't give up. I would not give up." Although this responsibility was specifically assigned to her by the superintendent, Dr. Luna took it upon herself to beginning the process of dismantling discriminatory practices as she stated "on the first day." Further, she strongly felt that it was her personal responsibility to directly confront the inequitable practices herself. She stated, "If I didn't take it on, it was not going to happen."

Dr. Luna felt satisfaction with the changes that she had implemented, thus proving to herself that she was a leader. Others' recognition of her leadership skills led to her placement in this position; however, it was meeting her self-imposed requirement of changing the school on "the first day" that convinced her of being a leader. Her next administrative position was as a district area assistant superintendent.

Consuelo Perez was an active and a visible teacher in her rural school district for more than four years. She became the president of the local teacher association and was instrumental in the negotiations of teachers' salaries and work conditions. In addition, she consistently attended the school board meetings and made concerted efforts to be vocal and recognized by the board members. Consuelo's initiation to leadership came when she was recruited directly by the superintendent and asked to be the head teacher of a small, out-of-town school. The position required that she be a teacher as well as the acting principal of the small rural school. However, her major responsibility while in this position was consolidating two schools into one.

When the superintendent asked her to fill the position, Consuelo accepted. Although the position was considered undesirable because there were drawbacks, she viewed it as an opportunity. "I said okay but that meant buying a second vehicle. It was expensive for me to take it." Mrs. Perez recognized that the task could be accomplished easily by merely decreeing a consolidation of the two schools as a district decision. However, she believed that the rural school community should be approached differently.

Consuelo described this task in the following way: "That particular school was not getting all the programs because there were only seventy-five students and because of that they weren't getting band, they weren't getting chorus, they weren't getting physical education. The district couldn't afford for all of those people to drive out there. If they consolidated the school with the new one in town, they would get all those services, a broader program, for their students." She placed upon herself the responsibility of convincing this established rural community of the advantages to closing its school and busing their students to the new, in-town school.

Consuelo accomplished her main task of closing the school and moving students to a new school with minimal community objection. She did this by communicating to the community the benefits of this change. In describing this accomplishment, she stated, "I think that particular community viewed me as a leader, and they trusted what I said. They believed in what I thought was good for students." By having met the responsibility of blending two very different communities into one in an amicable manner, Consuelo met her self-imposed requirement and thus proved to herself that she was a leader. Her next position was as an elementary school principal.

TRANSFORMATION OF SELF

Having accomplished their initiation to leadership, with its self-imposed qualifying task, the women now considered themselves leaders. What occurred next was a transformation of self, the middle phase of their redefinition process. It was a phase characterized by a major change in how these women viewed themselves, their skills, and their abilities—a change that ultimately led to them becoming superintendents. The transformation of self occurred in three distinct transitions. The first transition was marked by a decision to become a superintendent. The second transition occurred during the interviewing process. The final transition in the transformation of self took place when each was selected as a superintendent.

Decision

The first shift in the women's transformation of self began with a conscious, deliberate decision to become a superintendent. This decision was either inspired or provoked by events that led the women to reevaluate their abilities. In addition to reexamining their capabilities, they evaluated others who were either in the position or applying for a district leadership position and compared themselves to these individuals. The women concluded that they were just as capable or better qualified than those individuals. Therefore, they decided that they could and would be superintendents and began to actively seek this position.

For two women, the decision to become a superintendent was inspired by a female district leader. Ventura decided to become a superintendent when she was an adult; Consuelo was inspired when she was a young child. The other two women, Dr. Muñeca Guzman and Dr. Antonietta Vidal, were provoked into deciding to become a superintendent. All clearly recollected when their decisions were made.

The experience of Dr. Muñeca Guzman best illustrates being provoked into a decision. Having served as acting superintendent during a search for a new district leader, and having been ordered not to apply for the position herself, she became keenly aware of the applicants' abilities. As she carefully reviewed the applications submitted and seriously studied the information of the person selected for the position, she concluded that she had better qualifications. "When I began to look at the applications, I saw that I had a better packet in many cases. Since I helped with the process in selecting the applicants, I saw then that the people who were interviewed didn't have what I had. That's when it began to click, 'I can do this.' That's when I decided." Being told not to apply and determining that she was as qualified or better than some of the applicants, Muñeca decided that she would pursue the superintendency in another district.

Mrs. Perez's description of deciding to become a superintendent clearly illustrates the impact of being inspired to seek this position. Consuelo became aware of women as superintendents very early in her life. When she was in the second grade, she met the county schools' superintendent, who was a Hispanic female. Consuelo shared that when this happened, she became aware of the "pecking order," the hierarchy of positions, that existed in schools. She became aware that her teacher had "a boss," the principal. Further, she recognized that "then the boss had another boss," and it was a realization that the "other boss" was a *woman*—that was significant to her. It was an awareness of what she described as "a reversal of roles," compared to what she had seen in her family, specifically the role of her mother, which was important to Consuelo. This recognition of the "other boss" above the male principal being a Hispanic female instilled in her the inspiration to become a superintendent, and while Consuelo was a principal, this memory surfaced and triggered her decision to seek the superintendent position.

Each woman in this study described a specific event that led to her decision to become a superintendent. Once the decision was made, each proceeded to actively seek the superintendency and to assert that she was capable of leading a public school system.

Proclamation

The second shift in their transformation occurred as the women vied for a district leadership position. This shift occurred during these women's interviews for superintendency positions. Common to all four women in this study was their approach to the interviews. They used the forum as a means of practicing and refining their interviewing skills. None of the women believed that they would be selected. Dr. Muñeca Guzman's description of her approach to her first superintendency interview exemplifies sentiments expressed by the other women. She stated that she thought, "Well, why not apply? I'll probably get an interview, because I have a good packet, and it'll be a good experience, so that I can begin to prepare myself. One of these years I will be a superintendent." Indeed, two of the four women interviewed for more than two district leadership positions before being selected as the next superintendent. Despite their approach to using the interviews as a means of honing their skills, the interviewing process marked an important change in how these women viewed themselves.

The interviewing process had three characteristics. First, the interviews became a public assertion of themselves as women who could be district leaders. Even if the interview did not yield the selection of themselves as the next superintendent, it provided the women with opportunities to keep asserting themselves publicly as women capable of leading a district. Second, through the interviews, the women compelled a recognition of themselves as potential superintendents. Third, during the interviews that led to their selection, the women realized that the district was ready to accept a woman as a district leader. Illustrations of these three characteristics are provided next.

Dr. Ventura Luna and Mrs. Consuelo Perez described how the interviewing process served as a public assertion of their abilities to be a superintendent. During their interviews, both women were articulate not only about their skills and abilities to perform the responsibilities of the district leadership position but also asserted their willingness to carry out the duties inherent in the superintendency.

In describing the interview for her second superintendency, Consuelo Perez stated, "When they asked me what I could do for the district, I said, 'I have many contributions to make to the district that a person with less experience doesn't have. I still have many contacts in [the state department]. I'm good in school finance. I'm very strong in management. I know how to work with people and the community. I know how to motivate staff to do things and make them feel like it's their idea. I'll be good for your district because I have a good background.'" The interview served as a vehicle for Mrs. Perez to publicly declare her competence to be a superintendent.

Similarly, the interview process became forums for the women to decisively assert their abilities to perform the duties of the position. When describing her experience, Dr. Luna reported details of a particular question that she considered significant during her interview. "I was asked, 'Would you be willing to fire individuals within the [district] that were lacking in their performance?' and my answer was 'Yes.' Period. That's all I said and some people were shocked. I didn't give any qualifiers; I didn't say, 'Yes, however, blah, blah, blah.' In a real honest way, I just said yes. I didn't figure that there needed to be any more embellishment than that. I think that did surprise people."

One example of how the interviews allowed the women to compel others' awareness and knowledge of their competence to be a superintendent is the experience of Dr. Antonietta Vidal. After describing how she had asserted her skills to be a district leader during a superintendency interview, she related the following incident: "After my interview, I remember the president of [the] school board telling me, 'the best thing that came out of this interview is that the board members learned that you were very capable.' They didn't realize that I had the knowledge to be a superintendent. He said, 'What you accomplished is that they learned that you do have the skills to become a superintendent, and they were very surprised. They gained a new respect for your abilities and your skills.' I thought that was interesting." The other women also shared that similar remarks were made to them after they had interviewed.

Yet another significant quality of how the interviewing process promoted a change in these women's perceptions of themselves was that during the interviews they became aware of the school board members' readiness to hire a female as a superintendent. The women shared that during the interviews, they deduced or had an intuition about how the interviewers were responding to them as women seeking this position. When the women felt an acceptance of themselves or another female as the next district leader, they proceeded to continue confidently describing their knowledge and skills for the position.

As Dr. Antonietta Vidal stated, "I felt [this district] was ready for a woman. . . . The men were interested and open minded to elect a woman if the woman was ready. I sensed it, and I saw it. I think that made me even more comfortable. Later, they asked me, 'What do you want to know from us?' and I said,

'All I want to know from you is why are you, as an individual, serving on this board?' They were explaining why they were board members and what their goals were. As I listened to each individual, I knew I answered, basically, everybody's mission or goal. But I think knowing they were open to a woman made it easier to go through the process because I sensed that. . . . How could I sense it? Because of the openness of their questions. We ended up laughing and talking and having a conversation like we'd known each other for a long time."

Validation

The final shift in the transformation of self took place when the women were each selected to be a superintendent. Their selection as superintendents was a validation of these women as district leaders. Their selection, an affirmation of their competence, led the women to see themselves as individuals responsible for leading a public school system, as women capable of performing the duties of the position, and as women exemplifying the abilities of a female, and more important to these women, a minority female, to be a superintendent. The following descriptions of their first thoughts and emotions as they learned of their selection illustrate this final transition of their transformation of self and how this contributed to their redefinition of themselves.

Upon notification of being selected for her first superintendency, Consuelo Perez recalled that she quickly thought to herself, "I have taken on a big responsibility, so I better be willing to work twelve hours a day." Similarly, Dr. Muñeca Guzman reacted with these thoughts. "Oh my God, now I have this job. Now this district is in my hands. I'm now the person who's responsible to make sure that the discipline problems their high school was experiencing are resolved and that the teachers are motivated." She later described that although being selected was the achievement of a goal, her selection itself produced this reaction in her: "It's a responsibility. It's an *awesome* responsibility being a superintendent."

With their selection, the women viewed themselves as individuals with a significant responsibility but also as women able to do the job. When describing being offered her first superintendency, Muñeca recalled, "I thought, 'Oh my God' because, first of all, I did it. I got the superintendency. [An]other thought was that I had presented myself well to these board members and they liked what I had to offer. 'Yes! They saw potential in me.' So that validated what I knew I had in terms of my skills."

Consuelo Perez also reported similar emotions and ideas, as well as an alertness to what her selection indicated to herself and other women. She stated, "I felt 'They have faith in me and think I can do it.' I felt good, but in the back of my mind, I thought, 'I better not let them down.' . . . I was really scared, a little. It meant that I had to work twice as hard, so that I wouldn't blow it for other female candidates in other districts."

Being selected caused these women to change their self-perceptions from women with potential to women with the responsibility and capability of leading a district. Further, the women knew that their selection would be an example of women's, and especially minority women's, leadership abilities. Again, Consuelo's first thoughts upon being selected provided an illustration of this awareness. "I felt a lot of pressure at that time from within myself because I thought, 'If I blow this, I have blown the chances for other women.' So I had a lot of pressure on me as far as doing as good or better than the male superintendents."

When Dr. Antonietta Vidal first learned of her selection, among her first thoughts were, "I knew that I'd be seen as a role model. It was a little scary, because I knew that I needed to be a *good* role model. . . . This made it especially hard because, in my opinion, it was *harder to get in and important to be good.* Remember, I had a double whammy against me: number one being a woman and number two being a Hispanic." With their selection as the next superintendent, the women were aware that their performance in this position needed to be one that demonstrated themselves as minority women responsible for and capable of leading a public school system.

For each of the women, the transformation of self progressed from a private awareness to a public assertion and recognition of their knowledge, skills, and abilities to be superintendents. They were now superintendents; women assured of their competence, aware of their new responsibilities, and cognizant of being a role model. However, the women still continued redefining themselves as they entered the initial period of their superintendency. The final phase in their redefinition of self process was a metamorphosis into the position of a superintendent.

METAMORPHOSIS INTO THE SUPERINTENDENCY

This phase, metamorphosis to the superintendency, was the culmination of the women's redefinition process. A metamorphosis contains a significant alteration in character, and the alteration that these women experienced was more than a change to being a superintendent. Their alteration was an awareness and acceptance of striking differences in how they were perceived as they assumed the superintendency. This occurred early while in the position of being a district's main administrator.

Three significant realizations arose during this initial period that contributed to the final phase of these women's redefinition of self. First, the women became aware of differences in the types of interactions others had with them. People were either solicitous or aloof. Consequently, the women slowly recognized that as the superintendent they were now perceived as different because they were the superintendent. Closely related to this is the second awareness that these women described. They realized that they were now considered to be the position and not a person in the position. The women became cognizant that their personal self, the person they knew themselves to be, was subordinate to the title of superintendent. They were the position first and a person second. Finally, these two realizations combined to form the third understanding that these women experienced during the initial period of their superintendency. They became keenly aware that, as the district's leader, they were alone. Because of the differences in how others interacted with them and the perception of them as a title and not a person, the women recognized their isolation, their separation from others. Furthermore, the women accepted that the superintendency was a lonely position. What follows are descriptions shared by the women in this study of these realizations that led to their metamorphosis to the superintendency.

Dr. Muñeca Guzman's reflections on her superintendency illustrate the first recognition of the differences in interactions when being a superintendent. She shared that, "Some people shy away from you and other people want to politic you. The teachers are the same. Some just say, 'Oh oh, here comes the superintendent; I'm going to go the other way.' Other people are there at your door." The remarks of Dr. Ventura Luna also depict this shift in people's interactions when she stated, "[I]t's almost like the nature of the beast. I think it's not just superintendents, CEOs too, whoever it might be, that's what happens. People just treat you differently." This change in how others interacted with the women as they became a superintendent caused them to redefine themselves. The women now viewed themselves as being different, simply by having assumed the position of being the main administrator of the district. Furthermore, they also realized that not only were interactions now altered, but perceptions of them also had changed significantly.

The statements of Dr. Ventura Luna and Dr. Muñeca Guzman provide an illustration of how the women realized they were considered as the position first and a person second. Ventura shared that, "When you hit the superintendency, you have to realize that all of sudden you don't become a person, you become a title." In describing her two superintendent positions, Dr. Guzman stated, "You really become a different person when you become a superintendent. . . . Although I [was] my own person, I had the image that I was a different person to them. I can't explain it other than in terms of how other people viewed me. I [was] still the same person but other people viewed me through a different lens."

Last, because they were perceived and treated as different and as the title, not the person, the women came to the realization that they were removed and isolated as the district's primary administrator. They redefined themselves and the position as separate. When describing her initial experiences in her superintendency, Antonietta stated, "It [the isolation] makes it very difficult to shoulder sometimes; to coin an expression, 'it gets very lonely, very fast, at the top.' It's hard. You don't have too many people you can discuss some of these things with.

There are very few women out there in the [superintendency]." Similarly, when describing her first few months in the position, Dr. Luna stated, "You certainly feel the isolation."

Although Antonietta attributed her sense of isolation to the scarcity of fellow female district leaders, the experiences of Dr. Muñeca Guzman provide a different perspective. When reflecting on both of her superintendencies, she shared, "And you're very lonely. It's a lonely job. I used to think that it was a lonely job because I was in a small district, and I didn't have my support group around me. . . . But in between my superintendencies, I saw that even in the *men* superintendents. It's just a lonely job. You're just really alone; even if you're surrounded by a lot of good people, there's still something about that position that you're alone."

These realizations came as the women began their superintendency and finalized their redefinition of self. The women were now superintendents. Although they had not changed in terms of the person they knew themselves to be, they were now different because they assumed the mantle of the district's main administrator. These women viewed themselves and the position as being isolated and apart, but nonetheless they were confident in themselves to be responsible, and competent, models of minority women's ability to lead a public school system.

CONCLUSION

This study of four Mexican-American women's experiences while becoming superintendents revealed that they redefined themselves. Their self-perceptions moved from personally considering themselves leaders to privately acknowledging and then publicly proclaiming that they had the skills and abilities to lead a public school system to individually accepting that as a superintendent, they were now different. These women became the authors of their identity, constructing themselves according to their perceptions of themselves as being capable.

The process of redefining themselves put into play a sense of identity that emerged as the women became superintendents. However, for a redefinition to occur, an initial, defined identity was necessary. What was the initial identity the women changed? Was it a definition they had formed of themselves or one that others had given to them?

It is in exploring—as in this study—how minority women have become superintendents that begins to answer these questions. As stated earlier in this chapter, the superintendency is synonymous with white male educational leadership. Studies about women in educational administration indicate that the concept of educational leadership has been constructed by generalizations of gender attributes that define leadership, and thus define those who have or do not have access to leadership positions. What did the women in this study redefine, and how did they do this? This study asserts that they redefined themselves. They accomplished this by rejecting, asserting, and claiming. First, the women in this study rejected the definition of a superintendent as a white male. Moreover, they rejected an identity of themselves, whether self-imposed or other imposed, that placed the superintendency out of their realm of possibilities.

Second, these women asserted not only their competence to be a district leader but in doing so declared that the superintendency was a conceivable reality for themselves. Third, they claimed their definition of themselves as females, capable and empowered to be superintendents by having rejected the limiting perception of who can be a superintendent and affirming the district leadership position as a part of their identity and reality. The women not only redefined themselves but also redefined the superintendency.

REFERENCES

Adkison, J. A. 1981. Women in school administration: A review of the research. *Review of Educational Research* 51 (3): 311-43.

Armendariz-Housen, L. 1995. *Reflective narratives of eight Hispanic women administrators.* Unpublished dissertation, New Mexico State University.

Colon Gibson, F. 1992. *A profile of Hispanic women administrators in New Jersey public schools: Their entry and retention in educational administration.* Unpublished dissertation, Temple University.

Fernandez, M. A. 1989. *Hispanic women school administrators: Critical reflections on their success.* Unpublished dissertation, University of San Francisco.

Jones, E. H., and X. P. Montenegro. 1982. *Recent trends in the representation of women and minorities in school administration and problems in documentation.* Arlington, VA: American Association of School Administrators.

Ortiz, F. I. 1982a. *Career Patterns in Education: Women, Men, and Minorities in Public School Administration.* New York: Praeger.

———. 1982b. The distribution of Mexican-American women in school organizations. *Hispanic Journal of Behavioral Sciences* 4 (2): 181-98.

———. 1991. *Superintendent leadership in urban schools.* Paper presented at the Annual Meeting of the American Educational Research Association, Chicago, Ill.

Ortiz, F. I., and Y. Venegas. 1978. Chicana [female] school administrators. *Emergent Leadership* 2 (2): 55-60.

Texas Education Agency. 1993. Personal communication. Table I: Fall 1992-93 Personnel Roster. Austin, Tex.: Texas Education Agency.

Valverde, L. A. 1980. *Succession socialization: Its influence on school administrative candidates and its implications to the exclusion of minorities from administration. Final report.* Washington, D.C.: National Institute of Education.

Valverde, L. A., and F. Brown, F. 1988. Influences on leadership development among racial and ethnic minorities. In N. J. Boyan (ed.), *Handbook of Research of Educational Administration*. New York: Longman.

Yeakey, C. C., G. S. Johnston, and J. A. Adkison. 1986. In pursuit of equity: A review of research of minorities and women in educational administration. *Educational Administration Quarterly* 22 (3): 110–49.

CHAPTER NINE

Getting inside History— Against All Odds

African-American Women School Superintendents

BARBARA L. JACKSON

> When I referred to "blacks," it was in the generic sense of the term,
> for I still had no consciousness of black women. Women were out-
> side history. . . . black women were conspicuous by their absence.
>
> —Darlene Clark Hine, *Hine Sight*

Following in the footsteps of their sisters, African-American women superintendents are defying the odds and overcoming a long history that began in
slavery. While few in number, black female superintendents constitute a small
but determined lot who have gone virtually unnoticed and unchronicled. This
chapter, building on the work of others, starts to correct this oversight: detailing
the histories—or biographies, really—of these leaders, their lives, motivations, and
impact. The very act of "finding" living examples of current and retired female,
black school superintendents, interviewing them, and making sense of their
lives—all creates an important subtext for this analysis.

Black women superintendents grew up doubly marginal in society, as
females and African Americans. While women constitute about 70 percent of the
teacher force and 14.9 percent of the students attending public schools in 1996
were black, the number of female black superintendents apparently has never
reached fifty in any given year, although data since Jim Crow segregation
(1870–1960) are sparse and unreliable. Even though information on women and
minorities is often available separately, little research has been done on the com-

bination of race and gender. Although these women are few in number, they are living examples of human adaptability, strength, and accomplishment when opportunities for the position of superintendent do occur.

Four themes emerged from the interviews in this study:

1. These women, as they grew up, had the support and experiences which, unknown to them, prepared them for leadership. When opportunity knocked, they accepted the challenge, which was their due, only to find, like many white and male superintendents, that their time in power was limited and that turnover was high.

2. Although they all discussed the difficulties of staying in the job, they believed that they had and were making a difference for students. Optimism was their sustaining attitude.

3. All who survived came to realize that the superintendency is "life in a fishbowl" and accepted their new public persona.

4. Thus belying the popular misconception that African-American women were not as well prepared as others, their lives as young people and budding professionals amply demonstrated that they were ready for leadership (e.g., doctoral degrees, robust experience in the field, and good strong connections to their communities) and had meaningful life experiences as educators.

Most studies of black women are focused on specific issues or problems. A notable exception is Amie Revere's "A Description of Black Female School Superintendents" (1985), a comprehensive history completed in 1985. Since that history was completed close to ten years ago, it is time for a new study. This study is just that, an update on the African-American women superintendents in office in 1993–94 and as many former ones as were located. In it, thirty-two black women superintendents in office that year and forty-one former superintendents were identified. The difficulties in finding accurate data are described in the Data Collection Issues section.

Since it is not possible to include discussions of all four themes that emerged from the interviews and the problems the women faced, this study focuses on their personal experiences growing up. It is possible that their unique experiences as black women contributed to their leadership abilities and career patterns. This potential uniqueness is exemplified in a passage from an essay, "Black is the Noun," where Nikki Giovanni (1993) describes the original crew of Star Trek:

> Of all possible voices to send into space, the voice of the [b]lack woman was chosen. Why? Because no matter what the words, that voice gives comfort and welcome. The [b]lack woman's voice sings the best notes of which Earthlings are capable. Hers is the one voice

that suggests the possibility of harmony on planet Earth. . . . In order
to have a civilization, the [b]lack woman was needed. In order for one
day this whole mess to make sense, the [b]lack woman was needed.
So that one day forgiveness would be possible, the [b]lack woman
was needed. (Giovanni 1993, 118)

ORGANIZATION

This chapter begins with a section on data collection issues and selected facts and
figures about research on women school leaders in general and African-American women in particular. The next section analyzes the demographic data
received from the women who responded to contacts made in writing—twenty-
seven of the thirty-two superintendents identified in the 1993-94 year and fourteen of the twenty-one former superintendents contacted (no current addresses
for the other twenty former superintendents out of forty-one identified could be
found). Thus information from a total of forty-one women is presented—including information gathered in interviews with a subset of the total sample.

To learn from the women's "voices" about the experiences that contributed
to their ability to assume positions that defied the odds, a summary of the themes
from the interviews is presented, drawn from fourteen individual interviews and
a focus group of twelve. Nine of the interviews were with 1993-94 superintendents; two were with former superintendents; and three were taken from my earlier study (Jackson 1995).

Next, the chapter examines some of the reasons many superintendents did
not return to their positions and also examines their plans for the future. It
appears that at least eighteen of those in office in 1993-94 are no longer there.
This discussion also reflects some of the comments the women shared about
problems facing their school districts and about education in general.

The final segment offers some thoughts from these women on the dilemmas
of being both African American and female in positions of power (complexities
faced by almost all African-American leaders), and on how to be a part of the
black community and at the same time serve all the community's children. The
chapter concludes with suggestions for future research.

Data Collection Issues

To date, no one has compiled accurate, complete, and dependable information on women superintendents. In a field where statistics and numbers are kept
on almost all topics, it is disturbing to find so little "official" data on the gender
of superintendents. And for this study, where the "subjects" are not only women
but also African American, the difficulty is compounded. Shakeshaft (1989)
quotes from Hanson and Tyack's 1981 publication (p. 21).

> This proliferation of other kinds of statistical reporting in an age
> enamored of numbers—reports so detailed that one could give the
> precise salary of staff in every community across the country and
> exact information on all sorts of other variables—data by sex became
> strangely inaccessible. A conspiracy of silence could hardly have been
> unintentional. (Shakeshaft 1989)

Without accurate information, we cannot measure progress in equity or identify and thus remedy the conditions of underutilization of women school leaders.

A special effort was undertaken by the American Association of School Administrators (AASA) under the leadership of Effie Jones, former associate executive director of the Office of Minority Affairs, and with the help of Dr. Xenia Montenegro, to fill the void in information on the representation of women and minorities in school administration.

The first AASA survey, published in July 1982, was funded by the Ford Foundation. Updates were published in December 1985, August 1988, December 1990, and the more recent one following the same format in 1993 (although this last study reported by regions rather than states, making comparisons with the earlier studies more difficult). These studies depended on reports from state departments of education, which have certain limitations. The majority of states report gender and race (defined as minorities) but rarely combine the two. And the states generally do not separate elementary and secondary school principals. Even so, the AASA reports that focus on women and minorities provide the most complete information available on these groups.

These five AASA reports include data on principals and all central office personnel, but do not differentiate among school districts, that is county, K–5, or K–12. Mary Reese, who followed Effie Jones at AASA, provided invaluable assistance for the study I did in 1993–94 while I was a Scholar in Residence at AASA. This study, however, was not a direct follow-up to the earlier ones, since it only included African-American women superintendents, unlike the earlier, more inclusive, studies (see the References section for a complete list).

The AASA also publishes, at ten-year intervals, a survey of superintendents themselves. These surveys began in 1923 under the auspices of the Department of Superintendence of the National Education Association (NEA) and were continued by AASA beginning in 1953 (see References section for complete titles). Gender was not included as a category until the 1953 survey. Race, however, did not appear until the 1982 survey, and even then the more inclusive label of "minorities" was used.

The three most recent surveys (1971, 1982, and 1992) used a stratified sample to select the respondents, a change from the methodology used in the earlier surveys. Each used the classification by student enrollment prepared by the U.S. Department of Education: Group A with a student enrollment of more than

25,000; Group B with an enrollment of 3,000 to 25,000; Group C, with an enrollment of 300 to 3,000; and Group D, with an enrollment of under 300. The sample was weighted so that the number in each group reflected the total in each category. In the 1992 survey, a total of 2,536 superintendents were selected from the 15,499 school districts. The return was 1,724, or 68 percent–11 percent of all superintendents (AASA Study 1992, 6–7). Of those respondents, one hundred thirteen, or 6.6 percent, were women. (p. 9). The study reported that in 1952, 6.7 percent of the sample were women, many located in small rural districts. By 1962, the total number was down. In the 1992 survey, however, the percentage of women superintendents in large districts was greater than the national average–8.4·percent. My 1993–94 study supports this finding, showing a disproportionate number of African-American women in large urban school districts. With the stratified sample procedure, it is possible to miss some of the women superintendents, especially African Americans.

The other source of information was the National Alliance of Black School Educators (NABSE), especially from Dr. LaRuth Gray, who served as secretary of the Commission on Superintendents at the time, and Dr. Charles Moody, founder of NABSE. Even though one of the original purposes of NABSE was to maintain a data bank, this goal has not been pursued in a systematic way, thus the information is not easily available to researchers.

A dissertation by Blount (1993) documents the number of women superintendents in 1910, 1950, 1970, and 1990. Her data reveal a much larger percentage of women, especially at the county level, in the early decades of the century. But again, because the data did not include race as a variable, the results are not helpful to this study.

Selected Facts and Figures

The availability of consistent, reliable data on women superintendents is further complicated by various definitions of the superintendency and the changing configuration of school districts. Local school districts, while varying in student population from 300 or less to 1,000,000, always have a school superintendent and a school board. Local school districts also vary in grade organization, with some having only kindergarten through fifth, sixth, or eighth grade and sending their high school students to a consolidated high school district serving several communities. Many more school districts have grades K–12, with some now beginning with pre-kindergarten. Most states have an intermediate district between the state and local district, called different names and having various responsibilities. Given that each survey or report used a different combination of districts, it is difficult to make comparisons. Finally, the long-time practice of a state department's consolidation of school districts means that the configuration of school districts is constantly changing.

After reviewing all of the various reports, dissertations, and records, it is still difficult to state exactly how many African-American women superintendents there are now and how many there have been. Since many of the studies do not use names—this is appropriate and proper for the kind of research done—it complicates getting accurate numbers or comparing different studies, since the samples may be different. Revere, in her 1985 study, did list the names of the twenty-nine women that she included in her comprehensive description and history of black female superintendents. Bell and Chase (1993), in their research, do not list names but do have numbers of women—total and minority—listed by state. Alston, in her 1996 study, also lists numbers by state. I compared her figures with mine and found that we have slightly different numbers. It appears that in 1995-96 there may have been closer to forty African-American women superintendents than originally identified. Without one comprehensive list from all sources by name, we were not able to report precise figures for the current year, or for the earlier ones.

With all of these cautions, the following data from the national studies of women superintendents are reported, showing the total number of women superintendents. Table 9.1 shows the data and the gaps in information.

TABLE 9.1
Number of Women Superintendents and African-American
Women Superintendents Based on Research Studies

Year	#Districts	Women Supt. Number	Percent*	Black Women Supt. Number
1910	5,254	329	6.26	n/a
1970	10,380	71	.68	3
1982	13,715	241	—	11 (Arnez)
1983	n/a	n/a	—	15 (Ebony)
1985	16,000	—	—	29 (Revere)
1989	11,007[†]	284	6	14 (Bell and Chase)
1991	10,683[†]	424	5.6	19 (Bell and Chase)
1993	14,000[‡]	800[‡]	7.1	32 (Jackson)
1995	14,000[‡]	800[‡]	7.1	45 (Alston)
1996	14,000[‡]	800[‡]	7.1	33 (Jackson)

* Percent of all superintendents
[†] Bell and Chase (1993) used only K–12 districts in their studies
[‡] Approximate figures from AASA

WHO ARE THE AFRICAN-AMERICAN WOMEN SUPERINTENDENTS?

African-American women as teachers, administrators, and educators in general have been missing from much of America's history. Scholars are now adding to our knowledge and understanding of the significant role these women played in the past. We now know that even during slavery, black women had the courage to defy the law and teach slaves to read. They knew that the very survival of their race depended on education. Under segregation, these pioneering and courageous women continued the tradition of their predecessors as teachers and principals (dominated mostly by white men, some black men, and a few black women).

Black women not only played a significant role in education throughout history, but to use an idea from Hine's (1994) *Hine Sight*, they also worked "to make community." "Making community means the processes of creating religious, educational, health-care, philanthropic, political, and familial institutions and professional organizations that enabled our children to survive" (p. xxii).

Today's black women leaders continue to "make communities" wherever black people live. This same spirit is evident in the school systems that these black women now lead. They and other black women leaders do not use the phrase so dominant in the late nineteenth and early twentieth centuries, but their actions suggest the same idea: "Lift as we climb."

In the 1970s, women in general and African-American women in particular began to be appointed to the top public school educational position of superintendent of schools. Due to the research of Amie Revere (1985), a black woman superintendent was "discovered" in Boley, Oklahoma, an all-black community in 1944. She served until 1956, to be followed by her husband, who served until 1976 (p. 68). The number of women superintendents is still only about 7 percent, and the numbers of black women are too few to be a significant percentage.

The following data are from the women who responded to the current survey in 1993-94, and include educational preparation, experience, membership in organizations, years of appointment, and characteristics of the school districts they serve.

EDUCATION

Both the former and current superintendents indicate extensive educational preparation for high-level administrative positions. All forty-one respondents have master's degrees, with three having more than one; eight have the educational specialists degree or diploma. What is most significant is the number who have completed the doctorate: eighteen of the current women and thirteen of the former superintendents for whom information was supplied. Three indicated

that they have their course work for the doctorate and only need to write the dissertation. Thus, of the forty-one respondents, a total of thirty-one have the highest degree offered in the field. Almost all majored in educational administration;
two in psychology, and one in early childhood education for the doctorate.

The average time that lapsed between receiving their bachelor's degree and
doctorate was twenty years, with a range from seven to thirty-seven years. One
received her doctorate in 1990 and another in 1991. The others were evenly
divided between the '70s (eleven) and '80s (thirteen). No dates were given for the
others.

Most of the women received their doctorates from well-known institutions
such as the University of Texas at Austin; the University of North Carolina at
Greensboro and at Chapel Hill; Ohio State; the University of Minnesota; Rut-
gers; Michigan State, Virginia Polytechnic and State University, Wayne State,
and the University of Virginia.

Private universities included: Nova University, Teachers College Columbia,
Fordham University, George Washington University, the University of Chicago,
the University of Pennsylvania, Kent University, New York University and the
Union Graduate School.

The information on their undergraduate education shows a similar diversity
in institutions. Sixteen of the women attended black colleges: Alcorn (two);
Bishop, Hampton, Knoxville, Virginia State (two), North Carolina A & T,
Alabama State, Albany State, Johnson C. Smith, Norfolk State, D.C. Miner
Teachers College, D.C. Teachers College, Howard, and West Virginia State.
The others attended a mixture of public and private colleges. The undergraduate
majors show more diversity than the majors in their graduate work. Many
majored in elementary education (fourteen); early childhood education (two); the
sciences (five in math, science, psychology, biology); and the social sciences
(twelve in English, sociology, Spanish, music, speech, classical languages). The
others did not indicate their undergraduate major. The years they received their
bachelor's degree indicate that most of the women are in their fifties or sixties,
with only two reporting receiving their bachelor degree in the '70s.

EXPERIENCE

Not surprisingly, all of the women began their career in education as teachers,
serving from several years to as long as fourteen. Almost all followed the traditional career path to the superintendency by becoming principals. While most
were elementary school principals, several were junior or senior high school
principals. Their tenure as principals did vary considerably, with some staying
only a few years before moving to a central office position; however, some were
principals for as long as ten years. A fair number served as principals in more

than one school, and in some instances, in more than one school system. The offices held in the central office included director of elementary or secondary education, human relations or community relations, curriculum director, and head of school volunteers. At least half served as an assistant, an associate, or as a deputy superintendent, usually in the system in which they became superintendent. Prior to being appointed superintendent, a number held positions as state department administrators, or they were outside of the educational system in positions such as caseworkers, researchers, or even in business. At least two held positions with the U.S. Department of Education. These experiences are similar to other studies, which indicate a different career path for women and men—these women "compose their lives" rather than having a clearly defined path for their careers.

ORGANIZATIONS AND OTHER AFFILIATIONS

This group of women, both current and former, is quite active in both professional and community service organizations. Almost all belong to the major professional organizations, such as the AASA, the Association for Supervision and Curriculum Development (ASCD), Phi Delta Kappa, the National Alliance of Black School Educators, or an elementary or a secondary school principals' organization, and the local or state affiliates of these groups. Almost all are involved with local organizations that may influence school policy, such as the Chamber of Commerce, Rotary, Kiwanis, United Way, YMCA, and other youth-serving organizations, the local library, a hospital or mental health clinic board, the Urban League, the NAACP, and the League of Women Voters. Many mentioned membership in the major black sororities and a church affiliation, with a great number serving on governing boards.

YEAR OF APPOINTMENT

Of the twenty-seven superintendents holding office in the 1993-94 school year who responded to the survey, only four were appointed prior to 1990; in 1979, 1983, 1985, and 1989. Five were appointed in 1990, four in 1991, four in 1992, nine in 1993 (including one acting), and one in 1994.

SCHOOL DISTRICT CHARACTERISTICS

The school districts served by African-American women superintendents in 1993-94 ranged in size from Oberlin, Ohio, with approximately 1,300 students, to Chicago, with 409,730 students. Past studies indicate that women have tended to be appointed in small school districts. What is unusual about the black women superintendents is that a disproportionate number, both past and present, have served in major cities. The 1993–94 data indicate that African-American women were superintendents in Berkeley, Cleveland, Boston, Memphis, San Diego, Denver, and Chicago—all with student populations of more than 60,000, including three with more than 100,000. Former superintendents served in Philadelphia, Detroit, and Washington, D.C (which had two).

While some of the women work in districts that are majority black or minority, it is not true of all. For the districts for which this information was available, ten of the 1993–94 districts were comprised of 40 percent or more minority; in five, the minority student population was less than 15 percent. Seven served in large cities that all have a large percentage of minority students.

THEMES FROM THE INTERVIEWS

The themes that emerged from interviews with the 1993–94 superintendents, the former superintendents, and from additional conversations were similar to those found in several dissertations focused specifically on black women superintendents. Some used this "label," while others used African-American Woman and/or Females. The choice reflected in part the time during which the study was done, illustrating yet again the dilemma in America of what to call this group of Americans who are descendants from slaves (Revere 1985; Bulls 1986; Adams 1990; Watt 1995).

Since the focus of this 1993–94 research was on the "voices" of all of these women, and the questions were primarily about their "growing up years," it is not surprising that the themes of "family" and "church" emerged, along with "teacher/mentor," "role of the superintendent," "leadership style," "relationship with the school board," "politics and power," and finally, "gender and race."

Family

The women interviewed for the study described many experiences in their growing up years that nurtured their leadership development. They talked about their families and the high expectations parents and relatives had for them. More than one said that their families, their communities, and especially their churches "convinced them that they could do anything they wanted, be what they wanted to be." Several of the women mentioned the influence and expectations their fathers had for them as little girls. One said,

> My father—this was different than most of my friends at the time. My father made us take swimming lessons. I had piano lessons. But I just never thought I couldn't do what I could do because it was just the way it was in my family. I just didn't think about it. Are you going to college? Well, yes, I'm going to college, but I was never encouraged to go to college by counselors.

Church Involvement

Almost all of the women spoke of the influence of their church in growing up—mostly the "black church." It was not just the spiritual experience they recalled, but more important in their development as leaders was the emphasis on performing in the church play, participating in Sunday school pageants, speaking before the congregation, often at a very early age, or singing in the choir. Because of these experiences, these women developed self-confidence and self-efficacy, evident in the people who they are today—and their courage to defy the odds.

Teachers/Mentors

Several of the women found encouragement in the schools, especially if they attended segregated ones. Many of their teachers took a personal interest in the students. As one former superintendent said,

> The black teachers were in the elementary school, and they were very proud of their work. And they wanted you to make them very proud of you because they didn't want to damage the race. And you don't have that anymore. So these teachers were always urging me to do my best, to do better not just for my own edification and advancement but also because of their pride.

Those who had advanced degrees (which was most of them) mentioned the support and encouragement of their university professors. Several said that applying for the superintendency was the result of notice from their professors. Most of these supporters were male and white, though in at least two instances, the consultants for the superintendency searches were black.

Leadership Style

Several of the women were quite specific about their leadership style, "My style is participatory and inclusionary. I believe in a lot of involvement in decision making, which I find that people support . . . I don't make hasty decisions." Another superintendent, who made a practice of visiting schools, was surprised when many of the teachers and principals told her that they had rarely seen the former superintendent in the schools, for he never seemed to leave his office.

All of the women mentioned the children in their conversations. They were quite clear and explicit about the reason they were in the superintendency—it put them in a powerful position that could influence the lives of young people. One woman, who (like many others was trying to make a difference) was attacked regularly in the press, said, "I have to remain focused on the kids . . . I guess the kids were always at the bottom of this whole passion."

Boards, Power, and Politics

The women were clear that the relationship with their boards was critical to their success—even for their continuation as superintendents. Many recognized the importance of nurturing their boards. The composition of the board, either the gender or race mix, did not mean automatic support for the superintendent's ideas. Pursuing positive relations with the board forced the women into the political arena, a situation that most of them accepted as part of their jobs.

For these women, the idea of power was not foreign or uncomfortable. Those who mentioned the idea specifically saw "politics" as a way to achieve more for the children. As one said, "I don't see politics as a dirty word." Another stated that her doctoral program helped her gain "a better understanding of the political nature of the job . . . while we want children to learn and all of that, if we don't take care of the political piece, we don't get a chance to try to impact the children in learning." They were not hesitant to make their voices heard.

Gender and Race

All of the women with whom I talked seemed to be very comfortable with who they were—gender and sex were intertwined in their self-identity, and the various labels were not a concern. As a result, they had some difficulty in ascribing particular incidences or career decisions to their race or gender. It may be that their experiences, both growing up and during their careers, gave them the self-confidence and sense of efficacy that comes with both knowledge and acceptance of who they were.

Several did mention, however, that at times gender seemed to be more of a factor than race. Quite often they were the only woman present at meetings of their peers, and a black man would not have seemed "so strange" to the other men. As one said, "You better not be late because you are so visible." In at least two instances, gender was initially a negative factor in their appointment as a junior or senior high school principal, but they still got the job.

Several mentioned the support and caring they received from their husbands, despite the assumption that women holding powerful positions would not be able to sustain meaningful personal relationships. One mentioned that she and her husband had to leave town to have some privacy and vacation. Because these women were so "visible," they found it difficult to leave the job to relax. Even finding a new church home had political overtones—one stated that she visited all of the churches before making a decision about joining one because of her public position. And yet, they all enjoyed their jobs. While some of the women did have family support, others were either divorced or widowed, so that they no longer had this personal relationship.

In another interview, one superintendent commented on some of the personal concerns of women, which may not affect men at all.

> Going on trips and not knowing the agenda—men take their suits
> and they are through. . . . You have to know whether or not there
> are going to be evening affairs; what the temperature in the room will
> be. Whether you take a heavy coat—in winter they take a top coat, in
> the summer they take none . . . and what about the beauty parlor or
> times to travel so as not to arrive at night in a strange city.

How women are perceived may affect the success of the women in male
positions of power—especially African-American women. As one said, "They
expect us to be bodacious, beautiful, but not arrogant, which has a negative connotation for women." Often the first impression is critical—will they be perceived as caring and nurturing or officious and domineering? A former superintendent who did overcome the odds for at least a time, summed up some of
the problems women in general have experienced, perhaps even more so for
black women:

> I think life is difficult for anyone going into administration. The rea-
> sons are many, but the most important is the family. Women just do
> not want to uproot their family and their husband to quit jobs. So,
> it's a terrible strain on the women, so they tend to defer these kinds
> of options until after the children are at least out of high school. . . .
> The second thing is that women have a problem fitting in their long
> term study. . . . So they're not qualified to take advantage of some of
> the options when they have the experience and ability to do that. The
> third thing is the fear of not being able to do both, especially for
> young women.

SUMMARY OF INTERVIEW FINDINGS

The African-American women superintendents who participated in this research
project demonstrated that they possess the educational preparation and experience to assume the position of superintendent of schools. From their descriptions of their growing-up years, they had the family, church, and community
support to prepare them to take risks, to develop a self-identity, sense of efficacy,
and determination to accept the challenging job of leading a school system. They
were aware of the "fishbowl" existence they would have, but they accepted their
public role as being part of the job. They thought they were aware of the dynamics of the school, community, and especially school board politics, but some
found that it was impossible to be totally prepared for these critical relationships.
All had the children at the top of their agenda, and would continue to do whatever they could to prepare them for a productive future.

What has happened to those women who were superintendents in
1993-94? The next section provides some answers and suggests what still needs
to be done to learn more about the lives of these women.

WHY? WHERE? WHAT?

A recent survey and conversations with many of the women indicated that at least eighteen of the thirty-two identified in the 1993–94 study are no longer in office or left at the end of the 1996–97 year. Even with approximately nineteen appointed or identified since 1993–94, the number leaving means no net gain in the number of African-American women superintendents in these years. Why are they leaving, and what are their plans for the future?

Why Are They Leaving?

In the responses to the survey and in talking with many of the women superintendents, nine of the eighteen are retiring after many years of service. Most stated that they have devoted thirty to forty years to education, primarily in the same school system. They were promoted from within the system near the end of their careers and served as the top educational leader for a relatively short time.

A second group (seven of these) left for other reasons—generally a difference between them and their school boards. In at least two systems, the turnover of the board membership was constant, so that only one or none of those who hired the superintendent was still there at the end of their first term. As noted in many studies, when a school board changes, the new members almost always want to select their own superintendent. Two left due to changes beyond the school system—one due to a change in state law; the other due to a failure of voters to approve higher taxes and a lack of support by the mayor and city government. Neither completed their full term, which was true in several of the communities when the superintendent's departure was a result of a change in the school board.

Where Are They Going?

Of those not retiring, none has been appointed superintendent in another district at this time. Some of the former superintendents went on to a second or even third superintendency. However, very few of these women had multiple superintendencies, unlike men who are hired more often by another district, especially white men.

Those who are retiring after many years of service plan to travel, do volunteer work, spend more time with the church, or consult in order to share some of their experiences with others. One plans to move to Florida. Of all those who retired—for whom we have information—several have established their own consulting firms and specialize in superintendency searches. Only a couple of the women have moved to a university as professors, a move that is often the future career of retiring men superintendents. Private industry, such as publishing companies, attracted some of the retirees. To my knowledge, not one has written a book about her experiences (except Barbara Sizemore, as mentioned earlier). The others remain in the job market.

What Problems Were Identified By These Women?

The problems identified by a sample of the women in the study were similar, regardless of the size of the district. Student achievement was mentioned by almost all who responded—some specifically mentioned test scores. Staff development and the need to change attitudes also were listed, as were adequate funding, rising costs, and diminished resources, including federal funds.

A dominant concern was politics, with specific concerns about the relationship with the school board—the turnover, the lack of understanding the difference between policy and operation, and the intrusion with the management of the system were specifically mentioned. Involvement of parents and the community with the school system in order to build support for public education was mentioned by one. One stated that being a superintendent means living in a "fishbowl—it comes with the territory," so one should be prepared to be a public person.

RECOMMENDED FUTURE STUDIES

As Hine reminds us, black women have been absent from America's history. For women superintendents, it was not until the 1970s that they began to be appointed in any number, and still the percentage is less than 10 percent—for black women, the percentage is almost too low to calculate. These women are the needed role models in education, especially in public school positions of power and authority. The children are their concern. They recognize the importance of understanding the dynamics of their schools and communities. We have much to learn from these courageous women, who defied the odds by daring to lead.

As mentioned earlier, most of the recent studies of African-American women superintendents kept the identity of the women confidential, as it should be. While we have a great need to do in-depth studies of some of these women to make our history complete, stories are available of at least two of these women: Nancy Arnez's study (1981) of Barbara Sizemore's two years in Washington, D.C., as the first black woman to head a major urban system (1973-75), and Sizemore's own story (1981). Revere (1989) also has written about a real pioneer, probably the first black woman superintendent in the country—Velma Dolphin Ashley, 1944-1956. But other stories should be shared with a larger audience. What follows is a list of some of the retired black women superintendents, many of whom have served in more than one district:

Ms. Beauty Baldwin, Buford, Georgia

Dr. Constance Clayton, Philadelphia, Pennsylvania

Dr. Bernice Davis, East Orange, New Jersey

Dr. Evie Dennis, Denver, Colorado

Dr. Rosie Doughty, University City, Missouri, and East Cleveland, Ohio

Dr. Germaine Fauntleroy, Petersburg, Virginia

Dr. Edith Francis, Princeton Regional School District and Ewing Township, New Jersey

Dr. Edyth Gaines, CSD #12, N.Y.C., and Hartford, Connecticut

Dr. LaBarbara Gragg, Pontiac, Michigan

Dr. LaRuth Gray, Abbott Union Free School District, Irvington, New York

Dr. Drue Guy, East Orange, New Jersey, and Racine, Wisconsin (acting)

Dr. Lois Harrison-Jones, Richmond, Virginia, and Boston, Massachusetts

Ms. Argie Johnson, CSD #13, N.Y.C., and Chicago

Dr. Margaret Labat, Evanston, Illinois

Dr. Ruth Love, Oakland, California, and Chicago, Illinois

Dr. Betty Mason, Oklahoma City, Oklahoma

Dr. Deborah McGriff, Detroit, Michigan

Dr. Eloretta Dukes McKenzie, Washington, D.C.

Dr. Sammie Parrish, Cleveland, Ohio

Dr. Lee Etta Powell, Cincinnati, Ohio

Ms. Greta Shepherd, Plainfield and East Orange, New Jersey

Dr. LaVoneia Steele, Berkeley, California

Dr. Bernica Venable, Trenton, New Jersey

Dr. Judith Wilcox, Pleasantville, New Jersey

In addition to those who have retired, several who are now in office warrant an in-depth study. For example, Dr. Rosa Smith, who was named the 1997 Superintendent of the Year from the state of Wisconsin by the AASA (the first black woman), or Dr. Beverly Hall, who was appointed state superintendent in Newark, N.J., in 1995, after serving as Superintendent of one of N.Y.C.'s thirty-two Community School Districts and as Deputy Chancellor of the New York City Public Schools.

Another interesting study would be an investigation of the cities that have had more than one African-American woman superintendent. Those cities include (and several also have had African-American men superintendents): Washington, D.C.; Chicago, Ill.; Richmond, Va.; Oakland, Calif.; and Pleasantville, N.J.

A final recommendation is to compile a comprehensive list of all present and past African-American women superintendents. The dissertations and studies of recent years have some information to contribute to such a list. With the work that has already been done, we are in a position to tell a more complete story of all of these women leaders. We need to hear their voices loud and clear, "in order for one day this whole mess to make sense, the black woman is needed."

REFERENCES

Adams, B. 1990. *African American female superintendents: Perception of factors influencing their career success.* Unpublished dissertation, Lehigh University.

Alston, J. 1996. *Black female school superintendents and success: A study of perceptions regarding constrains and facilitators encountered en route to the superintendency.* Unpublished dissertation, Pennsylvania State University.

American Association of School Administrators, Office of Minority Affairs Reports. Arlington, Va.: AASA:
Perspectives on Racial Minority and Women School Administrators (1983)
Women & Minorities in School Administration (1985)
Women & Minorities in School Administration (1988)
Women and Minorities in School Administration: Facts & Figures 1989–90 (1990)
Women and Racial Minority Representation in School Administration (1993)

American Association of School Administrators, Arlington Va.: AASA. List of Reports on Superintendents:
The Status of the Superintendent in 1923
Educational Leadership (1933)
The American School Superintendent (1952)
Profile of the School Superintendent (1960)
The American School Superintendent (1971)
The American School Superintendency in 1982
The Study of the American School Superintendency (1992)
America's Education Leaders in a Time of Reform
(No survey was conducted in 1940–41 because of the war.)

Arnez, N. 1981. *The besieged school superintendent: A case study in school superintendent-school board relations in Washington, D.C., 1973–75.* Lanham, Md.: University Press of America.

Bell, C. and S. Chase. 1993. The underrepresentation of women in school leadership. In C. Marshall (ed.), *The new politics of race and gender.* The 1992 Yearbook of the Politics of Education Association. Washington: The Falmer Press.

Blount, J. C. 1993. *Women and the superintendency, 1900–1990: "Destined to rule the schools of every city . . ."* Unpublished dissertation, University of North Carolina at Chapel Hill.

Bulls, G. 1986. *Career development of black female superintendents.* Unpublished dissertation, University of Pennsylvania.

Ebony (June 1983), pp. 88–94.

Giovanni, N. 1993. Black is the noun. In G. Early (ed.), *Lure and loathing.* New York: Penguin Books.

Hine, D. C. 1994. *Hine sight.* Brooklyn, N.Y.: Carlson Publishers.

Jackson, B. L. 1995. *Balancing act: The political role of the urban school superintendent.* Lanham, Md.: University Press of America, in cooperation with the Joint Center for Political and Economic Studies, Washington, D.C.

Revere, A. B. 1985. *A description of black female school superintendents.* Unpublished dissertation, Miami University (Ohio).

———. 1989. Pioneer black woman superintendent: Velma Dolphin Ashley, 1944-1956. *Equity and Excellence* 24 (2): 62-63.

Shakeshaft, C. 1989. *Women in educational administration.* Newbury Park, Calif.: Sage Publications.

Sizemore, B. 1981. *The ruptured diamond: The politics of the decentralization of the District of Columbia Public schools.* Lanham, Md.: University Press of America.

Watt, C. 1995. *Urban school district African American female superintendents: Their levels of perceived self-efficacy and their leadership types.* Unpublished dissertation, University of Southern California.

Other References Not Cited in Chapter

Banks, C. 1988. *The black school superintendent: A study in early childhood socialization and career development.* Unpublished dissertation, University of Pittsburgh.

Chambers, R. C. 1979. *An identification and comparison of problems encountered by black and women superintendents.* Unpublished dissertation. The University of Iowa.

Costa, M. E. 1981. *A descriptive study of women superintendents of public schools in the United States.* Unpublished dissertation, Columbia University Teachers College.

Gabriel, S. L. 1981. *Urban school politics: A descriptive analysis of the political work environment as perceived by four urban school superintendents.* Unpublished dissertation, University of Massachusetts.

Hall, B. 1990. *Leadership: The black urban superintendent.* Unpublished dissertation, Fordham University.

Jackson, B. L. 1988. Education from a black perspective: Implications for administrator preparation programs. In D. C. Griffiths, R. T. Stout, and P. S. Forsyth (eds.), *Leaders for America's Schools* . Berkeley: McCutchan.

———. 1990. Black women as role models: Where can we find them? *Initiatives* 53 (1): 37-45.

Jones, E. H. 1984. *A survey of the problems and characteristics of school districts administered by black superintendents.* Unpublished dissertation, the George Washington University.

Moody, C. 1971. *Black superintendents in public school districts: Trends and conditions.* Unpublished dissertation, Northwestern University.

Payne, N. J. 1975. *The status of black women in educational administration.* Unpublished dissertation, Atlanta University.

Revere, A. B. 1987. Black women superintendents in the United States: 1984-85. *Journal of Negro Education* 56: 510-34.

Scott, H. 1980. *The black superintendent: Messiah or scapegoat?* Washington: Howard University Press.

Shepherd, W. R. 1996. *A study of the career ascendancy patterns of African-American superintendents serving in the United States from 1990-1996.* Unpublished dissertation, Clark Atlanta University.

Sizemore, B. 1986. The limits of the black superintendency: A review of the literature. *Journal of Educational Equity and Leadership* 6 (3): 180-208.

CHAPTER TEN

Dancing in Red Shoes

Why Women Leave the Superintendency

CYNTHIA BEEKLEY

Look at your shoes, and be thankful they are plain . . . for one has
to live very carefully if one's shoes are too red.

—Clarissa Pinkola Estés, *Women Who Run With the Wolves*

In the old women's teaching tale, entitled "The Red Shoes," as told by Clarissa
Pinkola Estés, a young girl becomes enamored with a magical pair of red
shoes. She puts them on against the warnings and disapproval of others, only to
be danced to near death by these shoes. At last she begs the executioner to cut
off her feet and the shoes so that she may escape. The girl ends up a cripple and
never again wishes for red shoes.

Women who aspire to the school superintendency run the risk of dancing
in red shoes. They can become consumed by the job, its visibility, and its vulnerability, which may cripple their power and energy. They seek the job out of
interest, confidence, and a desire to make schools better for children. Those who
leave the position before the end of their career to take a lower-level position feel
a loss and a sense of seeking something easier, less stressful, and more compelling. Why do women who come to the dance so enthusiastically leave before
it is finished?

Our society appears to be more willing than ever to accept women in many
top-level management positions (White 1992). The public school superintendency in the United States is typical; although it is an occupation dominated by
men, the number of women superintendents has nearly doubled, from about
4 percent in 1990 (Radich 1992) to 7.3 percent in 1992 (Montenegro 1993). The
pool of candidates for the superintendency is approximately 71 percent female
and mostly public school teachers (Dunlap and Schmuck 1995). With this large

candidate population and equal access to administrative opportunities, one would expect to see the ranks of women administrators swell appreciably. However, Gupton and Slick (1996) report that "they [women] are not retaining these positions as long as they once did" (p. 143).

Traditional ideas about leadership in schools assume a male-dominated perspective, knowledge base, and behavior model (Shakeshaft 1989). Feminist perspectives and multicultural viewpoints are rarely included in the preparation programs of educational administrators (Orenstein 1986). In fact, both men and women perceive social institutions through the cultural lens of gender, which automatically channels females and males into different roles (Bem 1993). In addition, women in educational administration do not have many female role models or support systems for their positions, since their numbers are generally small (Radich 1992).

Feminine voices about the superintendency would be valuable since women experience the role differently (Chase 1995; Hart 1995; Rosener 1990) and may perceive leadership as being more of a process than an issue of control (Burns 1978). Women have proven themselves to be effective school administrators; the research is overwhelming in pointing to ratings of women as being equal to or better than men in various administrative positions (Frasher and Frasher 1979; Shakeshaft 1989). Therefore, I undertook a study to determine why capable women who had attained a superintendency would leave it or exit—that is, to not seek another superintendency but to move to what, by the accepted male standard, is a lower-level position in the education hierarchy.

I sent letters to nineteen women who had been public school superintendents in the Midwest between 1988 and 1993 and who had left the superintendency voluntarily, requesting their participation in a study about why people leave the superintendency. Three of the women were not located; ten refused to talk about their experiences. Of those, several who would give reasons said it was "too painful to talk about," they would rather not "dredge all that up again," they had been "requested" not to talk about it, or they had made an "agreement" not to talk about it. These stories may have been more interesting than the ones that were told. The obvious pain of these responses, briefly witnessed, hints at tumultuous experiences.

Six women were interviewed about their experiences. One had been an interim superintendent for six months in a district in which she worked for twenty-three years. She was asked to apply for the superintendent's position by two of the school board members, but she felt she "wasn't ready" for the position and, therefore, did not apply. The other woman had sued her school board for a financial settlement, and they agreed not to talk about the case. The remaining four were used for case studies, which included interviews with school board members and other professionals in their school districts. Before the interviews were held, I reviewed school board minutes and newspaper articles about the women's work.

Though the number of cases is small, the research on women in the superintendency has been limited because there are so few of them, and many, such as these, choose not to discuss their experiences. Therefore, even a small sample can prove valuable to the understanding of why women would choose to leave this important position in education.

A review of the literature identified three approaches that were used to examine the experiences of these women superintendents: cultural/social, organizational/professional, and personal/family. The cultural approach is an all-encompassing perspective from which to understand issues in women's leadership. Male dominance and androcentrism contribute to a culture that has long placed women in secondary positions in terms of value and power (Mead 1935). This approach, which examines the basic values in our male-dominated culture, suggests that women's work is less valued and is often subsumed under male control. Estler's model, which suggests that it is not "Women's Place" to be in leadership roles, best exemplifies this cultural norm (Estler 1975). Dancing in red shoes can be seen as a metaphor for a high-profile leader's role, which is considered inappropriate cultural behavior for women in our society. Women are discouraged from seeking leadership positions and are made to feel unwelcome and even to endure discrimination when they attain top positions. Shakeshaft (1989) lists over thirty studies that document overt sexual discrimination against women in school leadership. In addition, women who attain leadership positions may not receive support from other women (Gupton and Slick 1994; Woo 1985). Women who move into positions of leadership may adopt the prevailing male culture and continue to support discrimination against other women (Klein and Ortman 1994). Cultural influences from our society as a whole are not supportive of women in leadership positions.

An organizational and a professional approach to examining women superintendents' work indicates that women in leadership positions often are isolated (Kanter 1977; Lynch 1990; Swiderski 1988). By numbers alone, women leaders remain in the minority. The "old boy network" has frequently been identified as excluding women from access to information (Armstrong 1990). Current research validates that this barrier continues to exist for women (Lourdes 1995; Beason 1992; Hawkins 1991). Sponsorship, mentorship, and networking control access for women and thus limit their power in organizations (Moody 1983; Ragins and Sundstrom 1989; Gupton and Slick 1996). Even service organizations such as the Rotary Club and Kiwanis have only recently admitted women; many golf clubs still limit playing times for women. For those women who do aspire to leadership, entrance continues to be a challenge. Women have to be asked to dance, and the dance is still male dominated and controlled.

The personal approach is strongly influenced by cultural norms. Those who take this approach suggest that women do not aspire to the superintendency because their priorities are with home and family. Kanter (1977) suggests that women do not aspire to high-level positions because they recognize limited opportunities for acceptance and advancement. This approach would indicate that the woman is to blame for own her lack of achievement (Schmuck 1986). In a world where status is defined by men to mean moving "up the hierarchy," administration is defined as being more important than teaching. Thus, women who choose to stay in teaching are defined as having low aspirations, when in fact they may simply prefer the job that they originally chose for themselves: working with children (Shakeshaft 1989). In addition, women in educational administration experience more personal stress (Scott and Spooner 1989) and higher levels of visibility (Tallerico, Burstyn, and Poole 1993) than men in similar positions. Each of these personal issues for women suggests circumstances that make it necessary to "live carefully" in red shoes.

CONTEXT AND PARTICIPANTS

The stories of four women superintendents who exited the superintendency— Diane, Barbara, Kathy, and Luci—are based on their own recollections of their experiences as well as those of their school board members, and on written records. The size of the school districts in which these women worked ranged from 1,200 to 7,000 students. All were in the Midwest. These districts represent attitudes and behaviors that can best be described as middle America: two were rural and two were small suburban districts; all were predominately white and middle class. These women are typical of those reported in a study by Gupton and Slick (1996), which found that only 5.3 percent of women superintendents were in urban districts. The women, all white, ranged in age from forty-five to fifty-five, supporting the research that most women are older than men when they enter the superintendency (Maienza 1986; Gupton and Slick 1995; Shakeshaft 1989). All were married with children. Two were first-time superintendents and insiders; that is, they were already working in the district when they were chosen to be superintendent. The other two women were outsiders, each having held one other superintendency before the position from which she exited. All of them followed male superintendents who had been in that district superintendency for at least ten years. With the exception of Diane, whose district had a woman interim superintendent for several months twenty years earlier, all were the first women superintendents their districts ever had. Their tenure as superintendents ranged from three and a half years to seven years. All left the superintendency of their own choice and moved to a lower-level position in the education hierarchy in another school district: one is now a principal, one a director of student services, and two are assistant superintendents. Two have doctoral degrees, one is All But Dissertation (A.B.D.), and one holds a master's degree. All are bright, friendly, dynamic, and appeared open and honest during the interviews.

All of the women were described as capable, effective school superintendents by their school board members. These women were described as "spunky," "doing a super job," "meeting problems head-on," and "paving the way for women . . . to assume administrative roles in education." Board members noted that these women were hard working, were knowledgeable about curriculum and instruction, were collaborative, provided leadership, and were intelligent and thoughtful. All had the political support of their school boards. All displayed collaborative leadership styles with a genuine interest in improving instruction to benefit children. Their resignations were voluntary: all had time left on their contracts; one had received an extended contract and a substantial raise right before she resigned.

Diane

Diane was a superintendent in a city school district of about 7,000 students. She had worked in the district as a teacher, principal, and central office administrator before becoming superintendent. Diane experienced discrimination against a woman in a leadership position from community members. She was not accepted by the local businessmen's organizations, the local newspaper, and the male leadership of the community. This attitude was reported by the board members as well as by Diane herself. As a member of the Rotary Club, Diane was never addressed by her first name, even though all male members were. She remembered, "At the second Rotary meeting the men held up a picture of a pinup girl in a bathing suit and said that was me." A board member verified this situation: "The guys would sort of chuckle at making off-color comments when she was there. Or calling her Mrs. when everyone else was on a first-name basis. Just little things like that. A few of the guys admitted it. They just took some pleasure in 'we're the old guard guys and it's our club—you're only here because we're told we have to—it's federal law.'" The local newspaper never used the title of "Doctor"; she was identified as "Mrs." The board president recalled a conversation with the head of a major corporation in the city who wondered how the schools could expect his support when they hired a woman to be their chief executive officer.

But perhaps most distressing to Diane was the man in the community who started a vicious campaign against her leadership. "Leon" began writing letters to the editor of the newspaper about a year after Diane became superintendent. Leon's attacks appeared to be directed at Diane because she was a woman. One male board member said, "One strike Diane had against her, and I didn't think it would be a problem (I had no problem with it), was that she was a woman." Another board member said, "Leon never made any waves against Frank [the previous superintendent] because he was afraid to, but as soon as Frank left, then he made accusations against Diane." Another comment was, "I think they [the power structure in the community] let it happen; they did not speak up you know, and as supporters they should have." It was unclear why the board members let it happen; apparently all of them knew what was going on, but no one made any attempts to address the problem.

And so it went on for two years. Diane remembered how painful it was: "I had never been attacked before in my professional life. I'd never been questioned like that . . . where my whole character and credibility were on the line, so I was not prepared for it, and I didn't know how to handle it. . . . He was horrible." He ran for the school board and was defeated. He continued a steady barrage of criticism against her until her resignation. He frequently attended school board meetings and criticized her leadership. He requested her resignation at the meetings. At one meeting, the entire school board walked out during one of his tirades. Finally, Diane resigned after three and a half years and got the board to pass the reorganization plan at her last board meeting.

In addition to discrimination in the community, Diane felt very isolated professionally as well. She stated flatly, "I didn't have a support system among superintendents." There was one male superintendent who was helpful and friendly to her. "He was wonderful," but she added, "There's definitely an 'old boy network'. . . . There were only three guys I ever felt were on my side."

Diane talked about "not really having a social life because even if you would go to gatherings, you are always the superintendent—you cannot escape the damn role. . . . I don't care what you're doing . . . you're on. People quote what you say—it doesn't matter what it's about." Two things helped Diane deal with the pressures of the job. She remembered, "I had about four or five people that I didn't have to be 'on' with inside the district." These people provided a haven for Diane to be herself. The other escape was her cottage: "I think the one thing that got us through all that frankly is that in 1978 we bought a cottage on a lake in a nearby state. I honest to God believe that cottage is what got me through the worst times as an administrator."

Diane left the superintendency after three and a half years. Her husband was transferred to another state. Actually, when the opportunity came up, she said she was "delighted. . . . I was looking for a graceful way to get out. . . . I knew I did not want to live that way much longer." Diane said her being a superintendent was "a bad match." She felt she was a doer and wanted to get the reorganization accomplished, but that change is very slow in education. She regretted her decision to be a superintendent because, she said, "It was a really bad way to end up in a place. I had gotten a lot of premiere things done there and had a very good reputation, and I hurt myself." She said she would never again be a superintendent. For Diane, the red shoes did not lead her to a satisfying dance, personally or professionally.

Barbara

Barbara served a longer tenure than any of the other women interviewed—seven years. Fowler was a small district of about 1,600 students with two elementary schools, one middle school, and one high school. Proud of its schools, Fowler was a bedroom community contiguous to a large Midwestern city. Barbara enjoyed being a superintendent in a small district where one "can know the students by name." She believed in "empowering people . . . to let people see that they do have the ability within themselves and help them have the confidence and skill and whatever else it takes to make things happen." Board members recognized that Barbara brought an improved climate to the district. A board member said that during her tenure, ". . . there was a real increase in the trust and communication between the teachers and administration." She negotiated a contract with the teachers that remained unchanged for eight years. When the one and only levy failure occurred, the newspaper reported that over 100 staff members in the district signed a letter of support for Barbara. But Barbara also faced the wrath of a man in the district who felt antagonism toward her visible, leadership role.

Barbara's harassment at the hands of a community member came when he was elected to the school board. He achieved a seat on the school board during the fourth year of her tenure. As in Diane's situation, male board members recognized the situation, "He had no trouble with any of the male people for some reason. He was a member of a religious group which has a different perception of women being in a leadership role. It was an unbelievable four years of absolute mistrust that he created in information being given to community people." Another board member recalled, "Barbara was constantly harassed by this guy in public."

Barbara blamed herself for "Elmer's" negativism at first. She tried to find ways to work with him. But nothing seemed to improve the relationship. She said, "The thing you found yourself doing was that you were blaming yourself . . . or there were some skills or something that you should be able to do to get things back together. You would try, but there seemed to be more determination that it wasn't going to work. . . . I refused to believe that there were evil people in the world until I had to deal with this man." His attacks were directed at other women administrators as well. At the time "Elmer" came on the school board, four of the five administrators in the school district were women. By the last year of his tenure, all of the female administrators, including the treasurer, had resigned and had been replaced by men. One of the board members commented

after Barbara left and the board was considering two finalists for the superintendent's position, one male and one female, "The female we thought was going
to be super, and we wanted her but if you don't go in 5 to 0, you're creating a
whole new set of problems for yourself. 'Elmer' made it a point that he 'wasn't
voting for no woman.' We gave in."

Barbara understood the importance of networking. She served as president
of the state association of school administrators. She knew superintendents all
across the United States whom she could call on for help. She understood the
importance of "politics." She said if she were preparing women to be superintendents, she would teach them ". . . the different levels of politics. Women seem
hesitant to play a game of 'political savvy' in recognizing who's on their way
where and hitching up. I know that sounds terrible, but that's how men play the
game. Women think it's dirty. I think it's foreign to them and it just doesn't
occur to them . . . understanding politics is not a dirty word. I think it would be
one of the key things . . . and then learning to play a damn good game of golf!"

Barbara knew she had to take the initiative to become connected to the power
in the community. She recalled, "There was a hesitancy on the part of the established men's groups to invite a woman, and I don't know that I was as forceful
in obtaining entree in some of those groups as I should have been. I served on
what were supposed to be important committees, but I wasn't so naive not to
know that there was nothing happening at those committees. It wasn't until I was
invited for beers after the meetings. So I did get it but it took me four years before
that happened." Barbara's experiences are a reminder that, for women, the organizational connections may take longer and women need to initiate invitations.

Barbara acknowledged the personal difficulties for women that the superintendency promotes. Although her husband was very supportive of her work, he
had to work through the changes and the problems it brought. Moving was one
of them. "Well, if we could have a wife, this would be so much easier. Some of
the fellas do, and just by nature there are some things they don't have to attend
to that women do." Visibility was a key issue of concern in her life as well. Barbara described it as "Being on, twenty-four hours a day, seven days a week. You
live in a fishbowl. Your private life is pretty much wide open. And I got tired of
that." A board member commented, "I think she really didn't like the negative
aspects of the limelight. She was much more interested in doing a job and getting it done." Barbara has taken off her red shoes in a new job as an assistant
superintendent. "Here, he, the superintendent, is the point person. I can go to
the grocery store and I don't know if people know me or not. I don't care."

Kathy

Kathy was the superintendent of a county or an intermediate school district.
The district of Burlington served three local school districts and provided con-

tracted services to two city districts, serving a total of about 2,600 children. Located in a rural area, the office consisted of only three people when Kathy became superintendent. Kathy gained community support by being visible and by initiating new programs. The district was financially stable, and there was no need to place levies on the ballot for support. Run by a conservative board of area farmers, the office had allowed its relationship with the districts it served to deteriorate. Kathy changed that relationship. She went out into the districts, met with area superintendents, asked what they needed, and provided those services. She increased the office staff from three to eleven. She established a gifted and talented program, a work-study program, a truancy program, and a preschool program. She said, "The job was a great deal more satisfying than I ever expected. There were three people employed when I took the job, and in five years I was able to build it with services this county had never seen before. I was able to do it cost effectively, as far as low cost to the schools involved. I was able to bring all schools to cooperate on some programs that they had not done before. I really found the job itself very exciting. "

Although Kathy did not experience discrimination against women leaders from the community, she experienced hostility from a member of her organization. Although Kathy worked with an all-male school board, her office staff was made up of all women. One of these was the treasurer, a woman who had been in the area for more than twenty years and had virtually run the office during the tenure of the last superintendent, who had pretty much been a figurehead. The treasurer did not like working with another woman in a leadership position. From the beginning, the two women butted heads. "Bonny" manipulated the men on the school board, who were all family friends or relatives. Kathy said, "They let her do whatever she wanted." One of the board members described the problem as a "chick thing."

Pretty soon the two women were not even speaking to one another. The men refused to become involved in the situation because they felt it was a "cat fight." One board member, who had worked with this treasurer in another district when he had been the superintendent, said that he had problems with her there as well. He simply went to the board and said, "Either she goes or I go." That board fired "Bonny." When he was asked why Kathy did not do that, he said she did not have the board support to do that, and the men did not want to become embroiled in what they perceived as a women's issue. He also added, "I don't think 'Bonny' would ever accept a female. No other female has ever come into her territory that she hasn't been able to tell what to do. When it comes to dealing with men, 'Bonny' was able to use her femininity to get her way with them. That didn't work with women." However, the board continued to be satisfied with Kathy's work and even gave her an extended contract and a raise the month before she resigned.

On the other hand, being one of few women provided visibility that could be beneficial, as Kathy pointed out: "It benefited me in some ways to be female . . . I was put on committees and things that I might not have been if I were just another superintendent." She felt the superintendents' organization was "welcoming," even though there were no other female intermediate super-intendents in the state. But board members noticed the difficulties that being female entailed. In Kathy's case, one said, "At first it was tough, the fact that she was a female and because superintendents for the most part were of the 'old school' so to speak. At times they looked down on her because she was female, and they were playing 'the good old boy system'—golf in the afternoons, and she wasn't part of that. That really made it hard to work with them, especially at first breaking in. But she got through that."

Kathy talked about how hard being a superintendent was on her personal life. "It was extremely difficult on the family, and that is a woman's issue too. If that had been reversed, it would be nice to have a wife too." Kathy said the thing "missing" from the job was ". . . direct contact with students. You do sit there and wonder how much of this paper pushing is worth it."

Kathy left the superintendency when the situation with "Bonny" became extremely strained. In addition, she felt she had lost control of the board. New members came on the board who had a "bad history" with one another. She said, "At board meetings more attention was paid to that end of the table [where they were] than my end—it was like a power struggle. If I wasn't their executive leader, then I didn't need to be going through the agony. I didn't think it was going to change real soon. So, board changes were part of the reason and rela-tionships were part of the reason. Maybe I didn't want to work hard enough to turn it around, or maybe I didn't know how. I don't think I knew how." Kathy worried about letting women down who might aspire to the superintendency and about proving everyone else right that she couldn't handle it. But she ultimately decided she had danced very well, and it was time to move on to new challenges.

Luci

Luci was the only one of these women who did not face a personal attack during her superintendency. She became superintendent of Woodville, with a student population of about 2,500, after a brief stint as a superintendent in a small, rural district of about half that size. Luci enjoyed being a superintendent. She stated, " I did not have one truly unpleasant moment. I mean it was really very challenging for me. I felt totally supported by the boards I worked with. It was a wonderful time for me. . . . Actually it was fun. . . . I even had fun in all the levy defeats we had. Even though we were getting defeated, I developed very close ties to the people who were working on it." According to all of the board members I interviewed, Luci was "very well accepted, very well liked in the community." Luci transformed school board meetings by instituting the televising of school board meetings over the local access channel. It became a big feature in the community on Monday night to watch the proceedings. Luci remembered, "Someone would run in and say, 'I just heard that on the cable and want to make a comment on it.'"

Discriminatory attitudes from both men and women were a small part of Luci's experience. Luci described the school board member who suggested that she did not need a salary increment because, "You don't need as much money because you are a woman." Luci described her feelings: "That is the only time in my entire career that someone has said something like that to my face. I said, 'Richard, I can't believe you said that.' He never apologized for it." A board member remembered complaints that she had not moved to town and had commuted for a while: "I think it came from people who didn't see a woman as superintendent. There were people in the community who had problems [with it]."

Luci felt support professionally since she knew other women and men superintendents whom she could call for advice and support. She learned early in her career the importance of networking. She said, " You have to be a network builder with all the internal and external groups in your community. To me that has to be the role [of the superintendent] and it is through the development of this positive network that the school positions itself." Luci also learned to use resources for information and support. She recalled, "One of my professors [from graduate school] lived in my district and I would call him . . . and he would always help me." Her networks included men as well as women; she recognized the importance of being what she called "proactive" in reaching out to as many networks as possible.

Visibility was the personal issue that affected Luci most intensely. Appearance is much more an issue for women than it is for men (Tannen 1993). Luci described it as making her "want to throw up. It's not that I don't like being active, but everything you do is always subject to scrutiny. . . . I don't mind running into Mrs. Jones, or that she wants to talk but not to have her wonder, 'My God, why does she have on those awful sweatpants?' I feel like I can't go around in my sweatpants, you know. I don't like feeling that I ought to take ten more minutes and get 'gussied' up' before I go to the drugstore. The kind of thing that restricts your behavior is what bothers me."

Luci's decision to exit was based on her desire to be more involved in her children's lives and to get out of the red shoes. In a small community such as Woodville, she felt she was always on display. She said, "Part of the reason I wanted to move this time and why I was fairly serious at looking at jobs that were not superintendencies is that . . . you have so much visibility. In a small town you are expected to do everything, be in everything, support everything. I finally said, 'I don't want this—visibility is not important to me. I want it if it helps the school but it isn't helping me personally. At this point, if I had to choose, I am going to choose to let somebody else do it . . . cause it's taking away too much of me." An important issue for her was whether she was letting down other women. She wondered if she was "abandoning the ranks" by leaving the superintendency. But she decided that her family and her privacy were more important and that maybe she would return to the position at a later time.

DISCUSSION

These women were all successful school superintendents, by every account. Every one of the board members who were interviewed described them as "the best" or "one of the best" superintendents with whom they had worked. Three of the four received community or state recognition for their work. These women faced many of the same problems that men face in the school superintendency: problematic school board relations, public criticism, time/stress management, and political and financial worries (Griffiths 1988). But their problems were compounded by gender issues, including discrimination, which led to extensive public criticism in two cases and internal conflict in another; marginalized status from a professional standpoint; and a diminished quality of personal life, which increased their stress.

Women who dance in red shoes appear to have lost a sense of "their place" in our society. Three of these women—Diane, Barbara, and Kathy—were confronted with noisome behaviors rationalized by beliefs, attitudes, and expectations that were not culturally supportive of the concept of women as leaders; it was the red shoes of leadership that made these women vulnerable. The noisome beliefs and aggressive behaviors discouraged them from remaining in leadership roles once they attained them. It is worth noting that none of these women verbally identified gender discrimination as a problem for them. Kathy, for example, described our interview as "a bit of catharsis just to talk about it." They saw their experiences as being isolated, unusual instances. This discrimination produced situations these women had never faced so directly before. They were surprised and uncertain, and unprepared to make an appropriate and effective response. The emotion and pain of the situations were more clearly described by the board members, who watched the problems unfold. The interviews with school board members suggest the gender of these superintendents made them fair game for attack and that little was done to help them. Board members were sympathetic, in retrospect, but not very helpful ("we gave in"). All three women, unable to resolve these attacks, lived with them for several years before they finally removed themselves from situations for which they could find no satisfactory solutions.

From a professional standpoint, all of these women were marginalized to some degree by their gender. They were one of few women on the dance floor, since they worked with all male or predominantly male school boards. Two of them, Diane and Kathy, knew no other women superintendents. The male superintendents they knew were described as being usually friendly and helpful when asked for assistance. But assistance had to be sought. All of these women understood the value of networking and appeared successful in gaining acceptance from their peers. However, the women had to work at it, understood that there were some barriers that would not be overcome, and had to accept the "benefit" the heightened visibility of the red shoes brought. All of the women acknowledged the lack of role models, a support system (with the exception of their husbands), and close friends among other superintendents.

These women were not "place bound," a criticism often given to females to explain the reasons there are not more women superintendents (Miklos 1988). In two cases (Barbara and Luci), the husbands moved when their wives accepted superintendencies. Barbara said, "The superintendency hasn't been without its price. When we moved for the first job, my husband couldn't give up the house. He stayed there and I moved." Each of these women acknowledged the importance of their supportive, adaptable partners to the success of their careers. One board member described Luci's husband as "Mr. Mom," since he worked flexible hours and was able to be home with the children while Luci was involved with her superintendent's duties. These women made adaptations within their family lives to accommodate the dance. But the amount of time the dance required, basically "all of it" as Kathy said, and the heightened visibility that they felt intensely as women made life increasingly burdensome. The personal lives of women are affected deeply by the time, visibility, and isolation from friends and family required by the superintendency. The cultural expectations for women's work to be centered around home and family are subtle but pervasive. Without the assistance of a supportive husband, these women believed that the dance of the superintendency would be much more difficult, or even impossible.

The results of this research validate much of the previous research about women in the superintendency. A central theme of this small sample is that capable women are exiting the school superintendency prematurely for reasons that primarily have to do with their gender. These capable women are disadvantaged as a result of various combinations of cultural and social discrimination, professional and organizational isolation, and a diminished quality in their personal and family lives. Dancing in red shoes provides a metaphor of what undermines the determination and drive of women who seek this top management position in education. Leadership is experienced as a visible, vulnerable dance in red shoes. These women wearied of the dance.

REFERENCES

Armstrong, M. D. 1990. An examination of public school superintendent interpersonal networks in Washington and Idaho. Paper presented at the annual meeting of the American Educational Research Association, Boston, Mass.

Beason, J. H. 1992. *Identification of career barriers faced and professional strategies used by female secondary school principals.* Unpublished dissertation. *Dissertation Abstracts Internationa,* 53 (03): 668A.

Bem, S. L. 1993. *The lenses of gender.* New Haven: Yale University Press.

Burns, J. M. 1978. *Leadership.* New York: Harper & Row.

Chase, S. E. 1995. *Ambiguous empowerment: The work narratives of women school superintendents.* Amherst: The University of Massachusetts Press.

Dunlap, D. M., and P. A. Schmuck (eds.). (1995). *Women leading in education.* Albany, N.Y.: State University of New York Press.

Estler, S. 1975. Women as leaders in public education. *Signs: Journal of Women in Culture and Society* 1 (3): 363–86.

Frasher, J. M., and R. S. Frasher. 1979. Educational administration: A feminine profession. *Educational Administration Quarterly* 15 (2): 1–13.

Griffiths, D. 1988. Administrative theory. In N. J. Boyan (ed.), *Handbook of Research in Educational Administration.* New York: Longman.

Gupton, S. L., and G. A. Slick. 1994. The missing pieces in emerging female leadership in the profession: Support systems, mentoring, and networking. *Mississippi Educational Leadership* 1 (1): 13–18.

———. 1995. Women leaders: Who are they and how do they compare. In B. J. Irby and G. Brown (eds.), *Women as school executives: Voices and visions.* Hunstville: The Texas Council of Women School Executives.

———. 1996. *Highly successful women administrators: The inside story of how they got there.* Thousand Oaks, Calif.: Corwin Press.

Hart, A. W. 1995. Women ascending to leadership: The organizational socialization of principals. In D. M. Dunlap and P. A. Schmuck (eds.), *Women leading in education.* Albany, N.Y.: State University of New York Press.

Hawkins, L. G. 1991. *Barriers associated with the limited numbers of females in public school leadership positions in South Carolina.* Unpublished dissertation. *Dissertation Abstracts International* 52 (12): 41630A.

Kanter, R. M. 1977. *Men and women of the corporation.* New York: Basic Books.

Klein, S. S., and P. E. Ortman. 1994. Continuing the journey toward gender equity. *Educational Researcher* 23 (8): 13–21.

Lourdes, C. R. 1995. Factors influencing the career development of community college women administrators. *Dissertation Abstracts International* 56 (12): 4630A.

Lynch, K. K. 1990. Women in school administration: Overcoming the barriers to advancement. *Women's Educational Equity Act Publishing Center Digest* (August): 2.

Maienza, J. G. 1986. The superintendency: Characteristics of access for men and women. *Educational Administration Quarterly* 22 (4): 59–79.

Mead, M. 1935. *Sex and temperament in three primitive societies.* New York: William Morrow.

Miklos, E. 1988. Administrator selection, career patterns, succession, and socialization. In N. J. Boyan (ed.), *Handbook of Research in Educational Administration.* New York: Longman.

Montenegro, X. 1993. *Women and racial minority representation in school administration.* Arlington: American Association of School Administrators.

Moody, C. D. Sr. 1983. On becoming a superintendent: Contest or sponsored mobility? *Journal of Negro Education* 52 (4): 383-97.

Orenstein, G. 1986. Is equality still inequality? *Journal of the National Association for Women Deans, Administrators and Counselors* 49 (summer): 22-28.

Radich, P. A. 1992. Access and entry to the public school superintendency in the state of Washington: A comparison between men and women. Paper presented at the annual meeting of the American Educational Research Association, San Francisco.

Ragins, B. R., and E. Sundstrom. 1989. Gender and power in organizations: A longitudinal perspective. *Psychological Bulletin* 105 (1): 51-88.

Rosener, J. B. 1990. The ways women lead. *Harvard Business Review* 68 (6): 119-25.

Schmuck, P. A. 1986. Networking: A new word, a different game. *Educational Leadership* 43 (5): 60-61.

Scott, N. A., and S. Spooner. 1989. Women administrators: Stressors and strategies. *Initiatives* 52 (2): 31-36.

Shakeshaft, C. 1989. *Women in educational administration.* Newbury Park: Corwin Press.

Swiderski, W. 1988. Problems faced by women in gaining access to administrative positions in education. *Education Canada* 28 (3): 24-31.

Tallerico, M., J. N. Burstyn, and W. Poole. 1993. *Gender and politics at work: Why women exit the superintendency.* National Policy Board for Educational Administration: Fairfax, Va.

Tannen, D. 1993. Wears jump suit, sensible shoes, uses husband's last name. *The New York Times Magazine* (June 20): 18-19.

White, J. 1992. *A few good women: Breaking the barriers to top management.* Englewood Cliffs: Prentice Hall.

Woo, L. 1985. Women administrators: Profiles of success. *Phi Delta Kappan* 67 (4): 285-88.

PART FOUR

"One's True Song"

Athenticating Research

C. CRYSS BRUNNER

> There are some good questions to ask till one decides on the song, one's true song: What has happened to my soul-voice? What are the buried bones of my life? In what condition is my relationship to the instinctual Self? When was the last time I ran free? How do I make life come alive again?
>
> —Clarissa Pinkola Estés, *Women Who Run With the Wolves*

When we ask questions of ourselves or others, we wish to hear the "true song." When we repeat what we have heard from others, we hope to repeat the "true song." To that end, this section includes three companion chapters that focus on uncovering a collective "true song" for women superintendents. With this focus in mind, the three interactive chapters examine how the research of two researchers relates to the lived experiences of a woman currently in the position of superintendent of schools.

The collaborative project began with a series of interviews with one woman superintendent—Debra Jackson. Interview questions were driven by prior research done by C. Cryss Brunner and Margaret Grogan on women superintendents. After transcribing the interviews, the researchers separately used different lenses for data analysis. Chapter 13, written by Debra Jackson, is her response to Brunner's and Grogan's analyses. The point of Jackson's chapter is to establish the usefulness and validity of the researchers' perceptions of women superintendents—in short, to authenticate research with an overlay of a practitioner's "own true song."

CHAPTER ELEVEN

"Back Talk" from a Woman Superintendent

Just How Useful Is Research?

C. CRYSS BRUNNER

Although empirical research in the area of educational administration is plentiful, often it seems to be of little practical use. In fact, I remember reading research when I was a public school administrator and asking myself, "How am I supposed to use this?" Thus, my goal as a researcher is to make my work useful and practical for the people I study. To that end, the purpose of this chapter is to examine the usefulness of a framework that emerged from my interpretations of data gathered in qualitative research (Brunner 1997). The original study drew on the insights of twelve women superintendents who were considered successful in their roles by those around them. The framework I developed emerged from the data gathered and defined "strategies for success" for women superintendents.

To begin testing the practical usefulness of the "strategies for success" framework, I enlisted the assistance of a woman superintendent not included in the original study—Dr. Debra Jackson. I designed a single-case qualitative study to capture her reaction to the framework. This chapter reflects changes in my thinking that were provoked by her "back talk." My purpose in doing this is to begin a larger conversation with practicing women superintendents articulating useful "collective solutions" (see Chase 1995) for the individual gender-related problems that they face while in their positions. The framework and Dr. Jackson's "back talk" is a beginning point for that conversation.

A SINGLE-CASE QUALITATIVE STUDY

In doing this study, my intent was to gather narrative data in the same manner as in my earlier interviews. First I interviewed (twice) a woman superintendent,

Dr. Debra Jackson, who was not a subject of the first study. I used the same non-standardized, free-flowing format (Patton 1980; Guba and Lincoln 1981) that I used in the original study.

Next I gave Dr. Jackson a copy of her two transcribed sixty-minute interviews so she could reshape her responses if she wished. Finally, I gave her a copy of a paper that reported the results of my interpretation and organization of her data. This completed the first part of the study.

The Participant

At the time of the first interview (April 1996), Dr. Debra Jackson, a Hungarian-Italian American, was forty-one years old. She had been superintendent of a Northeastern school district (800 students) for four years. At the time of the second interview (fall 1996), she had been hired to head a district, in the same region, which had 1,600 students. Her career history followed this path: admissions counselor (1977-78), art teacher (1978-80), project director in gifted education (1980-82), curriculum coordinator (1980-83), elementary school principal (1984-89), assistant superintendent of schools (1989-92), and superintendent (1992 to present). She earned her master's degree in administration, policy, and urban education in 1981 and her doctorate in education in 1990.

I selected Dr. Jackson as the participant because of her interest not only in my research, but also because of her interest in research in general. In addition, collaboration with her was logistically convenient because she and I attend research organizations such as the University Council of Educational Administration and American Educational Research Association. Further, she is quite active in professional organizations, including the American Association of School Administrators. Because of her intellectual contribution to organizations that focus on both theory and practice, she was an ideal participant.

The Analysis

Because the framework of strategies for success had been established in the original study, I was able to go directly to the stage of categorizing units of the new data gathered from Dr. Jackson. The second stage of analysis was done collaboratively by Dr. Jackson and me. This collaborative analysis (Lather 1991) emerged during in-depth discussions (recorded and transcribed) and was focused on the usefulness of the "strategies for success" framework as collective solutions for all women superintendents. These discussions—labeled "Researcher/Practitioner Dialogue"—are also reflected in this chapter. (One of these discussions was held at the annual meeting of the University Council of Educational Administrators and is explained in depth in chapter 12.)

THE FRAMEWORK—STRATEGIES FOR SUCCESS

I began my original research with women superintendents (Brunner 1997) by suggesting that there is a need to identify strategies for success specifically for women superintendents. "Success"—for the purposes of the study—was defined as "being not only capable and effective in the role, but also well liked and supported by others who knew or worked for the superintendent." Using qualitative methods aimed at understanding the narrative data, the study drew on the insights of twelve women superintendents and twenty-four people who knew them. The study yielded seven significant findings, in seven "strategies for success" found in the practice of women superintendents. While many of these findings may be sound advice for anyone wishing to succeed in an administrative position, each is specifically related to gender as an issue associated with the position of superintendent of schools. The seven strategies for success were drawn from the work the women superintendents in the study had done to manage the complex expectations confronting women in the superintendency (p. 31).

The seven strategies arrived at in the original study were stated as follows:

1. Women superintendents need to learn to balance role-related expectations with gender-related ones.
2. Women superintendents need to keep their agendas simple in order to focus on their primary purpose: the care of children, including strict attention to academic achievement.
3. Women superintendents need to develop the ability to be "culturally bilingual."
4. Women superintendents need to "act like a woman."
5. Women superintendents need to remove or let go of anything that blocks their success.
6. Women superintendents need to be fearless, courageous, "can do" risk takers. At the same time, they need to have a plan for retreat when faced with the impossible.
7. Women superintendents need to share power and credit. (Brunner 1997, 31)

Drawing on what I learned from the original study, I concluded "that although on the surface women in the superintendency did not appear to be paying attention to the fact that they are women, [the] study found the reverse. The women in the [original] study articulated and carried out gender-specific strategies which created, in part, their support while in the superintendency" (p. 31). My findings agreed with the assertions of Susan Chase (1995), who found that "women superintendents fully acknowledge their continuous subjection to gendered and racial inequalities in the profession . . ." (p. xi).

DR. DEBRA JACKSON AND "STRATEGIES FOR SUCCESS"

The following section of the paper shares Dr. Debra Jackson's narrative data, organized under the seven categories and compared and contrasted to the narratives of the women superintendents in the original study. (Note that Dr. Jackson's narratives are in italics.)[1]

Strategy 1: Learn to Balance Role-Related Expectations With Gender-Related Ones

The women in the original study, in one way or another, communicated that one requirement for succeeding in the superintendency was a keen awareness of what they were expected to do and be. They repeatedly discussed the importance of knowing that expectations included not only those required of all superintendents, whether male or female, but also additional ones related to their gender. The women in the study said that to be successful, they must address both sets of expectations—expectations that often resulted in contradictory experiences of power and subjection (Chase 1995). As I learned in the study, their ability to recognize and reconcile contradictory expectations and experiences was the ground on which they constructed their individual strategies for success. A woman from a large district spoke directly to this point:

> I think that expectations of the people around me are different [because I am a woman]. I think when you put a female in a position that has been predominantly held by men, the expectation in the business community is to see a man. And when they see a woman, their expectation is that she is to do everything the female of the culture has always done—that is, to pay attention to detail, to be caring, to do everything you would expect a female to do. Plus, the expectation is that she will also do what you expect the man to do. And I think a board member will ask a female superintendent to do things he/she would never even consider asking a male superintendent to do.

Researcher/practitioner dialogue. While Dr. Jackson agreed that Strategy 1 was useful in specific settings, she was not convinced that it held true in all situations. She gave specific examples of when she felt the force of these expectations. She believed, as did the women in the original study, that during group meetings of superintendents, there were things expected of her that were not expected of her male colleagues. She often was the only woman in the group, so differences in expectations were obvious to her. She also felt that requirements for women during the selection process were different than those for men. Other areas where Dr. Jackson noted gender-related expectations as well as role-related expectations are reflected in her narratives analyzed under the other six strategies for success.

On the other hand, she believed that the role-related expectations were the same for both men and women. That is, that they were not altered because a woman was in the position. As she said:

> I think on the job, I don't believe there are differences with regards to requirements.

Strategy 2: Keep Your Agenda Simple in Order to Focus On Your Primary Purpose—The Care and Development of Children, Including Strict Attention to Academic Achievement

The women superintendents in the original study repeatedly emphasized how they had to simplify their work and lives in order to focus on their primary purpose for being in the position—children. A statement by one woman superintendent that is representative of the other women in that study follows:

> I measure success by the fact that 73 percent of the kids in our city graduated from high school the year I came, 81 percent graduate today. I measure success by the fact that we have many alternative schools where kids are getting degrees now instead of being out on the streets or in the jails. I don't feel successful because too many youngsters who have not been successful in academic areas are minority youngsters. I am still having real difficulty in getting our people in our elementary schools to believe that poor youngsters can learn. . . . I worry . . . about the children—somebody's got to be responsible.

Dr. Jackson's primary purpose in her position was the same as that of the women in the original study. She focused on the children in her district. Everything on her agenda came back to that, and she kept her agenda simple:

> I make decisions based on how we can best make a difference for students. I bring everything back to that all the time.

When talking about making decisions based on what is best for the students, she noted the source of her motivation:

> [A]ctually I make decisions based on my belief system. . . .

Dr. Jackson also reported that decisions made based on "caring for children" were often not easy to make:

> I've made some very tough decisions as superintendent, and it comes down to [students] every time. Not what everyone might have to say, but what is best for those students.

Like the women studied in my original research, Dr. Jackson's agenda was simplified by viewing everything through the lenses of "what best served the students":

> Being a superintendent means doing what's best for the students in the
> district.

Researcher/practitioner dialogue. Dr. Jackson was in agreement with my
analysis of her narrative. She believes that this strategy is central to her role as
superintendent, in fact, central to the role of superintendent whether a man or
woman is in the position.

Strategy 3: Develop the Ability to be Culturally Bilingual

This strategy is complex and disturbing. Due to space limitations, the discussion in this section is only a brief summary. (For a fuller discussion, see the
paper devoted entirely to this strategy, Brunner 1996.)

The differences between men and women associated with communication
require women to be what I termed *culturally bilingual* in the original study. I
defined this term to refer to women's ability to remain "feminine," in the classical
sense, while communicating in a "masculinized" culture. The women superintendents in the original study agreed that they were expected not only to know the
somewhat foreign male-defined language in the primarily male culture of the superintendency in order to meet role-related expectations, but also to communicate in
a "feminine" way in order to meet gender-related expectations (Bolinger 1980;
Gilligan 1982; Reardon 1995; Tannen 1986, 1990, 1994a, 1994b; Wolfe 1994).
Data related to communication in the original study fell into four categories: (1)
Silenced by the Term "Power;" (2) Overt Silencing; (3) Listening/Silence; and (4)
Ways of Communicating to be Heard. The last two categories reveal ways that the
women superintendents were communicating in a masculine culture while remain-
ing feminine.

Listening/silence. Most of the women in the original study used silence (did
not talk as much as they would have liked) to be accepted by their male peers,
and they listened because they believed it was respectful and important for gathering input. Consider the strategy used by one women in the original study:

> When I was first in administration, I found myself mainly in the
> "quiet persistence" category. All of my colleagues were the 'good old
> boy' type males. That was the way to get an entry—was to attend the
> meetings. . . . They didn't know how to deal with me. So I found
> that what was most useful was to sit and listen. Then quietly persist
> in getting my point across. For example, I would say, 'We talked
> about doing so and so, and if we should. . . .' And I would repeat
> what I wanted to say—persistently pursue—what I thought was
> important.

Dr. Jackson also spoke of the need to listen to people, specifically in order
to get their input. She stated that others viewed her as someone who was "*always*

ready to listen." She also talked about her natural tendency to be quiet, "*I'm a very quiet person. I am someone who really is probably more introverted than extroverted.*" She elaborated:

> My decisions are usually based on what's best for students and from the perspective of listening to others and gathering as much information about other's standpoints as I possibly can.

Ways of communicating to be heard. Even with the complications around silence and voice, women superintendents in the original study had ways to be heard. First, they stated that being "direct" was too harsh. One woman said, "Women can't be directive or before long they are called bitches. So if women want to stay in power they have to find a way to circumvent by using a softer style." Dr. Jackson also talked about the association between "being direct" and being authoritarian:

> I'm not seen as being authoritarian or direct. I associate "direct" with being authoritarian.

Second, they talked about using others (men) as spokespersons in order that their voices be heard. A woman in the original study talked about how she used men to speak for her when the mayor would not listen to her because she was a woman:

> The mayor that came in was much more adversarial toward the school district and the gender issue was difficult. I'm really not sure how comfortable he is working with a woman in authority, so I've tried to utilize the building-and-grounds people (men) to network with him in order to find his comfort level. And there's been much more progressive, positive communication between the two groups lately.

Dr. Jackson mentioned a similar strategy:

> And sometimes the approach is to get other people involved when you know that certain things need to come [from someone else] because that's part of what they want. They become the spokesperson on this issue that we worked on. I get them to be the voice if necessary. It's [the spokesperson is] not always me.

In this particular comment, Dr. Jackson separated herself from the notion that her voice needed to be used to express her idea. She stated that "the voice was still heard. It wasn't silenced." This separation may have allowed her to discount the fact that someone else's voice expressed her idea and, in the end, may have been credited for the idea. Although, I would have categorized the need to have someone else speak for me as "overt silencing," the woman in the original study and Dr. Jackson viewed it as a strategy for being heard.

Researcher/practitioner dialogue. I asked Dr. Jackson to talk about the notion of the need for women to be culturally bilingual because of all the issues around talking and being heard. She noted that anything she did—if it was being culturally bilingual or anything else—was "just her" rather than a conscious effort. This was true for the women in my previous study as well.

On the one hand, Dr. Jackson did not think that she was culturally bilingual, because she paid attention to the type of language that other people used and she was different than the men around her. She said, "There are people out there who use a real business language, and I absolutely work against that." In this case, she misunderstood "culturally bilingual" to mean that she spoke the same style of language as the male culture of the superintendency—"a real business language."

After thinking about Dr. Jackson's response to the term *culturally bilingual*, I decided that it was too laden with other meanings and, therefore, unclear. Since clarity is essential when communicating with others, I decided to articulate differently. I stated it as follows: Women superintendents need to develop the ability to remain "feminine" in the ways they communicate and at the same time be heard in a masculine culture.

Strategy 4: Women Superintendents Need to Remember to "Act Like a Woman"

Success Strategy 4 describes the ways in which women in the original study incorporated their traditionally feminine behavior into their roles as superintendents. They acknowledged that their roles as superintendents were most often defined by "masculinized" (in the classical sense) behavior and that it was easy to be confused about what behavior was expected of them—whether they should behave in a "feminine" or "masculine" way. It was crucial to resolve this dilemma. As one woman flatly stated, "Women who act like men: it doesn't work." Once aware of this "truth," the women in the original study recognized that they needed to be "comfortable with the fact" that they were women in male roles, but they continue to "act like women" anyway. Role-related expectations were subordinated to gender-related expectations as the strategy for success. As one superintendent put it:

> I believe people who are here [in this position] are comfortable with
> the fact that they are women by the time they have reached the posi-
> tion. They have foregone the struggle with believing that they must
> be thinking like or looking like a man.

Dr. Jackson's comments lead me to believe that she agreed with the women in the original study. When talking about whether she felt that she needed to "act like a man" in her position, she stated, "I don't. If anything, that would tend to be more of a problem for me than it would seem." She asserted that instead of thinking about how a man would act in the position of superintendent, she felt that women just had to have very strong belief systems to drive their actions:

> *I think there are people out there who are always going to pull at what you're not. But I'd say that it would be a problem for me to [act like a man]. Especially when it would mean that I'm not true to myself. . . . I believe being yourself is really being strong about what you believe you need to do in order to accomplish what your tasks are. . . . But I don't think that means acting more like a man. Although I've heard that time and time again.*

Some of the women superintendents in the original study were more vehement than Dr. Jackson about this topic. They not only expressed that it did not work to "act like a man," but they also stated that it was important to "act like a woman." Dr. Jackson, on the other hand, continued to come back to "being herself" as the measure of what was appropriate.

In the original study, one of the most important ways in which the women superintendents "acted like women" was articulated by a woman superintendent in a discussion about relationships. She said "that a female . . . is responsible for the caring of all employees and students." Most of the women in the original study strongly emphasized the high priority they placed on caring relationships[2] (Beck 1994; Noddings 1984; Purpel 1989) with and among their employees, colleagues, parents, and students. One woman revealed:

> The members of the staff are so dear [original emphasis] to me. For the most part I guess my success is in being able to hang on to the development of some kind of relationship in this crazy time in public education.

Her next comment made it clear just how much she relied on her relationships with the people in her district. She said, "If I am successful, I really believe it is because I have such [original emphasis] successful people that make me look good."

Dr. Jackson had another view. She thought that paying attention to relationships was a role-related expectation rather than a gender-related one. She believed that men superintendents whom she knew paid as much attention to relationships as she did. For example:

> *In one of my previous job interviews, the acting man superintendent was sharing with me that he has taken some time off just to spend some time with a staff member who was really upset and really just needed to have him be an ear. You know lots of times we're an ear for someone, we're a help. I mean this gentleman was an ex-coach, ex-tough guy, and it was still a big part of what he did.*

What I learned from Dr. Jackson was that, from her perspective, attention to relationships was an important part of the role of superintendent. She cast it in the set of expectations related to her role rather than in the set of expectations related to gender. The women in the original study would probably agree with her, with the additional note that they felt that they were expected to attend to relationships more than men superintendents, thus casting this expectation in the gender-related category as well.

Researcher/practitioner dialogue. Dr. Jackson was uncomfortable with this strategy, even though she agreed with the women in the earlier study that "acting like a man" did not work. I suspect for her the key word was "acting." I came to understand that she did not want to "act" like anyone or anything, she just wanted to "be herself," which for her meant being a professional woman superintendent—a complex description. To be told to "act like a woman" by society or anyone else was not, it seemed, to her liking.

Perhaps this strategy needs to be expressed differently. Certainly the women in the original work were not "acting" when they were "being women." It is helpful to understand that they too were expressing the complexity of being women in a male role. Most agreed, however, that "acting like a man" did not work. The only other choice is to "act like a woman," or perhaps more correctly stated, "to be the woman you are."

I have come to understand that in order to remove the uncomfortable and oppressive language, this strategy should be articulated as follows: Women superintendents need to disregard the old myth that they must "act like a man" while in a male role. It does not work.

Strategy 5: Remove or Let Go of Anything That Blocks Your Success

While the role-related expectation to "remove or let go of anything that blocks your success" is appropriate for anyone wishing to succeed in the superintendency, additional gender-related blocks for women in the original study existed and needed to be addressed. I learned that one potential block involved the risk of damage to their dignity and integrity because of issues related to sexual conduct. They understood that their presence in what had been commonly called the "old boy network" created some discomfort for their male colleagues. Rather than allowing complexity to develop around issues of sexual conduct, they set the ground rules in a simple, straightforward way from the beginning in order to remove any potential threats to their reputations and future success.

Some of the women talked about the things that they "let go of" as part of this strategy to be successful superintendents. For example, the most common focus of discussions was the difficulty faced in intimate relationships. Several of the women told me, with sadness, about their marriages—and in several cases, the demise of their marriages—and the dilemma facing the men in their lives. The women felt that because of societal expectations, most men had difficulty accepting the fact that their "wives" were filling the masculinized role of superintendent of schools and often were primary wage earners. Because of this difficulty and others, for some women, "letting go of blocks to their success" meant losing their husbands or partners rather than giving up their careers to save their marriages or intimate relationships.

Fortunately, Dr. Debra Jackson has not faced a divorce because of her career choice. In fact, she talked about her husband's understanding of her need to have a certain kind of life or career when she said,

> But, I do know one thing. I think he [her husband] recognized early on that I have to do certain things or I wouldn't be happy. And I think he's just sort of accepted that as what comes with the territory [being married to her].

She did, on the other hand, talk about the workload she faced at home. Dr. Jackson works at home and in the office. Her work at home is gender and role related. Women in the home have a role as a mother and a wife—a gender-specific role. She is "on duty" at home and at work. While this analysis is not meant to cast a negative light on Dr. Jackson's husband, her comment about juggling caused me to understand that doing all that she does is not easy, and a portion of what she does is done because of gender-related expectations at home.

In one sense, what women "give up" to be a superintendent is the comfort of society's approved roles. "Letting go" of this form of comfort or socialization is one way they remove barriers that have the potential to block their success as superintendents.

In the original study, many of the women had been through divorces because they were forced—most often by their husbands—to choose between their lifetime desires to have substantial careers and their desires to have traditional marriages. Many of the women superintendents in my studies who had faced this difficult decision "let go" of their marriages to become superintendents. On the other hand, I will never know how many women "let go" of their dreams of becoming superintendents and chose to stay in marriages that blocked their career goals.

Ultimately, I came to understand that the core of this strategy is to "remove or let go of" anything that blocks success—even at a great emotional cost—in order to meet role-related expectations. This is one time when gender-related expectations took a back seat.

Researcher/practitioner dialogue. In terms of intimate relationships, Dr. Jackson agreed that women face gender-specific expectations in marriage relationships that make a career choice to become a superintendent even more difficult. She understood how other women found themselves divorced in order to remain superintendents.

Strategy 6: Remain Fearless, Courageous, A Risk Taker, a "Can Do" Person and, at the Same Time, Have a Plan for Retreat When Faced with the Impossible

The notion that anyone in the superintendency must be fearless, courageous, a risk taker, and a "can do" person is no surprise to anyone familiar with the role-related expectations of the position, but most often these descriptions have been reserved for men in our culture. Almost all of the women in the original study referred to their risk-taking attitudes, noting that most often they were influenced by important people in their lives to be courageous.

Dr. Jackson certainly presented evidence that she was a "risk taker." Her risk-taking behavior usually related to decisions she made that impacted the students in her district. At one point she told a story that revealed the extent of her willingness to take risks.

> I'm working now with an inner city. My business administrator said, "Debra, you're not really going to go ahead with this project with the inner city district. You know, we know what people are going to think and say." And I am going ahead with it because, truthfully, students of this community really do need to have other insights and other views and learn to live with others and understand differences. But those are the kinds of decisions that limit the tenure of a superintendent in a particular district.

Dr. Jackson was willing to risk her job to implement a program that she believed served the students of her district.

The women superintendents in the original study reported that strong influences in their lives helped them develop the ability to be risk takers and "can do" type of people. The strong influences they referred to were fathers, mothers, grandfathers, bosses, or mentors. For example, one woman stated:

> I am the oldest of four children and I always have believed in the impact of the father/daughter relationship. My father said you can do or be anything you want, and I mean I set my goals!

Dr. Jackson did not have a story like the one above. In fact, she felt her childhood had contributed to just the opposite self-image for her:

> I had the complete opposite experience. I was in what was then called a large high school, an accelerated program. And if anything, in that group of twenty kids, I always felt like the bottom of the barrel, as someone who couldn't do. Those kids were absolutely brilliant. I didn't know where I fit in. In fact, I know my parents expected me to have a job when I graduated, and at sixteen I was expected to be able to deal with that. But when you graduated in New York state from this accelerated track, you didn't have any skills.

I pressed Dr. Jackson to recall what created her "can do" attitude, her willingness to take risks, even though her background did not create it. She replied:

> *I think of it as more of a personality trait than something that I've picked*
> *up along the way. I still don't like being told that I can't do something. . . .*
> *Some of it was just a reaction to circumstances.*

I came to understand that Dr. Jackson felt that she learned to be independent because of the circumstances of her childhood. She did not like anyone to tell her that she could not do something. Her independent and determined nature created her willingness to take risks, to believe that she could do whatever she wanted, even when other people told her she could not. Dr. Jackson was influenced by circumstances rather than by particular people. I learned that she was a product of adversity rather than support.

Clearly, Dr. Jackson was a risk taker, someone able to face adversity and impossible odds. The women in the original study also were able to face adversity and impossible odds, one of which was the fact that they were women. Being a woman was "always an issue." As one woman from the original study stated:

> You're not a male. That's never going to happen. You're always
> going to be a female in that group. It's never not [original emphasis]
> an issue. You're always a female in a group of males and you're never
> neuter—that just doesn't happen either.

At times, this fact created frustration and added more difficulty to the women's already challenging lives. Planning ways to retreat and regain strength, then, was critical for women in the position. Hill and Ragland's (1995) research on women in educational leadership positions showed that these individuals take time for stress-relieving activities. The women in the original study planned ways to retreat into the cracks and crevices of their busy lives, because they recognized that their own private selves must remain extremely private. When sharing this part of their practice, the women appeared to be slightly uncomfortable. It was my sense that this aspect of their lives was almost too private to share. They were so accustomed to measuring their worth by their task-oriented behavior that they seemed reluctant to admit that life held more than focused work. Once they began sharing the information, however, it was clear that this private space was extremely necessary for their own well-being, and, in fact, for their continued excellent performance in their positions.

Dr. Jackson also talked about the way she found time for herself—and the necessity for that private time. She talked about three different types of "retreat time." First, she spoke of private time with her family:

> *There's the time for getting away with your family. Part of that kind of*
> *time is to make sure everybody is away from things they normally do so*
> *that we really have some time together.*

Next, she talked about the type of private, reflective time she needs to "come back stronger" on the job:

> The district just sent me to Harvard for two weeks, and that was really time to reflect and think. There's a need for finding time to really think about what we do and reflect about it, write about it [undirected, on your own time]. There's a need to spend time reading what's current, thinking about what's current and almost getting my whole belief system and value system sort of regenerated.

Finally, she talked about the type of " solo retreat time" that she needed to stay physically, emotionally, and spiritually healthy:

> I absolutely need a physical type of down time. I think it's truly just knowing that we come back stronger. We think clearer when we take care of our bodies as well as our minds. And for me it has to be a solo activity for it to work.

As I said, this strategy has two parts. My cross-data analysis of the women in the original study led me to conclude that when the two parts work together, women in the superintendency are successful.

Researcher/practitioner dialogue. While Dr. Jackson had no mentor, she felt strongly that she was a risk taker. She affirmed that although the cause of risk-taking behavior is not always the same, the behavior is very important for all superintendents. She also believed that for women to be superintendents at all was a risk and required courage. And, as indicated, she spoke strongly about the need for retreats of all types.

Strategy 7: Share Power: Share Credit

This strategy reflects how the women in the original study specifically defined and used power (see Brunner, chapter 4, in this book for a fuller discussion of power theory). In order to understand how they viewed power, I turned to some of the literature on the subject. Nancy Hartsock (1987) began her discussion of power by associating it with gender. She asserted that power defined by white male intellectuals is dominance, strength, force, authority, and violence. Cantor and Bernay (1992) concluded that unconscious practices and social norms support the perception that power is masculine. This is a standard line of thought.

The women in my original study, however, did not practice or define power as dominance, authority, or power over others. Instead, they used a collaborative, inclusive, consensus-building model of power. They worked in concert with others rather than in authority or dominance over others. This collaborative action was comfortable for them, because they did not view themselves as being powerful in the traditional sense. In turn, this nontraditional view and use of power was a strategy for success because it met gender-related expectations—that women are not to be dominant or in charge—while at the same time meeting role-related expectations—they got the job done.

Several of the women had difficulty talking about power because their views of power were so different from the dominant definition. One woman flatly stated, "Actually, I never think of the superintendency in the sense of power. . . ." I believe the following statement regarding power reveals a transformed sense of the word, and was representative of the women in the original study:

> In a position of power you really are in a position of servant leadership. Your leadership should be to help other people accomplish goals and objectives in the mission, in the vision of an organization or a school system, or whatever. I mean that's really what it is to me. Power means assisting other people to accomplish their goals, and that means a lot of collaboration and linking and linkage and bringing people together. That's what power means to me.

This compares with the definition shared by Dr. Jackson, who defined power as follows:

> I define power as the ability to empower others. . . . Power for me is getting others to understand that they can really make a difference, and working that through so that there's a sharing of what we do.

Dr. Jackson defined power as shared, as people working together to accomplish things. She believed that part of her work was to help others understand how important they were in accomplishing what everyone wants to get done. I asked Dr. Jackson to go further with her discussion of power and to tell me how she worked with others. ˙

> I also am very willing to hear what other people have to say. So my decisions are usually based on what's best for students and from the perspective of listening to others and gathering as much information about others' standpoints as I possibly can.

In the statement above, Dr. Jackson identified her view of collaboration—working with others. When I mentioned to Dr. Jackson that I heard her talking about collaboration, she wanted to make clear her specific use of the term. She began with the comment:

> I start having discussions in many different ways to talk to people who might see things very differently than I. And then from that I, well, more than likely build in a process. It's probably not in my nature to build any process, but I do. And sort of get some "buy in" along the way from some-

> one that usually has a direction when I'm moving forth. But I'm also someone who has—from meeting with people and hearing other pieces—changed in some ways. I try to learn as much as I can in that process.

Dr. Jackson was working to let me know that how I defined collaboration was important to her. She viewed herself as being collaborative, but did not want me to get the idea that she delegated decisions to committees or was not involved in the process herself. As she put it:

> I'm definitely collaborative. What I was trying to communicate is that there's a difference between being a collaborative leader—I am definitely not an authoritarian leader. No one would say that about me. But on the other hand, I don't abdicate the decision process. I don't just say here is this group and whatever you come up with is fine. I really see it as my role to give every bit of information to a collaborative group. And if it means we all have that information among us that's fine, but if we don't, it means getting out there and getting that information to that group. But to me there's a leadership piece there. I see it as a responsibility. Now if someone else in that group can do that, that's fine. But probably just my involvement is important.

At that point in the interview, I began to understand that Dr. Jackson did not want me to view her as someone who turned decisions over to a group. I responded, "Maybe this will be helpful, maybe it won't be. But the difference I see between collaboration and what you're talking about—just turning the decision over to a group—that to me is delegation." Dr. Jackson replied, "Yes, okay. And that's not what I do at all." She said that although there were times when she was a delegator, she was not a delegator when it came to collaborative decision making. She continued by stating her agreement with my assessment, that delegation to a committee was not collaboration. She said:

> That's probably the difference, yes. I think I need to be an active contributor to a group. So collaboration for me is to bring what I have to bring and help other people bring what they have to bring.

At that point, I asked her if others viewed her as a collaborative leader. She replied:

> Oh yes. If you ask people—I can say that very distinctly because we just had a visitor here and that's exactly how I was described. I was described as someone who looks at bringing together others ideas and pulling together a direction and helping people implement what it is they're trying to do.

This notion of collaboration parallels the definition of power as shared. Dr. Jackson did not delegate her individually held power to a group so that they could make a decision. She viewed the people in the group as being powerful in their own right. But she was an active part of the group and the collaborative process. She shared power with those in the group, and those in the group shared power with her. They made decisions together. This distinction in the definition of collaboration is important. Dr. Jackson was not powerless, but she did not hold all of the power—evidence that her definition of power is a part of her practice.

In all of the narratives in the original study, the women separated themselves from the definition of power as control, authority, or dominance over others. I came to understand that perceiving the self as separate from the dominant culture's notion of power as "power over" seemed to be necessary for a woman to be truly collaborative, thus successful. Genuine collaboration occurs when all participants are considered equals. This attitude and practice was reflected in all of the narratives of the women superintendents.

Researcher/practitioner dialogue. Dr. Jackson believed that this strategy was accurate and important. She reflected on a dilemma that she faced with a board of education member who sometimes thinks that she is too strong in her leadership style and too weak at other times. She did not alter my interpretations in any way. Her discussion of collaboration added to my understanding of the nuances related to its definition.

CONCLUSION

The purpose of this chapter is to examine the usefulness of a framework of collective solutions for women superintendents—strategies for success. This examination was important because it not only altered the framework, but also added additional understanding to the original interpretations. After the "back talk" from Dr. Jackson, the strategies were altered to read as follows (changes are in italics):

1. Women superintendents need to learn to balance role-related expectations with gender-related ones. *There are numerous approaches to balancing these two.*
2. Women superintendents need to keep their agendas simple in order to focus on their primary purpose: the care of children, including strict attention to their academic achievement. (no change)
3. *Women superintendents need to develop the ability to remain "feminine" in the ways they communicate and at the same time be heard in a masculinized culture.*
4. *Women superintendents need to disregard the old myth that they must "act like a man" while in a male role. It does not work.*
5. Women superintendents need to remove or let go of anything that blocks their success. (no change)

6. Women superintendents need to remain fearless, courageous, risk takers, and "can do" people. At the same time, they need to have a plan for retreat when faced with the impossible. (no change)

7. Women superintendents need to share power and credit. (no change)

In conclusion, these altered strategies could begin the construction of collective solutions. Sadly, some of the strategies may reify current gender bias (see Strategies 1, 3, and 5). These strategies tend to insist that women continue to behave in the limited ways dictated by the dominant masculine culture. Other strategies, however, are promising transformations of the role of superintendent. All, at a practical level, appear to be important for women who are succeeding as superintendents. Similar findings are contained in the literature on women in educational administration (see Adler, Laney, and Packer 1993; Edson 1988; Schmuck 1975; and Shakeshaft 1989), but the findings in this case have been reexamined by someone in the field for their potential usefulness as collective solutions to the gendered problems facing women in the position.

Contrary to common sense, the positional power of the superintendent does not eliminate the need for gendered strategies for successful women in the position. This fact makes collective solutions for women especially important, as the negative effects of gender bias appear to be greater rather than lesser for women who occupy the most powerful administrative office in public schools.

NOTES

1. Small portions of the text in this section are taken verbatim from an earlier manuscript—the write-up of the original study (see Brunner 1997).

2. Some feminists have been critical of the views of women and caring held by Gilligan (1982) and Noddings (1984, 1992). These feminists are critical of any essentialized notion of women (Weiler cited in Ladson-Billings 1995) and suggest that no empirical evidence exists to support the notion that women care in ways different from men or that any such caring informs their scholarship and work (Ladson-Billings 1995, 473).

REFERENCES

Adler, S., J. Laney, and M. Packer. 1993. *Managing women: Feminism and power in educational management.* Philadelphia: Open University Press.

Beck, L. 1994. *Reclaiming educational administration as a caring profession.* New York: Teachers College Press.

Bolinger, D. 1980. *Language—The loaded weapon: The use and abuse of language today.* New York: Longman.

Brunner, C. C. 1995. By power defined: Women in the superintendency. *Educational Considerations* 22 (2): 21–26.

———. 1996. Searching the silent smiles of women administrators: Did you say something? Paper presented at the annual meeting of the American Educational Research Association, New York.

———. 1997. Women superintendents: Strategies for success. Paper presented at the annual meeting of the American Association of School Administrators, Orlando.

Cantor, D. W., and T. Bernay. 1992. *Women in power: The secrets of leadership*. New York: Houghton Mifflin Company.

Chase, S. 1995. *Ambiguous empowerment: The work narratives of women school superintendents*. Amherst: University of Massachusetts Press.

Edson, E. D. 1988. *Pushing the limits: The female administrative aspirant*. Albany, N.Y.: State University of New York Press.

Gilligan, C. 1982. *In a different voice: Psychological theory and women's development*. Cambridge: Harvard University Press.

Guba, E., and Y. Lincoln. 1981. *Effective evaluation*. San Francisco: Jossey-Bass.

Hartsock, N. 1987. Foucault on power: A theory for women. In L. Nicholson (ed.), *Feminism/postmodernism*. London: Routledge Press.

Hill, M. S., and J. C. Ragland. 1995. *Women as educational leaders: Opening windows, pushing ceilings*. Thousand Oaks, Calif.: Corwin Press, Inc.

Ladson-Billings, G. 1995. Toward a theory of culturally relevant pedagogy. *American Educational Research Journal* 32 (3): 465-91.

Lather, P. 1991. *Getting smart: Feminist research and pedagogy with/in the postmodern*. New York and London: Routledge.

Noddings, N. 1984. *Caring: A feminine approach to ethics and moral education*. Los Angeles: University of California Press.

———. 1992. *The challenge to care in schools: An alternative approach to education*. New York: Teachers College Press.

Patton, M. Q. 1980. *Qualitative evaluation methods*. Beverly Hills: Sage Publications.

Purpel, D. E. 1989. *The moral and spiritual crisis in education: A curriculum for justice and compassion in education*. New York: Bergin & Garvey.

Reardon, K. K. 1995. *They don't get it do they? Communication in the workplace—closing the gap between women and men*. New York: Little, Brown, and Company.

Schmuck, P. 1975. *Sex differentiation in public school administration*. Arlington, Va.: American Association of School Administrators.

Shakeshaft, C. 1989. *Women in educational administration*. Newbury Park, Calif.: Sage Publications.

Tannen, D. 1986. *That's not what I meant! How conversational style makes or breaks relationships*. New York: Ballentine Books.

———. 1990. *You just don't understand: Women and men in conversation*. New York: Ballantine Books.

———. 1994a. *Gender and discourse*. New York and Oxford: Oxford University Press.

———. 1994b. *Talking from 9 to 5*. New York: William Morrow and Company.

Wolfe, N. 1994. *Fire with fire: The new female power and how to use it*. New York: Fawcett Columbine.

CHAPTER TWELVE

A Feminist Poststructuralist Account of Collaboration

A Model for the Superintendency

MARGARET GROGAN

What is it like to be a woman and superintendent of a K–12 public school system? This chapter develops ideas gained in ongoing research I have been conducting with current women superintendents and another researcher. My work has been directed by a strong wish to make a theoretical approach to the superintendency accessible to practicing superintendents. As a researcher, I read transcripts of interviews, hear stories, listen to comments, and make sense of these using an analytical framework that helps *me* understand better what is going on in the worlds of these superintendents. But I wonder how much help the theory is to superintendents. To me, one of a researcher's challenges is to analyze data using a theoretical framework in such a way that practitioners understand better what is happening to them. In order to meet that challenge, researcher Cryss Brunner and I designed a study that would ensure discussion and dialogue between participants and researchers (see Brunner's conclusions in chapter 11 and Jackson's in chapter 13 in this book).

DESIGN AND METHODOLOGY

In 1996, Brunner twice interviewed superintendent Debra Jackson. The interviews were taped and transcribed and read by both researchers. After an initial analysis of the data, we arranged an opportunity for "back-talk" and public discussion of our interpretations of the data at the 1996 Annual Meeting of the University Council of Educational Administrators. Jackson, Brunner, and Grogan were joined by a room full of conference attendees in a session chaired by Charol Shakeshaft (*Women in Educational Administration*, 1989). The session was taped and transcribed and contributes data to this research. An additional Brunner interview of superintendent Carol Lewis (a pseudonym), taped and transcribed, completes the data set. What follows is my analysis of the whole data set, using a feminist poststructuralist framework. As researchers engaged in the same project, Cryss Brunner and I read each other's interpretations but, since we took different theoretical approaches, our conclusions are not exactly the same. We believe this to be a strength of the study: our analyses offer complementary views of the same data.

We designed the study to try to find out what it is like to be a woman superintendent. The interviews probed issues such as the definition of power, the influence of gender, the connotations of authoritarian versus collaborative leadership, the career path to the superintendency, and moral and ethical dimensions of leadership. The questions encouraged anecdotal responses from the participants and focused on their own lived experiences. What emerges most clearly from the data is a picture of contemporary women superintendents. How much of the discourse in which they are immersed is shaped by their gender and how much by the superintendency itself remains unclear. Further research is necessary to explore the issue. However, many insights into a woman's experience of the superintendency are gained from a feminist poststructural analysis of the data.

In this chapter, I first outline the basic assumptions underlying the theoretical framework. I discuss briefly what feminist poststructuralism is and how it provides the kinds of insights it does. Second, I describe the model of the superintendency that emerges from the themes recurring in the data. I then illustrate the themes with quotations and discuss them in light of feminist poststructuralism, which helps us understand *why* this model is adopted by the women superintendents in the study. I conclude with some thoughts on how the theory informs my understanding of what it is like to be a woman superintendent.

A FEMINIST POSTSTRUCTURAL FRAMEWORK

Feminist poststructuralism blends a commitment to social change with a sense of shifting perspectives. This framework is based on the feminist view that women and others similarly situated on the fringes of power have not been served as well as the middle- and upper-class white male, who has traditionally wielded the most power. Feminism motivates us to seek ways to disrupt the social structures that have reproduced the patterns of domination and subordination in our everyday lives. What shapes the way we live our everyday lives? The tools of deconstruction, made available by Derrida (in Sarup 1988) and Foucault's (in Gordon 1980) insights into power, knowledge, and the effects of one's life situation, have provided us with the concept of discourse. Discourse means the collective knowledge of a social institution that is handed on to us by those who have the power to shape the practices and beliefs that form a particular institution. We learn it through the language that is used to describe how we should think and what we should be like as participants in social situations. Kress (in Davies 1994) defines discourse as "a systematically organized set of statements which give expression to the meanings and values of an institution" (p. 17). There are many discourses in which we could be immersed. As mothers, we are formed by one discourse; as educational administrators, we are formed by another. The family provides us with yet another discourse, just as law, religion, and commerce do. While there are many concepts discourses can have in common with each other, each has its own set of rules, body of knowledge, and beliefs and values.

Poststructuralism reveals that individuals are *positioned* in discourses. Our positions in a discourse are determined by our race, class, gender, sexuality, and abilities or disabilities. Positions are dominant or subordinate. The understanding that we are not all equally well positioned in a discourse is important for us to make sense of what otherwise seems to be simply personal failure. If women still make up the majority of the teaching force from which administrators are drawn, and if women are becoming the majority in university preparation programs (Shakeshaft 1989), why else are administrative positions not equitably distributed among men and women? For various reasons, the discourse has served men better than women up until now. The most helpful realization is that *all* who have been immersed in the discourse have accepted the discourse as being legitimate and good, men and women alike. What points to this most clearly are the concepts of "barriers to success" for women or "the glass ceiling" that women are supposed to reach on their way up the administrative ladder. To look at what is happening in this way, to see obstacles in the path up the ladder, is to approve of the path.

Feminist poststructuralism allows us first to see the path more clearly and second to question it. Feminist poststructuralism offers a means by which we can examine the various discourses within which we are positioned and the relative positions we occupy. Levine (in Davies 1993) compares it to a process that makes material like glass opaque, so that we can no longer see *through* it but must look *at* it. Words and other signs are often thought of as having no substance themselves but are simply conveyors of meaning. To question this notion, we must investigate language and other signifiers in depth. Who is best served by what is approved of in a discourse? By becoming critically aware of language and other signifiers, we can discover the taken-for-granted assumptions that have grounded us in each of the discourses within which we find ourselves. This is particularly helpful because such assumptions are hidden. For instance, although it is quite common to hear the term *woman superintendent*, it is not at all common to hear of a *man superintendent*. The idea that superintendent is synonymous with man has emerged in the discourse of educational administration, due to the over-

whelming number of men who have held the job and the association of traditional male leadership attributes with the role.

A feminist poststructuralist approach adds to what is already known and
understood in the social sciences. There are many theories in the social sciences:
some explain what is going on in the social world, some prescribe better courses
of action to follow, and others simply describe the world. Feminist poststructuralism can be used both to explain and to change current practices. This theory
expands views offered by other theories and provides different insights into what
is happening. Cautioned by Lyotard's (1979) exposure of the "grand narrative," I
do not argue that feminist poststructuralism provides the final word. Rather, the
theory suggests that we avoid all efforts to discover the final word. Instead, its usefulness is in its provision of a temporary handle on what is going on so that we
can bring about changes to the current way of doing things. If changes were to
occur, for example in how to access high level positions in educational administration, then other things might be going on, and we would have to try to find
out what they were. For instance, it is possible to imagine that the job of superintendent might become devalued in terms of power, or scope of responsibilities,
thus allowing it to turn into a "lesser" position in educational administration—one
that is more associated with women. If that were to occur, we might be turning
our attention to how and why the position itself had changed. I imagine no end
to the process of trying to understand more fully what is going on in a discourse.

However, I anticipate that the insights I offer from this perspective will provide opportunities for change. The power of seeing how a discourse shapes a person is the power to alter that mold. As a researcher, I cannot alter it, but the one
who is being shaped can. Davies (1994) states that "power comes from being
able to see the effects of discourses upon those who are constituted through
them" (p. 26). Once individuals have understood how words, images, and symbols are used to position them in any given discourse, they can negotiate that discourse in a much more effective manner. This is especially relevant in a discourse
such as educational administration. If men currently hold over 90 percent of the
superintendencies in the United States (Blount 1993; Glass 1992; Montenegro
1993), it is important that women who wish to be successful as superintendents
understand how the discourse works so that they can shape their responses to
their advantage. It is an invitation to women to be smart, not to imitate what has
worked best for men in the past.

A CLOSE LOOK AT THE DATA

At the outset, the theoretical perspective I have chosen to use forces me to take
notice of the kind of questions we asked superintendents Jackson and Lewis. Feminist poststructuralism acknowledges researcher influence in framing interview

questions (Lather 1992). Most important is the knowledge of the field of educational administration and the superintendency that we bring to the study. Already well informed of current research on the topic and informed by previous studies of our own (Brunner 1995, 1996, 1997a, 1997b, 1998; Grogan and Henry 1995; Grogan 1996; Grogan and Smith 1996), we contributed to the superintendents' answers inasmuch as the interviewer directed the discussion and responded to their comments in particular ways. In the "back talk" session, although the discussion ranged quite freely among the three presenters, the chair, and all of the attendees, the researchers again provided the context for the discussion by choosing to focus on particular quotations from Dr. Jackson's interviews.

However, analysis of the data identifies three dominant themes that recur in all of the discussions: (1) concepts of power; (2) beliefs about decision making; and (3) notions of leadership. These themes are intertwined and often merge with one another. But what becomes clear upon close inspection is how collaboration connects all three. In other words, for the superintendents in the study, power, decision making, and leadership all depend on collaboration. Dr. Jackson and Dr. Lewis define those concepts in terms of collaborative practices. It is important to note that they do not claim that all of their decisions are collaborative ones. They describe collaboration as their preferred mode of operation, and they seek collaboration on as many issues as possible.

This is the model that emerges from this study (see Fig. 12.1). Influenced by Capper (1993), I have called it a model of *Empowering Leadership* to characterize it as representing the kind of leadership that is the outcome of a respect for collaboration. In the model, decision making flows from the superintendent's collaboration with other members of the community, which leads to empowerment of others rather than to the concentration of power in the hands of the superintendent. Collaboration is identified with the practices of sharing information, coalition building, shaping direction, and appreciating diversity of opinions and ideas. This in turn becomes the foundation for leadership. Strong beliefs and resistance to being silenced by the traditional discourse or "voice" strengthen the model.

One of the most valuable contributions feminist poststructuralism can make to our understanding of what it is like to be a woman superintendent is to make the traditional discourse visible. Earlier, I referred to the theory's potential to provide a medium through which words, images and other signifiers could be revealed for close inspection. We need to be able to "see," in a literal sense, which phrases, which concepts, have had the most effect on Dr. Jackson and Dr. Lewis as they live the life of a superintendent. From their responses to the questions, we come to understand how they deal with the expectations others have of them as superintendent, and of those they have for themselves.

A glance at the literature on the superintendency reveals that the position has not been researched much until relatively recently (Crowson 1987; Hord 1993).

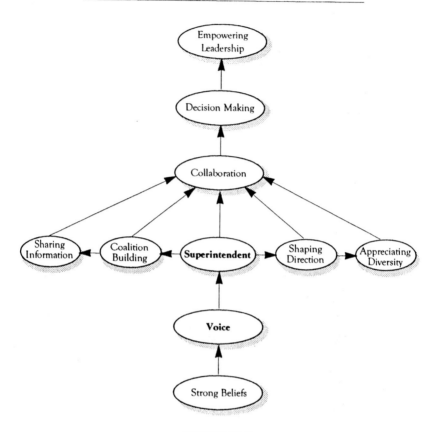

FIGURE 12.1

Thus, the kind of insights we gain by analyzing narratives such as the ones provided here are extremely helpful in building a picture of the lived experiences of a superintendent at the end of the twentieth century. Not only that, but since so few women have been in the position, we also need to hear their stories. If there is to be any chance of a more equitable access to superintendencies in the future, then every attempt must be made to learn what it is like to be a woman superintendent. As the discourse is revealed, more women who aspire to the position will be able to imagine what it is like and to picture themselves in it.

CONCEPTS OF POWER

Asked to define power, Dr. Jackson goes into some detail. As she elaborates, it becomes clear that she wishes to distinguish her use of the word from the way others might use it.

> I define power as the ability to empower others. I define power from a perspective of how you can change thinking and change dialogue. Power is not a word that's regularly in my vocabulary. Power for me is getting others to understand that they can really make a difference and working that through so that there's a sharing of what we do. And there's an understanding of where we are headed. People in power have the power to educate others to a way of thinking.

Jackson states that "power is not a word that's regularly in her vocabulary." One reason that she might not use it is that is has most often been associated with force. A common definition of power is the capacity to make others do what they would otherwise not do. If this is how superintendents have come to understand it through exposure to the discourse of educational administration, then it is not surprising that a woman superintendent wishes to dissociate herself from its traditional connotation. Many women leaders have resisted the male images of domination and aggression. The power-driven male models, found at least in the early literature about the superintendency, have conflicted with the relational dimension of many women's traditional experiences (Belenky et al. 1986; Edson 1988; Glazer 1991; Grogan 1996).

Aside from that, Jackson's comments about power as a form of empowerment are very much in line with recent leadership literature, even if the term *empowerment* is not used (Aburdene and Naisbitt 1992; Brunner 1995; Capper 1993; Dunlap and Schmuck 1995; Hill and Ragland 1995). To empower others is to shift the focus from a top-down model of leadership to a model that is web-like in its structure. Brunner (1995) writes of such approaches to power as those "which stress collaboration, inclusion, and consensus building" (p. 24). Jackson's statement about using power to "get others to understand that they can make a difference" is reminiscent of the feminist desire to flatten the hierarchy of organizations (Ferguson 1984; Mills and Tancred 1992). This is particularly helpful if members of the organization are to become truly empowered in the sense of owning decisions and being accountable for them. I understand it to mean sharing power, not giving it away.

Empowerment in the minds of these superintendents is associated with the kind of guidance and direction that they can give as expert educators who are cognizant of "the big picture." For instance, Jackson states that "people in power have the power to educate others to a way of thinking" and that "power is . . . a way of looking at how things work and how we want them to work." The use of "we" in the latter quote certainly suggests that it is a shared power if "we" means the superintendent and community together. But the superintendent certainly helps shape the direction. Dr. Jackson sees this as a major responsibility. It does not, however, lead to unilateral decision making. When used as she describes it, this kind of power stimulates the community to work together at decision making.

When asked the same question, Dr. Lewis defined power similarly as

> the ability to influence the process that leads to the accomplishment
> of a desired outcome. It does not matter who gets the recognition as
> long as the desired outcome is realized. All of the superintendent's
> victories are achieved through the work of other people. Power is the
> ability to successfully facilitate and direct the work of others.

This reminds us of the context of the superintendency. If the average tenure of a superintendent is 6.47 years (Glass 1992), then a superintendent who wants to achieve some if not all of his or her goals has to garner support quickly and effectively.

In sum, both superintendents describe their power as being able to "direct and facilitate the work of others." On a challenging note, at the back talk session, the question of "power over," meaning the use of force, versus "power to," meaning shared power, provoked a lively discussion. Members of the audience argued, and Dr. Jackson herself acknowledged, that superintendents use positional power differently under different circumstances. The resolution of certain issues such as legal, financial, and student safety is not one over which the superintendent delegates power. Not only that, but superintendents also have the power to determine the context of many conflicts. As Lewis says: "Superintendents have the power and opportunity to predetermine how the battle will initially be framed and defined. This determination can limit the span of the battle." Thus the kind of empowerment that emerges from collaboration is probably best discovered in selected administrative arenas.

BELIEFS ABOUT DECISION MAKING

The second theme centers more precisely on decision making, another concept associated with the superintendency that receives a lot of attention in the current literature (Brandt 1993; Grogan and Smith 1996; Henderson 1993; Konnert and Augenstein 1990; Leithwood 1995; Lilly 1992; Murphy 1993, 1994; Walker 1995). The superintendents were asked how they made decisions. Jackson said,

> I'm not someone who believes you throw decisions out to a committee and they all work with that. I believe it's important for me to have a very strong belief system. My board informs me I have a very strong belief system . . . what happens is that I work with people. They always know where I stand and I also am very willing to hear what other people have to say. So my decisions are usually based on what's best for students and from the perspective of listening to others and gathering as much information about others' standpoints as I possibly can. But in the end, and I've made some very tough decisions as superintendent, it comes down to me every time. . . . I make decisions based on my belief system.

Firmly student centered, Dr. Jackson draws attention to how her decisions are grounded in her beliefs. Dr. Lewis is equally vehement about her beliefs. Lewis said,

> My attempts here are to focus everything on what I believe is our primary purpose—student achievement . . . being a superintendent is more like a mission than anything else for me. I have intentionally devoted my work to children in urban public schools. I believe that people like me are needed in these districts if all children are to succeed. Therefore, I must accept that there may be others who may not be interested in the success of all children and will (fight) me in many creative ways.

In the context of public education in the nineties, this stance can be seen as courageous. Dr. Lewis argues for the success of all children, despite the opposition she encounters from those who battle her in "many creative ways." We would encourage administrators to appreciate multiple points of view, but that also necessitates a deep respect for the issues of diversity. The challenges of celebrating a pluralistic society appear to caution administrators against adopting a particular posture. However, both superintendents seem able to forge strong positions based on their beliefs. Dr. Jackson emphasizes how her own collaborative strategies and values are intertwined. In a second comment, she says,

> I always try to see it from everyone else's (perspectives). I try to see it from a political perspective . . . if we need to make a decision . . . the political piece has to be considered . . . one of the first things I do is look at that political landscape. Second, I would say that within that I probably weigh how important is this in the overall piece. . . . I look at who it will affect and then from there I look at students in terms of what we are really trying to do . . . there's a lot of reflection in place.

Her reference to the value of reflection is informative. It is not the kind of reflection that paralyzes the superintendent, that renders her unable to make a decision. In comparing herself to her predecessor later in the discussion, she makes the point that he "was seen as someone who had difficulty making decisions. [He] would listen to everyone and never bring it to closure." In contrast, Dr. Jackson goes on to state that she is seen by others as "someone who's very decisive, who can make decisions." The way she describes the process of decision making is also instructive. One key to her approach is her political astuteness, a recommended attribute for superintendents (Blumberg 1985; Boyd 1974; Burlingame 1981; Cuban 1976; Johnson 1996). However, unlike the traditional notions of the political dimension of the superintendency, which suggest a certain amount of "wheeling and dealing," Jackson's political sense is geared toward coalition building and mustering support for what the district is trying to accomplish.

Feminist approaches to leadership have encouraged these strategies as being consistent with the relational aspects of many women's administrative styles (Hill and Ragland 1995; Grogan 1996; Shakeshaft 1989; Scherr 1995).

Indeed, both Dr. Lewis and Dr. Jackson connect their approaches to decision making to their attitudes toward leadership. As the aforementioned illustrates, they see themselves as leaders who guide and offer direction, not as leaders who make unilateral decisions. But they also go to some length to lay the groundwork for good decisions. This is consistent with their rejection of power as a tool to enforce their will on the community. As Lewis puts it,

> I work hard to be inclusive in seeking input from others and dele-
> gating decision making to others. What I understand from experi-
> ence is that people accept this style easier from women, and there-
> fore, it generates more commitment and success.

Gilligan's (1982) findings demonstrated that women have been socialized to value their sense of connection to others and to maintain relationships with others. These findings are reflected in the ways in which women deal with the issue of being heard. When the superintendents discussed the question of how they contribute to decision making in mixed peer groups, it became clear that both women experienced being silenced. In the first instance, for Dr. Lewis, it was silencing by exclusion. Lewis said,

> . . . it was a critical issue for the board [of a community service orga-
> nization on which she serves because she is the superintendent] and
> as I sat around the table, I was the only female there that morning,
> I quickly realized that most of the men had already been [telephoned]
> on the issue and had discussed it. Normally, I'm very supportive of
> the person who was chairing this, but, I thought, 'Well, I'll be!' I
> thought, 'I'm out of the loop . . . maybe just because I'm a
> female' . . . you know I could have done nothing. But I decided to
> say right there in front of everybody in as diplomatic a way as I could,
> 'Given that I haven't had an opportunity to be consulted on this
> issue before, I can't really speak to where I think I'll be on it.'

For Dr. Jackson, it was a matter of being ignored. Jackson revealed,

> At an executive meeting of which I am the only female and there's
> maybe ten of us in that group, I will have an idea and talk about it
> and say this is something we need to consider and no one will say
> that's a good idea, bad idea, discuss it with me, or dialogue about it.

Dr. Jackson goes on to say that sometimes her point does get taken up, particularly if a male colleague repeats it. Under such circumstances, she believes that she is not silenced, because her perspective has been appreciated, even if the group "heard the idea through someone else's voice."

At our conference session, there was much discussion of this experience. Why was she ignored? As Jackson points out, she knows the language of the superintendency; she has learned it on the job. My interpretation of her experience is based on understanding that the discourse has been created by the male voice in language that is most often associated with men and delivered in authoritative tones. So it has more to do with how she delivers what she wants to say. She might have been better heard if her speech were more aggressive, for instance. Charol Shakeshaft, a female participant in the session, made an interesting observation on the experience of being silenced. Charol said,

> Although I've studied a long time and even written about women who have this experience happen to them, . . . what interests me in my own life is that it's never happened to me. And I can't figure out if it's because I'm so insensitive that I just don't code it because I'm so focused on what I want people to know. If I want you to know something, I'll just keep on it until you have to give in. . . . But I often leave the group feeling humiliated and ashamed of myself, and not good.

Therefore, from a feminist poststructuralist point of view, it seems clear that what is happening is that women can find themselves immersed in conflicting discourses. The partnering, caregiving discourses that encourage women to maintain relationships by supporting the ideas of others or keeping their ideas to themselves are in direct contrast to ones like the superintendency that reward more outspoken, assertive forms of expression. Women can certainly adopt such behaviors but, for some, it is at the expense of feeling comfortable. That is why Jackson feels content to be heard through others at times, and why Lewis decides to stall the decision making in the experience she related. Women can choose among a number of strategies, including using approaches more traditionally associated with men. The key is to realize that being heard takes some effort, and that the status of superintendent does not carry with it a gender-equal guarantee of success. The more subordinate that one's position is in a discourse, the less likely that one's ideas will be heard. What complicates the issue here is that the position of superintendent is not a subordinate one, unless the female gender renders it so. Women administrators are seen first as women and second as administrators (Grogan 1996).

Another dimension to Dr. Jackson's decision making is her ethical stand. She talks of two or three instances where she was prepared to risk losing substantial support for the sake of hearing all voices. One divisive issue in the community concerning diversity actually pit her against the majority of her board. Jackson argues:

> I really saw it as not letting a minority of people who have this elitist attitude make a decision for this community . . . so I now have five members on the board who are not happy with the fact that I opened it up.

What drives Jackson in these cases is the conviction that the students benefit from including all perspectives. An example she provides is "developing programs and doing work with the inner city." Despite the lack of encouragement from a major sector of the community, Dr. Jackson moves ahead with the plan. Her sense of direction is clear here. Jackson says,

> I am going ahead with it because, truthfully, students of this community really do need to have other insights and other views, learn to live with others and understand differences. So we're moving ahead with that.

The superintendent is fully aware of the potential cost to her of taking this position. She admits that "those are the kind of decisions that limit the tenure of a superintendent in a particular district." But it is a matter of opening up the decision-making process. Instead of simply making the decision herself ("I don't have the power control, and I don't want the power control to make the decision"), she strives to provide all of the possible information so that an informed decision can be made. Once again, it comes down to a strong belief system. Jackson sums up:

> To me I had to do as much as I could to open that process up. To me there was no choice. Part of my belief system . . . this was a matter of doing what I felt was absolutely important to do.

NOTIONS OF LEADERSHIP

The following discussion of leadership was prompted by a question asking the superintendents whether they considered themselves collaborative leaders or authoritarian ones. Both see themselves as being highly collaborative leaders. Dr. Lewis talks about how she developed her collaborative strategies. Lewis says,

> I needed a way to work with people to get a job done that (required) expertise that I didn't have, and I needed to work with them in such a way that we could all get the job done. Part of being collaborative from my perspective is recognizing and respecting the strengths of other people.

To get the job done, Lewis says,

> I make sure that everyone understands the big picture, how the "thing" fits into the strategic plan, how it supports our stated beliefs about children—and then delegate the work with ample support, to the person whom I feel has the highest potential for getting the job done.

Jackson says,

> I'm definitely collaborative. . . . I'm definitely not an authoritarian leader. No one would say that about me. But on the other hand, I

> don't abdicate the decision process. I don't just say here is this group
> and whatever you come up with is fine. I really see it as my role to
> give every bit of information to a collaborative group. [I see my role
> as] getting out there and getting that information to that group.
> There's a leadership piece there. I see it as a responsibility. Now if
> someone else in that group can do that, that's fine.

At the outset, Dr. Jackson explains that she does not "abdicate the decision process." She wants to distinguish between abdicating responsibility for the decision
and initiating a process to gather information. As a leader, she directs the process. Jackson elaborates,

> I think that you look for leadership in a group, in many ways and it's
> not always me. But I think I need to be an active contributor to a
> group. So collaboration for me is to bring what I have to bring and
> help other people bring what they have to bring . . . they know from
> working with me and from that trust piece that I expect them all to
> contribute their thoughts and ideas.

Again, this is consistent with both superintendents' beliefs on empowerment,
which undergird many of these remarks. As the person with the big picture of
the district, they see themselves as catalysts, as initiators who set things in motion
but who expect others to pull their weight. The collaborative model that Jackson
describes allows her to guide the district, secure in the knowledge that she leads
from a position of strength, stemming from her openness. Her ideas are aired in
discussion and shaped accordingly. Jackson says,

> I'm not someone who just picks up and goes to a committee model.
> I start having discussions in many different ways to talk to people
> who might see things very differently than I. And then from that I
> more than likely build in a process. And sort of get some buy-in
> along the way from someone that usually has a direction when I'm
> moving forth. But I'm also someone who has, from meeting with
> people and hearing other pieces, changed. I try to learn as much as
> I can in that process.

Her political skills, already mentioned, prompt her to "get some buy-in along the
way," but she does not force an issue. Again we hear echoes of the use of coalition building as a political maneuver to remain on course and to accomplish the
district's goals. The attention both superintendents pay to hearing opinions that
differ from theirs also reflects the sensitivity they have developed to the inclusion
of multiple perspectives. From a feminist poststructural view, this is an example
of an appreciation of diversity of opinions and ideas. A more traditional superintendent often surrounds himself or herself with others who share their con-
victions. Not necessarily a deliberate practice, it more than likely results from the

power of the discourse, which in the past at least was dominated by the view that a superintendent's capacity to lead depended on the extent to which he or she could maintain control. This often required the hiring of individuals who shared the same beliefs and ideas the superintendent had.

In contrast, true collaboration includes the possibility of dissensus. And if a superintendent's ideas can change as a result of deliberately exposing herself or himself to dissensus, it is a very different approach to conflict from those advised in the past. For instance, many of the most influential voices on the superintendency warned of the tough skins and ruthless determination to be developed by successful candidates for the position (Blumberg 1985; Boyd 1974; Burlingame 1981; Cuban 1976). But it was a *forceful* stand that they were encouraging superintendents to take, one that supposedly guaranteed the success of the superintendent's ideas. Jackson's and Lewis's openness to conflict and discord reflects a wish to hear all voices, not to stifle any. Indeed, the desire to encourage debate and dissensus (Capper 1993) is perhaps at the heart of a feminist poststructural approach to leadership. This is precisely the opposite of the urge to find consensus at all costs, an administrative skill that often is advocated by traditionalists who have not experienced the silencing effect of the process.

It is interesting to note how vehemently Jackson rejects the idea of an authoritarian approach to leadership. This can be explained, on the one hand, by the evolution of transformational leadership (Bass 1985; Bennis and Nanus 1985; Burns 1978; Leithwood and Jantzi 1990; Sergiovanni 1991). The literature on leadership, in general, has abandoned any approach that is blatantly top down. On the other hand, "authoritarian" is closely associated with the male images of leadership, mentioned earlier as those discarded by many women administrators. Thus Jackson is revealing both influences—of the current discourse surrounding the superintendency, and of gender. She says she was recently described as being

> someone who looks at bringing together others ideas and pulling together a direction and helping people implement what it is they're trying to do. I am viewed as a collaborative leader. Someone who is always willing to listen. Someone who is very creative and is willing to take other's ideas and help them form the process. What I think is a collaborative leader.

Therefore, it is clear that Dr. Jackson's notion of leadership is to work through others. Her image of "pulling together a direction and helping people implement what it is they're trying to do" in the aforementioned quote expresses it for me. This view is similar to Dr. Lewis's. She describes her part in maintaining the kind of collaborative leadership that "recognize(s) and respect(s) the strengths of other people." It is what I have called "empowering leadership." Lewis says,

One of the things that I think happened is that the people who worked in my division saw me as protecting them . . . when the person came to beat up on somebody they had to come through me first. And normally they wouldn't get through. That allowed everybody else to do their stuff. You know, to work and flourish.

This means that these superintendents advocate a flattened model of governance, one that is consistent with the feminist poststructural endeavor to dismantle the hierarchical structures of educational administration. The alternative to the bureaucratic approach is to acknowledge that leadership is a capacity-building enterprise that promotes growth throughout the organization, similar to Burns (1978) notion of transformational leadership. It is not, as both superintendents explain clearly, an abdication of responsibility. Nor is it an encouragement of "swaying in the wind," an image of an organization without a mission or a clear set of objectives. Dr. Lewis explains succinctly that the fundamental measure of whether the district is headed in the right direction is "that I can demonstrate to my community that children are learning more."

CONCLUSIONS SUGGESTED BY THE THEORETICAL FRAMEWORK

In summary, the picture that emerges in these interviews is one of top-level professional educators who care deeply about providing the best education possible for the students in their charges. Dr. Lewis and Dr. Jackson help us understand how they must adapt the administrative and political strategies of coalition building, garnering support, and managing conflict so that they are comfortable as women as well as superintendents. While there appear to be some contradictions in their lives as a result of having to balance the demands made on them as women and as superintendents, they are grounded firmly in their own beliefs. Where I sense they have the most difficulty is in reconciling their wish to empower others with their responsibility for maintaining direction in the district. Although they strive not to impose their direction on others, they nevertheless prepare the groundwork thoroughly for the kinds of decisions with which they are happiest.

Most important, the two women have been shaped by the superintendency. Again, despite their arguments to the contrary, they have power, even if they decide to give it away. Indeed, empowerment results from one "in power" sharing power. The superintendency is a position of power that contrasts with the kinds of subordinate positions women have traditionally held in the education profession. As teachers, and even as middle-manager principals, many women's voices have been silenced when their ideas have conflicted with the dominant ones. Dr. Jackson knows that she is not voiceless. Jackson says,

Keep in mind in a superintendency you're a voice in your community. . . . You're not silenced. . . . If I have something that I want brought forth to the board, I generally know [how to do it].

As exemplars for future superintendents to follow, then, Dr. Jackson and Dr. Lewis show how they can both empower others to make decisions and to lead others. Often it is in the direction that they have hammered out together with their constituents, but they use their own good judgment to prepare the way. In other words, they have learned enough from the traditional discourse of educational administration to be able to achieve what is expected of them as a superintendent of schools. And at the same time, they achieve it in a fashion that does not threaten their sense of who they are. While both women expressed certain frustrations with being women in the superintendency, both argued that the combination was a good one for their districts.

REFERENCES

Aburdene, P., and J. Naisbitt. 1992. *Megatrends for women*. New York: Villard.

Bass, B. 1985. *Leadership and performance beyond expectations*. New York: The Free Press.

Belenky, M., B. Clinchy, N. Goldberger, and J. Tarule. 1986. *Women's ways of knowing: The development of self, voice, and mind*. New York: Basic Books Inc.

Bennis, W., and B. Nanus. 1985. *Leaders: Strategies for taking charge*. New York: Harper and Row.

Blount, J. 1993. *The genderization of the superintendency: A statistical portrait*. Paper presented at the annual meeting of the American Educational Research Association, Atlanta, Ga.

Blumberg, A. 1985. *The school superintendent: Living with conflict*. New York: Teachers College Press.

Boyd, W. 1974. The school superintendent: Educational statesman or political strategist? *Administrator's Notebook* 22: 9.

Brandt, R. 1993. On restructuring roles and relationships: A conversation with Phil Schlechty. *Educational Leadership* 51 (2): 8-11.

Brunner, C. C. 1995. By power defined: Women in the superintendency. *Educational Considerations* 22 (20): 21-26.

———. 1996. Searching the silent smiles of women administrators: Did you say something? Paper presented at the American Educational Research Association, New York.

———. 1997a. Exercising power. *The School Administrator* 6 (54): 6-10.

———. 1997b. Working through the 'riddle of the heart': Perspectives of women superintendents. *Journal of School Leadership* 7 (1): 138-64.

———. 1998. Can power support an "ethic of care?" An examination of the professional practices of women superintendents. *Journal for a Just and Caring Education* 4 (2): 142-75.

Burlingame, M. 1981. Superintendent power retention. In S. Bacharach (ed.), *Organizational behavior in schools and school districts*. New York: Praeger Publishers.

Burns, J. 1978. *Leadership*. New York: Harper and Row.

Capper, C. April, 1993. "Empowering" leadership: Similarities and contradictions in critical, poststructural, and feminist/"otherist" perspectives. Paper presented at the annual meeting of the American Educational Research Association, Atlanta, Ga.

Crowson, R. 1987. The local school district superintendency: A puzzling administrative role. *Educational Administration Quarterly* 23 (3): 49–69.

Cuban, L. 1976. *Urban school chiefs under fire*. Chicago: The University of Chicago Press.

Davies, B. 1993. *Shards of glass: Children reading and writing beyond gendered identities*. Sydney: Allen & Unwin.

———. 1994. *Poststructuralist theory and classroom practice*. Geelong, Vic.: Deakin University.

Dunlap, D., and P. Schmuck (eds.). 1995. *Women leading in education*. Albany, N.Y.: State University of New York Press.

Edson, S. 1988. *Pushing the limits: The female administrative aspirant*. Albany, N.Y.: State University of New York Press.

Ferguson, K. E. 1984. *The feminist case against bureaucracy*. Philadelphia: Temple University Press.

Gilligan, C. 1982. *In a different voice* (new ed.). Cambridge: Harvard University Press.

Glass, T. 1992. *The 1992 study of the American school superintendency*. Arlington, Va.: American Association of School Administrators.

Glazer, J. S. 1991. Feminism and professionalism in teaching and educational administration. *Educational Administration Quarterly* 27: 321–42.

Gordon, C. 1980. *Power/Knowledge: Selected interviews and other writings 1972–1977 by Michel Foucault*. New York: Pantheon.

Grogan, M. 1996. *Voices of women aspiring to the superintendency*. Albany, N.Y.: State University of New York Press.

Grogan, M., and M. Henry. 1995. Women candidates for the superintendency: Board perspectives. In B. Irby and G. Brown (eds.), *Women as school executives: Voices and visions*. Huntsville, Tex.: Texas Council of Women School Executives.

Grogan, M., and F. Smith. 1996. Exploring the perceptions of superintendents: Moral choices or procedural alternatives. Paper presented at the annual meeting of the American Educational Research Association, New York.

Henderson, J. 1993. A climate for change. *The Executive Educator* 15 (9): 30–31.

Hill, M., and J. Ragland. 1995. *Women as educational leaders*. Thousand Oaks, Calif.: Corwin Press.

Hord, S. 1993. Smoke, mirrors, or reality: Another instructional leader. In D. Carter, T. Glass, and S. Hord (eds.), *Selecting, preparing, and developing the school district superintendent*. Washington, D.C.: Falmer Press.

Johnson, S. 1996. *Leading to change: The challenge of the new superintendency*. San Francisco: Jossey-Bass Publishers.

Konnert, M. W., and J. J. Augenstein. 1990. *The superintendency in the nineties: What superintendents and board members need to know.* Lancaster, Pa.: Technomic Publishing Co.

Lather, P. 1992. Critical frames in educational research: Feminist and poststructural perspectives. *Theory into Practice* 31 (2): 87–99.

Leithwood, K. 1995. Toward a more comprehensive appreciation of effective school district leadership. In K. Leithwood (ed.), *Effective school district leadership.* Albany, N.Y.: State University of New York Press.

Leithwood, K., and D. Jantzi. 1990. Transformational leadership: How principals can help reform school cultures. *School Effectiveness and School Improvement* 1: 249–80.

Lilly, E. 1992. Superintendent leadership and district wide vision. ERIC Document (ED 343222).

Lyotard, J. 1993. *The postmodern condition: A report on knowledge.* (Translated by G. Bennington and B. Massumi). (9th ed.). Minneapolis: University of Minnesota Press. (Original work published in 1979.)

Mills, A., and P. Tancred(eds.). (1992). *Gendering organizational analysis.* Newbury Park, Calif.: Sage Publications.

Montenegro, X. 1993. *Women and racial minority representation in school administration.* Arlington, Va.: American Association of School Administrators.

Murphy, J. 1993. Changing role of the superintendent in Kentucky's reforms. *The School Administrator* 50 (10): 26–30.

———. 1994. The changing role of the superintendency in restructuring districts in Kentucky. *School Effectiveness and School Improvement* 5 (4): 349–75.

Sarup, M. 1988. *An introductory guide to poststructuralism and postmodernism.* New York: Harvester Wheatsheaf.

Scherr, M. 1995. The glass ceiling reconsidered: Views from below. In P. Dunlap and P. Schmuck (eds.), *Women leading in education.* Albany, N.Y.: State University of New York Press.

Sergiovanni, T. 1991. *The principalship: A reflective practice perspective.* (2d ed.). Boston, Mass.: Allyn and Bacon.

Shakeshaft, C. 1989. *Women in educational administration.* (Rev. ed.). Newbury Park, Calif.: Sage Publications.

Walker, K. October, 1995. Ethical grounds for superintendents' decision making. Paper presented at the annual meeting of the University Council for Educational Administration, Salt Lake City, Utah.

CHAPTER THIRTEEN

Thoughtful Practice

Responding with Questions
from the Superintendency

DEBRA JACKSON

This chapter is my response—a practitioner's response—to the two chapters by researchers C. Cryss Brunner (chapter 11) and Margaret Grogan (chapter 12) in which they interpret the narrative data from interviews conducted with me. Beyond the actual "talking out" of the interpretations of my narratives, as recorded in Brunner's and Grogan's chapters, I believe the greatest benefits of researcher/practitioner interactions are the resulting questions built on the foundation of such a dialogue.

The new questions created by our dialogue allowed me to more deeply examine my practice. For example, the mere fact that interpretations of my narratives were the basis for discussion intensely drew my attention to the way I "talk." This event of attention allowed a moment in which the material of my narratives became opaque so I could no longer see *through* it but had to look *at* it (Levine in Grogan, chapter 12).

This chapter provides me with an opportunity to reflect on two critical questions about "talk" that I pondered as I attended in this new way. My new questions provoked and evoked "thoughtful practice."

NEW QUESTIONS

Grogan's feminist poststructuralist approach to my narratives asked that I consider my position in the discourse of practice. When so doing, I discovered two questions.

First, I considered one facet of my discourse on power. I, even while in a powerful position as a superintendent, was uncertain about how to talk about power (as is found in Brunner, this book, chapter 11). A new question erupted as I reflected further on my uncertainty. *Can the ability to live with uncertainty be learned?* I recalled that I was reluctant to talk about power because I was, in a certain way, self-conscious. This self-consciousness went deeper than either gender- or role-related expectations alone (Brunner, this book). Perhaps it was a combination of both, with an added element. I felt, and continue to feel, a strong need to pursue the "swamp" (Schall 1995)—a strong need to avoid the security of certainty.

It is certainty in what I say as a superintendent that often is interpreted as *the* course of action. People want to feel safe, and expect safety, security in certainty, from their leaders. Yet, in my view, the greatest learning does not occur in a safe environment. This implies that superintendents, women or men, who are focused on learning, need to develop an internal capacity to live in the swamp or with trepidation. My "talk," then, reflects uncertainty. My privileged position as a superintendent in the discourse becomes one of creating the swamp. I must guard against advancing one agenda. For example, I have changed positions on issues in discussions—especially when I notice a group looking for my position on a topic. By switching my position midstream and asking questions, other individuals begin to support their own positions. Their articulated positions change the look and sound of the discourse. My position—as woman, as superintendent—may *shape*, but does not have to *determine* certainty in the discourse.

Pathological certainty stands in the way of an understanding that everything is learning. The leadership challenge may be to interrogate "certainty" and to inquire why we insist on it. Unfortunately, this thinking is in direct opposition to scientific method, where one goal may be to move from uncertainty to certainty. Given our privileging of science, this goal makes a belief in uncertainty more difficult to support. Nonetheless, I believe we can help move the discourse to one of uncertainty so that learning can flourish. Catherine Marshall (1995) offered a helpful perspective. She suggested that we develop an image of leadership without the baggage of past practice and theories, one with schooling/learning at its core.

Paradoxically, as I write about uncertainty, I again sound certain. And, further, I am certain about the importance of learning and the type of environment necessary for its occurrence. This paradox shaped my second question: *If uncertainty in discourse is important for learning, of what can superintendents, educational leaders, be certain—what certainties can be retained for practice?* Grogan's and Brunner's analyses were helpful as I sought a preliminary answer.

From Grogan, I was reminded that I *may* avoid all efforts to discover the final word, I *may* remain uncertain—I *may* be satisfied to hold a temporary answer, to be temporarily certain that learning is important, and I *may* change the discourse to reflect that certainty. From Brunner, I was reminded that successful women superintendents tend to keep their agendas simple. My temporary certainty—that learning is important—in fact reflects my simple agenda. The discourse I shared with Grogan and Brunner was not only shaped by us but shaped us. The temporary answers reached during such a dialogue were tremendously helpful in my professional practice. They do not remain in books on my shelf, but become a part of my living work.

Attention to the discourse among public school educators is not enough. The same attention must be given to the discourse among researchers and practitioners, as in the case of these interactive chapters. For example, when university researchers conduct seminars for superintendents, they generally protect the certainty of the dominant discourse in educational administration. Most often, the content of the seminars is comfortable and designed to help participants sort through current practices. The certainty of the content prevents any challenging of status quo thinking and, in my opinion, prevents learning.

I end this brief chapter with the plea that other researchers—such as Brunner and Grogan—share space with other practitioners of educational administration—like myself—in the discourse of the swamp in order to advance and support learning. Is that not the goal of education, after all?

REFERENCES

Brunner, C. C. (See ch. 11 in this book.)

Grogan, M. (See ch. 12 in this book.)

Marshall, C. 1995. Imagining leadership. *Educational Administration Quarterly* 31 (3): 484-92.

Schall, E. 1995. Learning to love the swamp: Reshaping education for public service. *Journal of Policy Analysis and Management* 14 (2): 202-20.

Epilogue

SUSAN CHASE

> Let us admit it. We women are building a motherland; each with her
> own plot of soil eked from a night of dreams, a day of work. We are
> spreading this soil in larger and larger circles, slowly, slowly. One day
> it will be a continuous land. . . . This world is being made from our
> lives, our cries, our laughter, our bones. It is a world worth making,
> a world worth living in, a world in which there is a prevailing and
> decent wild sanity.
>
> —Clarissa Pinkola Estés, *Women Who Run With the Wolves*

This book takes a confident step in the slow but steady process of building a
motherland out of the institution of public school education, a land
enriched by the deepest care for all children who come to school as well as for
the teachers who facilitate their learning. The motherland metaphor is apt, not
because we want to create a world populated by female persons, but because we
know that schools are at their best when the needs of children come first. Perhaps all superintendents say they care for children, but the test lies in their
actions. How are their day-to-day decisions and the policies they negotiate with
school boards grounded in that care? And how do they decide what is best for
children in the first place? Do they listen to teachers, to parents, to the children
themselves? How wide and deep is the plot they cultivate before making their
decisions and implementing their policies?

The research presented here strongly suggests that when women lead
schools, these questions are likely to be pondered carefully. Such a statement
should not be confused with the useless argument that caring is an inherent
female quality. More sensible and fruitful is the idea that women's familiarity
with the work of caring for others at home, in schools, and other work places—
a familiarity produced by historical, structural, and cultural conditions—helps
women educational leaders prioritize children's needs.

Each of the authors in this book has cultivated a plot of her own, and each contributes to the development of a world worth living in, a healthy, vibrant educational institution. Jackie Blount connects the past to the present by providing us with an understanding of the history of women superintendents in the United States. This history offers both sobering and inspiring lessons about the relationship between earlier women's movements and women superintendents' progress, reminders of the pivotal connection between broader social forces and women's drive for access and success in a particular profession. Marilyn Tallerico links past research on women in the superintendency to our current needs in terms of research, and she points out that many questions remain to be answered.

In the middle sections of the book, eight chapters pull together the experiences of those few women who have managed to gain access to the top leadership position in public schools. Here we listen to the stories—the lives, the cries, the laughter—of women who struggle with persistent racial and gender barriers; who develop strategies for surviving and sometimes thriving in an unwelcoming world that does not acknowledge its hostility; who seek from family and friends the sustenance they need to continue in a job that is overwhelmingly exhausting, even while it offers satisfaction; and who decide to leave superintendencies as a result of discrimination and unresolved traumas. All of these stories need to be heard, especially by women who are just now daring to think about leadership positions for themselves. These stories bring together women who are already in the superintendency and women who need information in order to act on their thoughts and dreams of leadership.

Finally, Cryss Brunner, Margaret Grogan, and Debra Jackson break open the usually insular dialogue among researchers to create conversation among themselves as researchers and practitioners. This innovative, even radical, work ensures that research truly is for the people—the practitioners—it purports to serve.

The deepest connection among the individual plots developed in this book is somewhat implicit, not fully emergent, yet that connectedness represents the world worth living in that we must all keep working on collectively, even as we continue cultivating our individual plots. The rewards reaped through the hard work of prying open the doors of the superintendency, offering much-needed information to aspiring women, learning from the past and past research, and creating dialogue between researchers and practitioners are all for naught unless we keep daily in our minds and hearts our commitment to an educational institution that offers equality for all who learn and work within it.

How do we keep this world worth making in our minds and hearts? By remembering that getting women into the superintendency both represents and serves a larger purpose. That larger purpose is hinted at in the school-based reforms that Cryss Brunner discusses in her introduction to this book. Controversies certainly abound concerning which reforms are best for children and most supportive of teachers, as well as how, where, and when the needed changes should be implemented. Nonetheless, it is the collective push for social justice at all levels in public schools that constitutes the world worth making, the world worth living in.

By no means do I intend to suggest that women who dream of becoming superintendents should suppress that desire in the service of some supposedly distinct greater good. That notion—although prevalent in movements for social change, including the school reform movement—produces a false dichotomy between the individual and her community. Rather, I mean to point to an alternative to narrow careerism on the one hand, and blind self-sacrifice on the other hand. The alternative consists of understanding the connections among all forms of inequality in public education: the small number of white women and people of color in leadership positions; funding, curricula, and employment policies skewed to the interests of white, middle-class boys and men; and sexual and racial harassment experienced by students, teachers, and administrators.

In other words, a woman's dream of becoming a superintendent—of challenging the sexist and racist barriers that make that a rarity—can and should coexist with her desire to create the conditions all teachers need in order to help all children thrive. A woman who aims to become a superintendent and to survive once there can and should see in the strife she faces a reflection of the everyday struggles endured by teachers and students in an unjust institution. A deep commitment to prioritizing children's needs does not mean ignoring one's own desires. It means embracing, in Estés words, "a world in which there is a prevailing and decent wild sanity." In our contemporary times, decency and sanity are found in the wild idea that there are connections among all of us.

Contributors

Judy A. Alston is an assistant professor in the educational leadership and cultural studies department at the University of Houston. She received her Ph.D. at the University of Houston in 1996. She teaches courses in multicultural education for prospective teachers and administrators, in addition to organizational behavior. Her research areas include women and minorities in educational administration.

Jackie M. Blount is an assistant professor in the department of curriculum and instruction at Iowa State University. She completed her doctoral studies in the social foundations of education at the University of North Carolina at Chapel Hill. She is the author of *Destined to Rule the Schools: Women and the Superintendency, 1873–1995*, as well as of numerous articles and book chapters.

C. Cryss Brunner is an assistant professor in the department of educational administration at the University of Wisconsin-Madison. She completed her Ph.D. at the University of Kansas in 1993. Her research on women, power, the superintendency, and the gap between public schools and their communities has appeared in such journals as *Educational Policy, The Journal for a Just and Caring Education, The Journal of Educational Administration,* and *The Journal of School Leadership*. She is a 1996–97 recipient of the National Academy of Education's Spencer Fellowship for her work on the relationship between superintendents' definitions of power and decision-making processes.

Susan Chase is an associate professor of sociology at the University of Tulsa and the author of *Ambiguous Empowerment: The Work Narratives of Women School Superintendents* (1995) and numerous other journal articles. She is currently working on two projects: a qualitative study of college students' understandings of race, gender, and sexual orientation, and a text reader on feminism and motherhood.

Margaret Grogan is an assistant professor of educational leadership and policy studies at the Curry School of Education, University of Virginia. Resident in Tokyo for seventeen years, she served as a teacher and an administrator at an international school there. She received her Ph.D. in educational administration from Washington State University in May 1994. Her recent research into women aspiring to the superintendency, *Voices of Women Aspiring to the Superintendency* (1996), focuses on a feminist poststructuralist account of what it is like to be a woman in public school administration.

Barbara L. Jackson is professor and chair of the division of administration, policy, and urban education at the Graduate School of Education, Fordham University, in New York City. Dr. Jackson came to Fordham in 1987 after serving as professor and dean of the School of Education at Morgan State University, Baltimore, Maryland. She received her doctor of education degree from the Harvard Graduate School of Education in 1970. Her most recent publications include her book *Balancing Act: The Political Role of the Urban School Superintendent* (1995) and "Black Women Role Models: Where Can We Find Them?" in *Initiatives* (1990).

Debra Jackson is superintendent of schools of North Salem Central School District in New Jersey. She received her doctorate in education in 1990. She is active in the University Council of Educational Administration and American Educational Research Association, where she has presented papers on women superintendents.

Estelle Kamler is superintendent of schools in New York. She had served as an assistant superintendent for curriculum and instruction, a director of curriculum, an elementary principal, and an administrative assistant, as well as an elementary school teacher for eleven years. She also is an adjunct professor for the department of curriculum and teaching at Hofstra University.

Sylvia E. Méndez-Morse is an assistant professor in the bilingual multicultural education program at Eastern New Mexico University in Portales, New Mexico. She began her career as a bilingual education teacher, working with language minority students in Texas, New Mexico, and Arizona, and eventually became involved in the administration of programs serving this population. She has done research in educational leadership and educational reform, focusing on administrators leading educational change to improve the instructional needs of language minority students.

Flora Ida Ortiz is professor of educational administration at the University of California, Riverside. She specializes in organizational theory, socialization processes, and women and minorities in educational administration. She has authored books such as *Career Patterns in Education*, *The Superintendent's Leadership in School Reform*, and *Schoolhousing: Planning and Designing Educational Facilities*. Many of her works deal with Hispanic female superintendents and women's ascent to executive positions.

Barbara Nelson Pavan, professor of Educational Administration at Temple University, teaches principalship, organizational theory, and research and supervision courses. Her doctorate was earned at Harvard University. In addition to her book, *Nongradedness: Helping It to Happen*, and several book chapters, she has been published in *Educational Leadership*, *Elementary School Journal*, *Phi Delta Kappan*, *Principal*, and *Urban Education*.

Patricia A. Schmuck is a professor and chair of the department of educational administration at Lewis and Clark College, Portland, Oregon. She has authored books and articles about women in educational administration, including *Women Educators* and *Educational Policy & Management: Sex Differentials*.

Charol Shakeshaft is a professor and chairperson of administration, policy studies, and literacy at Hofstra University. She has studied gender issues in schools for nearly a quarter century. Her book, *Women in Educational Administration*, is in its fifth printing.

Marilyn Tallerico is an associate professor in the teaching and leadership program at Syracuse University. Her research centers on gender issues in educational leadership and the politics of education. Recent publications have appeared in the *Educational Administration Quarterly*, the *Journal of Staff Development*, and *Educational Considerations*.

Index

Printed in the United States
1075600005B/238-252